IMAGES
of America

ALONG THE CATAWBA RIVER

IMAGES FROM THE WINTHROP UNIVERSITY ARCHIVES

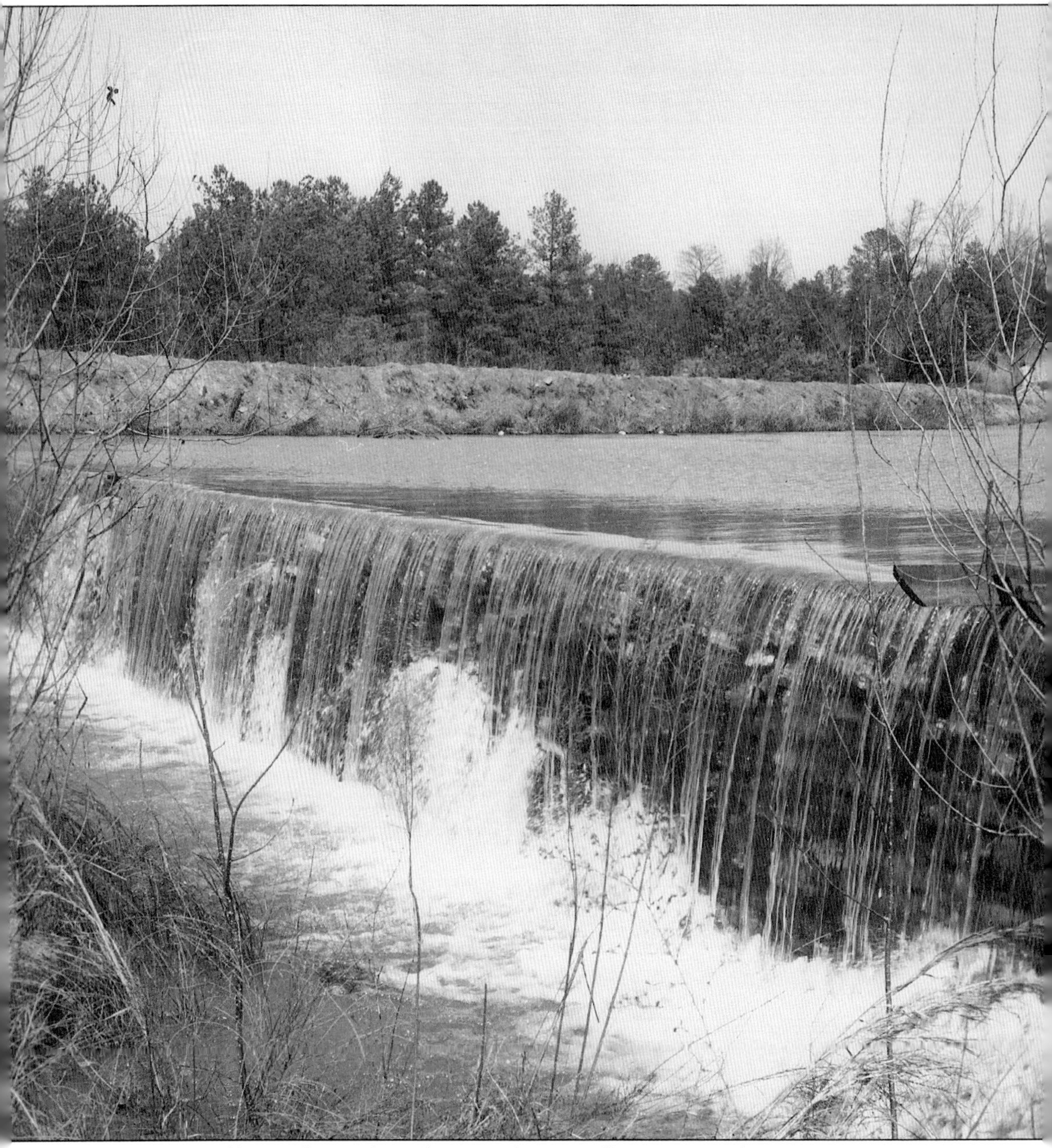

Near Great Falls, South Carolina, the Catawba River flows across a dam.

IMAGES
of America

Along the Catawba River

Images from the Winthrop University Archives

Ron Chepesiuk, Gina Price White,
and Edward Lee

ARCADIA
PUBLISHING

ISBN 978-0-7385-0291-5

Published by Arcadia Publishing
Charleston, South Carolina

Printed in the United States of America

Library of Congress Catalog Card Number: Applied for.

For all general information contact Arcadia Publishing at:
Telephone 843-853-2070
Fax 843-853-0044
E-Mail sales@arcadiapublishing.com
For customer service and orders:
Toll-Free 1-888-313-2665

Visit us on the Internet at www.arcadiapublishing.com

To Ann, Elizabeth,
Magdelena, and Russ.

Contents

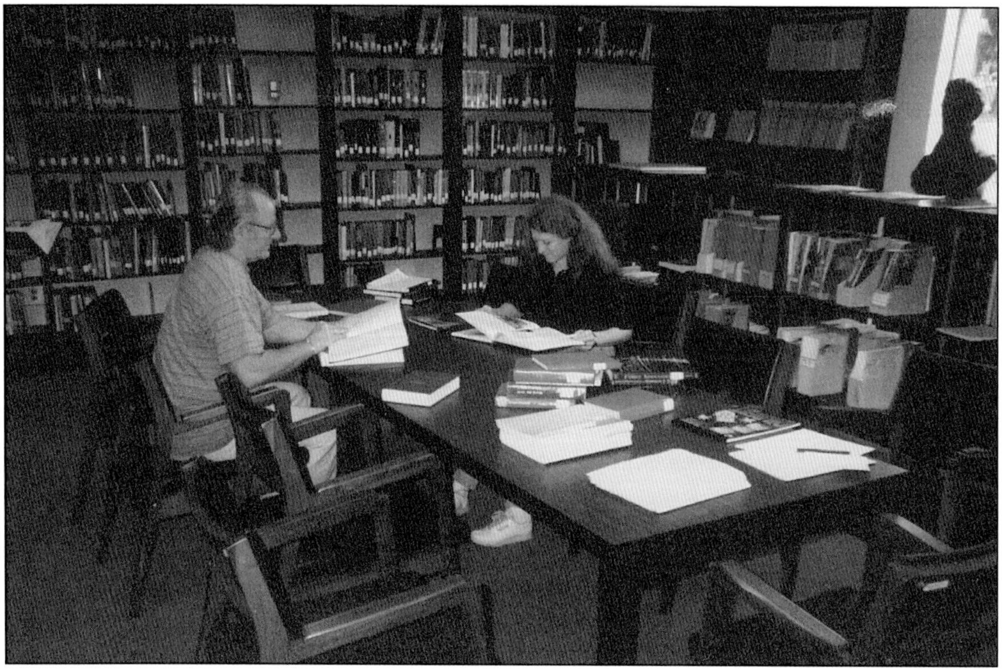

ACKNOWLEDGMENTS

The authors would like to thank the following people and institutions for their help with the book: Rachel Johnson, Clinton College, York Technical College, Russell and Company in Chester, and Sharon Jenkins and Elaine Nichols of Clinton College. Special thanks to Tyre Lee and to Billy Boan, whose hard work and diligence helped add a special touch to the book, and to the many donors who have generously given material to the Winthrop Archives.

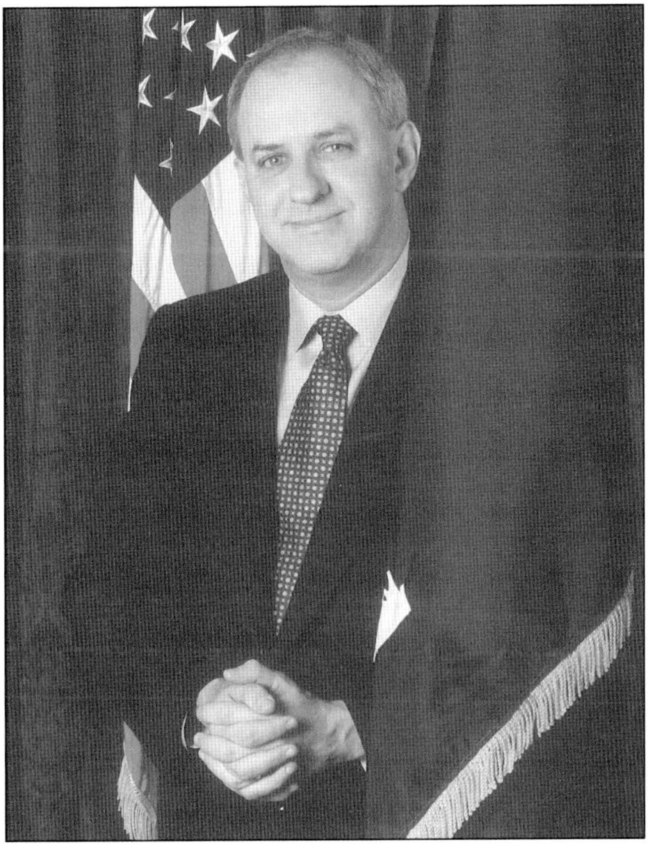

A Message from the Governor

South Carolinians have a unique sense of place that binds us to our small towns and communities. When we move to the big city, we still subscribe to the hometown paper. We use a small county store as a landmark when giving directions in rural areas. Entire towns cheer for the local football team on Friday nights.

This sense of place is certainly evident in Lancaster, Chester, and York Counties. The Tri-County area has a rich history and a unique identity, from its earliest days—as the tribal lands of the Catawba Indian Nation, the birthplace of Andrew Jackson, and the launching pad from the Springs' textile empire—the Tri-Counties have seen their share of history.

Today, the Tri-Counties continue to exhibit the charm, sense of community, and pride that distinguish the Piedmont region of South Carolina from the rest of the state.

The rich history and unique identity of Lancaster, Chester, and York Counties is captured in the book you are now holding. This book, a collaborative effort by the staff of the Winthrop Archives and a member of the Winthrop history department, sketches a lively portrait of the people and places of the region.

From the White Homestead to the Peach Stand, from Landsford Canal to the Aaron Burr Rock, the Tri-Counties have much to offer. As a native son of the region, I invite you to explore the history of *Along the Catawba River*.

Sincerely,
Jim Hodges

Introduction

Our River

Carved into the red clay of upstate South Carolina, the Catawba River flowed untouched under a canopy of luscious green for a thousand years. Then, gradually, the people of the river came. The first were members of the Catawba Indian Nation, filtering down from the icy prehistoric link with Asia. These proud individuals honored the river with its teeming fisheries and rich soil. From the river and the blue sky came life.

In five waves, spirited Scotch-Irish immigrants trekked hundreds of miles down the Great Wagon Road from Pennsylvania, bringing with them Presbyterianism and community names such as "Lancaster," "Chester," and "York." Freedom lovers, they clashed with their Loyalist neighbors, winning independence at bloody sites like Buford's Massacre, Hanging Rock, and Kings Mountain.

African Americans, snatched from their homeland and sold into bondage, came to the river in the 1800s. They worked daily from "can see" to "can't see" in the heat of cotton fields and tobacco barns. They lived, sang, and dreamed in the cabins of Van Wyck, Lowrys, and Brattonsville.

The people of the river are multi-hued. They are a colorful mosaic that stretches from red to white to black and includes every shade in between. They toil in mills, fields, factories, offices, schools, and homes sprinkled across Lancaster, Chester, and York Counties. These people are hard working, freedom cherishing, and independent minded. They worship from AME, Baptist, Episcopalian, Roman Catholic, and Methodist pews. They compete on the gridiron and boast of victory or vow "wait until next year." Their voices resonate across the stages of the Chester Little Theater, McCelvey Center, and the University of South Carolina Lancaster (USCL). They have defended liberty in faraway places named Normandy, Iwo Jima, Inchon, Hue, and Kuwait.

These people share a panorama of historic places like Forty Acre Rock, Brainerd Institute, People's Free Library, Andrew Jackson State Park, Bethesda Church, and Nation Ford. These people are, because of the unique place they call home, all sons and daughters of our Catawba River.

One

HOME, FAMILY, AND FARM

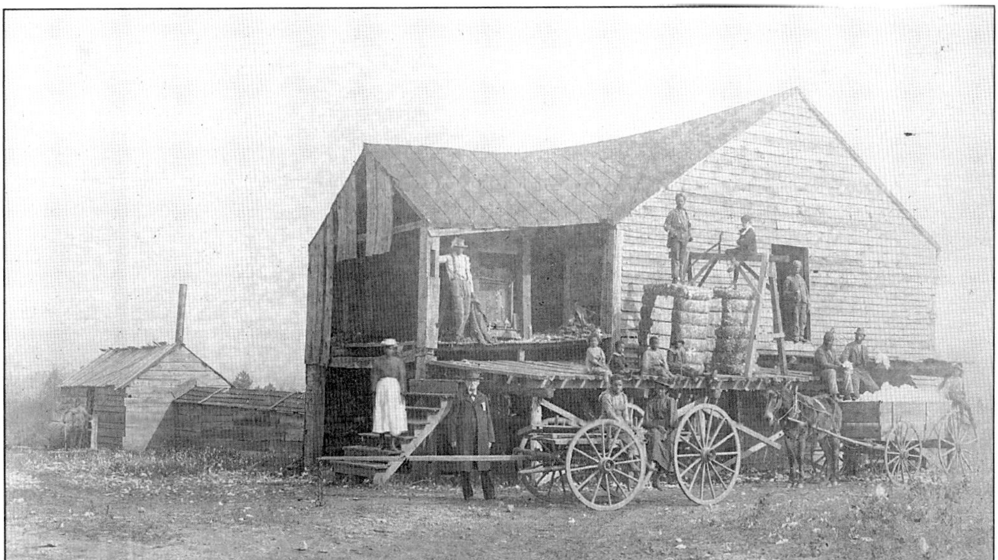

The Catawba region was primarily an agricultural area for most of its existence, and cotton, of course, was the most favored crop. This photograph, dated 1843, shows the Strawberry Hill Plantation that was owned by Capt. Iredell Jones and located near present-day Rock Hill.

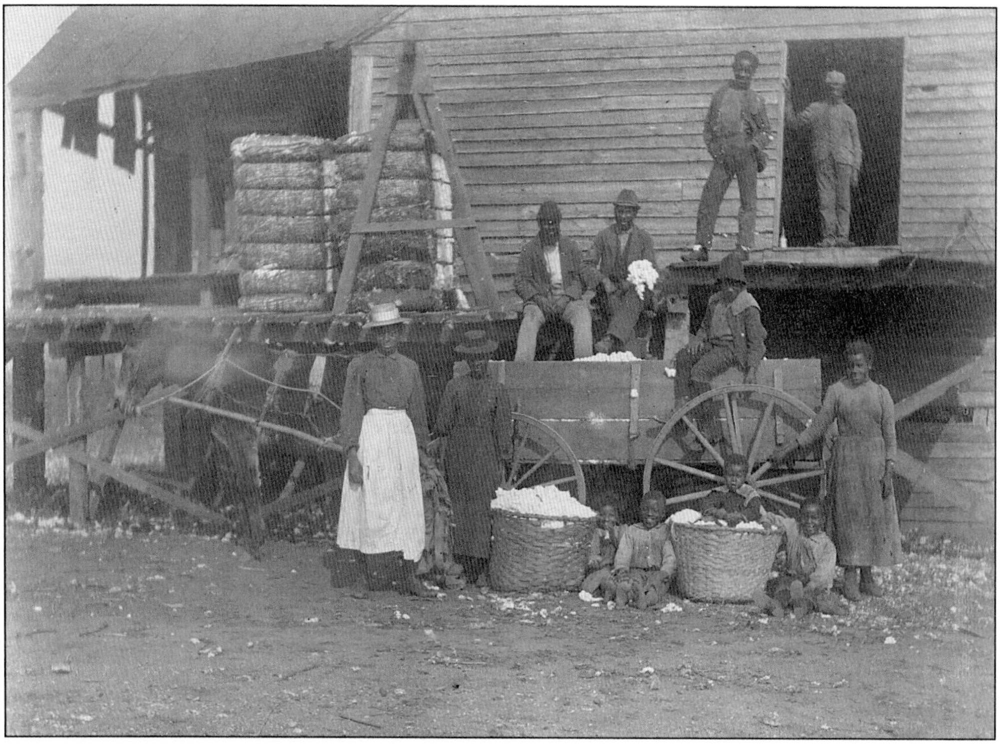

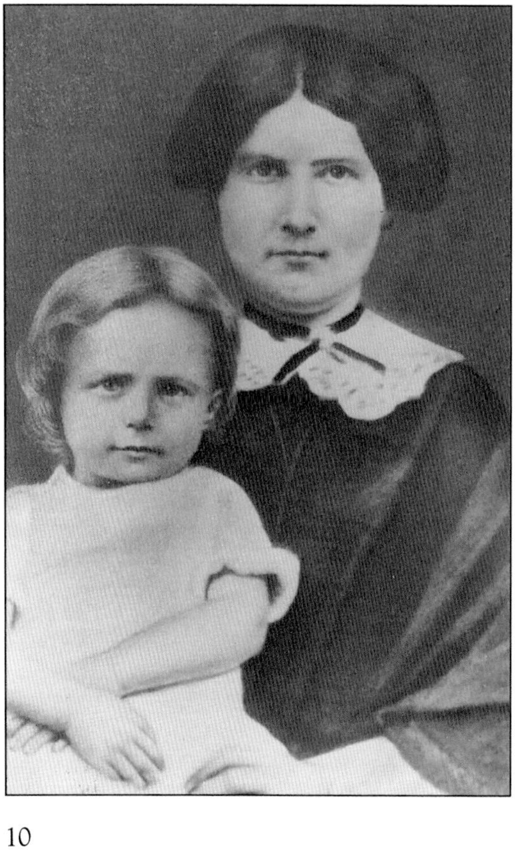

Like the previous photograph, this 1843 photograph shows the Stawberry Hill Plantation.

This photograph, taken in 1858, is of Rebecca Narcissa Poag Hicklin (1820–1879) with her son James Albert Roswell Hicklin (1852–1928) of Richburg.

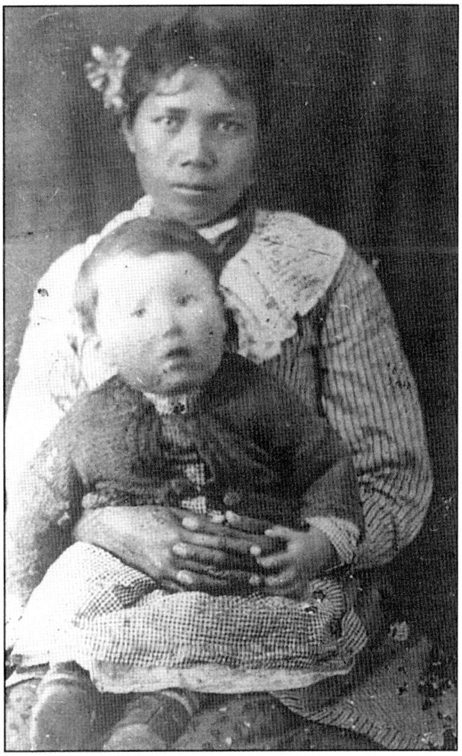

The first inhabitants of the area surrounding the Catawba River were members of the Catawba Indian tribe. The Catawba people migrated to this area hundreds of years before the first Europeans came. This is an unidentified Catawba woman and her child, *c.* 1870s.

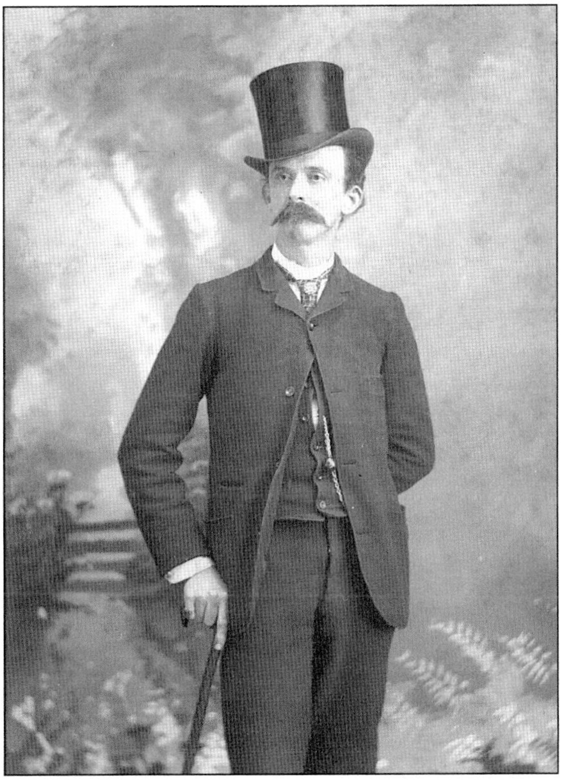

Having your portrait taken by a photographer was a popular pastime in the early 1880s. This gentleman posed for John R. Schorb in Yorkville. In 1853, Schorb moved to Yorkville, New York, opening a studio on his property on West Liberty Street. Schorb practiced photography until he was almost 90. He died on November 5, 1908, and is buried in Rose Hill Cemetery in York.

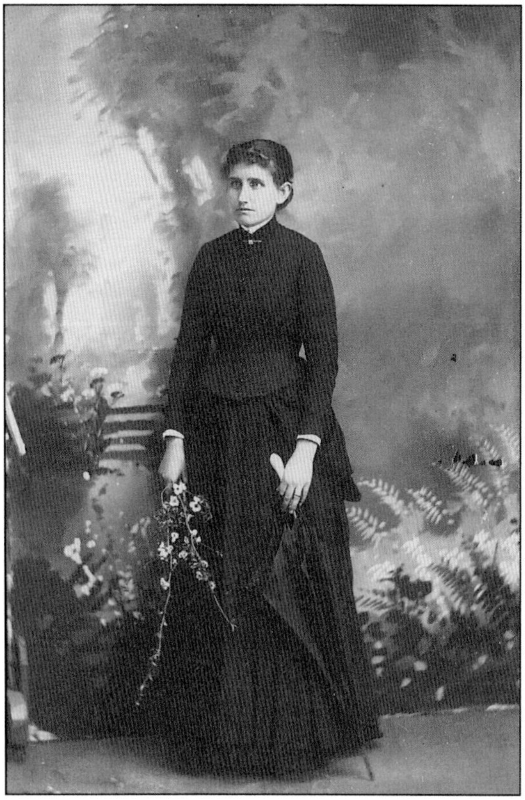

This *c.* 1880 portrait of an unidentified young woman was also taken by John Schorb. Notice the painted backdrop. Schorb built or painted all of his props.

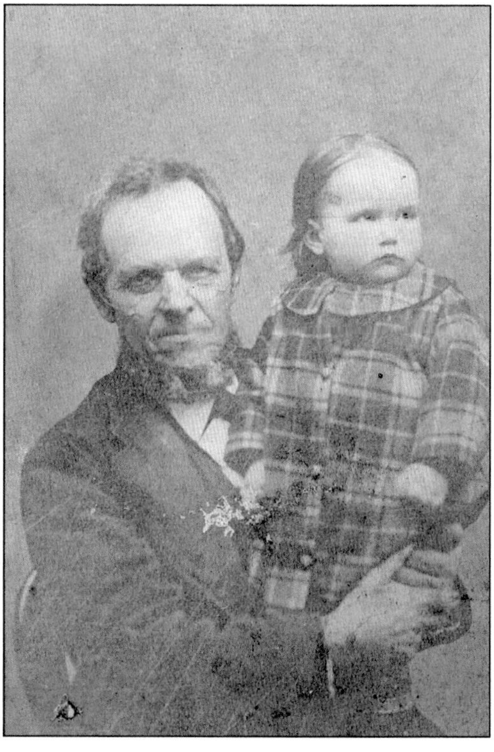

John R. Schorb and Mary Schorb are pictured here, *c.* 1874.

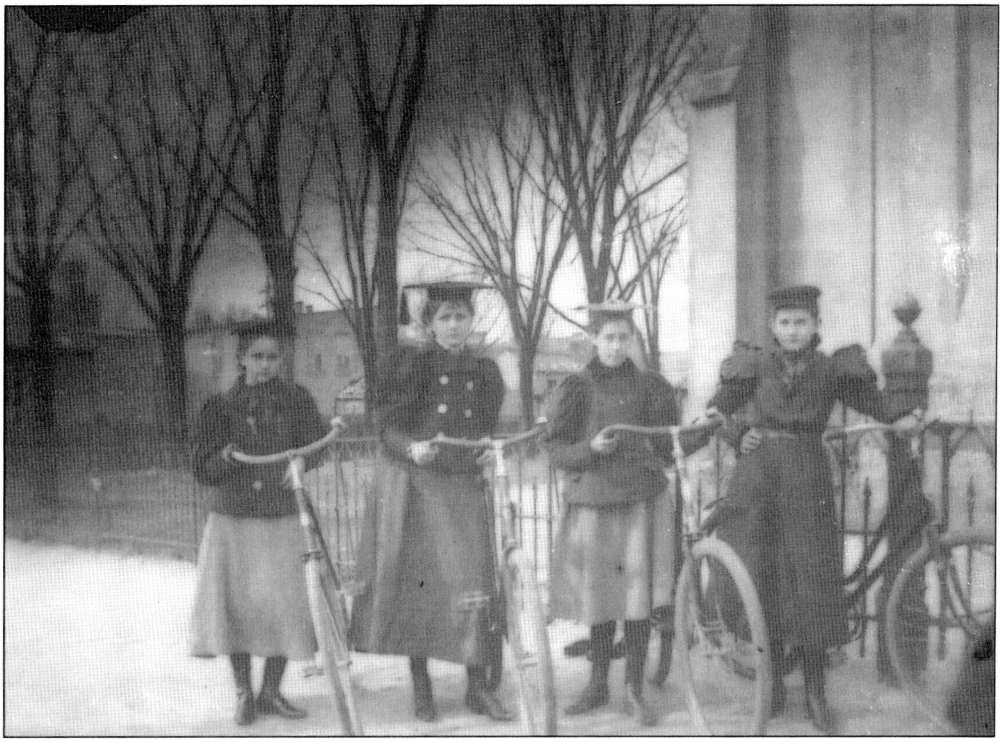

Four girls with their bicycles pose by the First Presbyterian Church in York *c.* late 1880s.

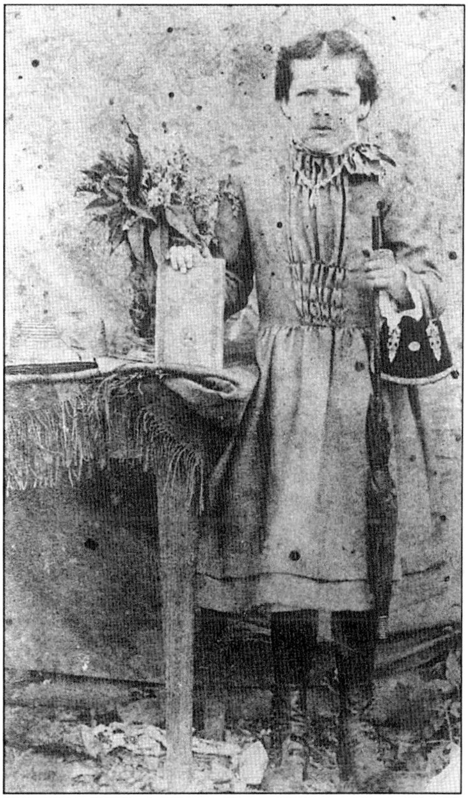

A young Native American girl of the Catawba people had her portrait taken *c.* 1880s.

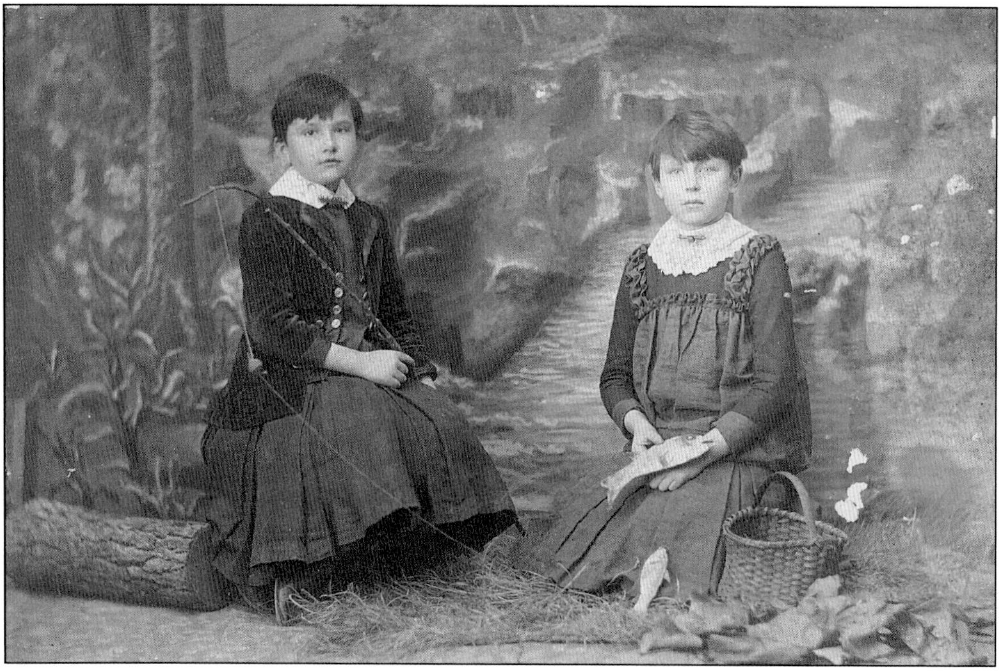

In the 19th century, boys were often dressed in skirts until the age of five or six. John Schorb photographed these two boys with fishing gear in 1885. We can discern that they are boys because their hair is parted on the side. Girls' hair was parted in the middle.

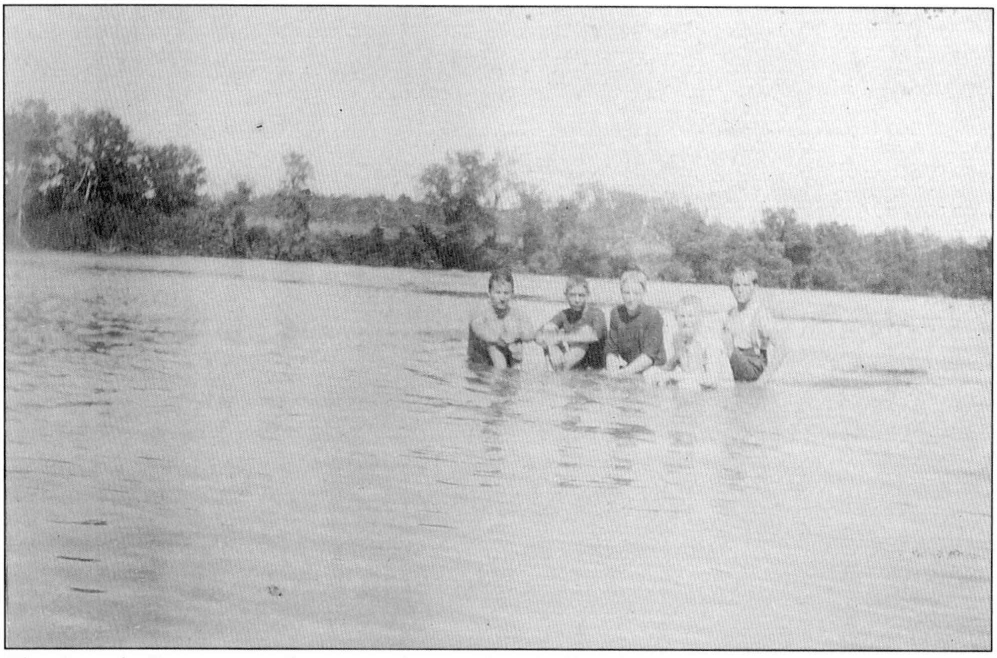

The Catawba River was a place to explore and cool off on hot days in 1897. In the river above the old mill are, from left to right, David Hope Sadler, Frank Culp, J. Hutchison, Eugene Hutchison, and Bob Tompkins.

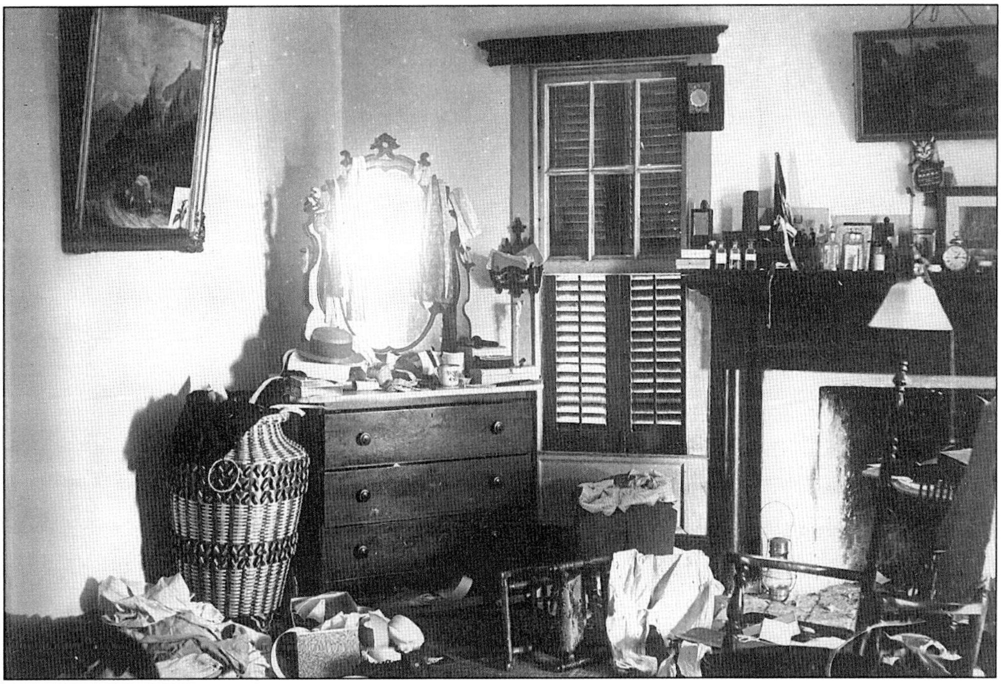

This is James S. Whites's bedroom at his parents' home in Rock Hill in 1897.

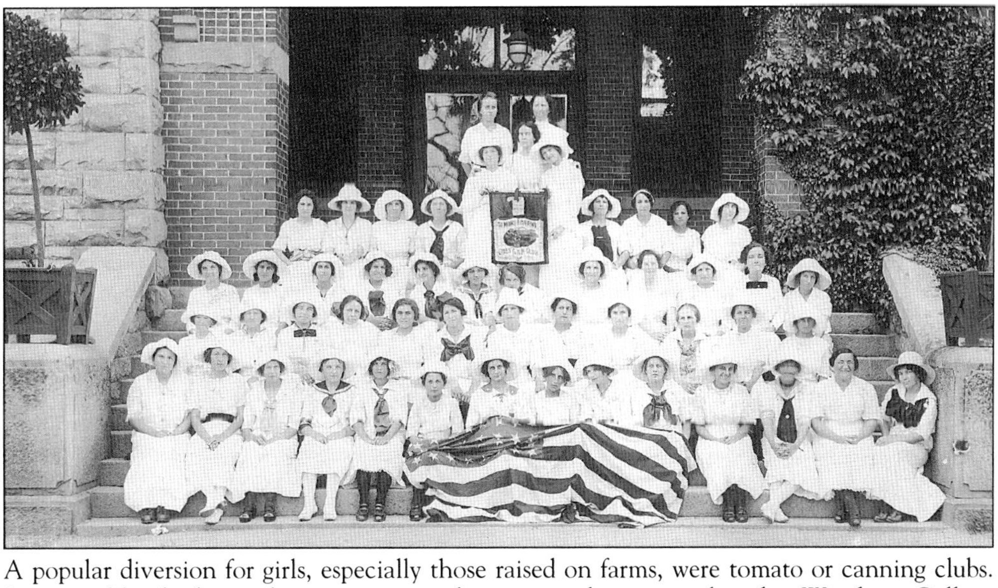

A popular diversion for girls, especially those raised on farms, were tomato or canning clubs. Sponsored by the home demonstration and extension department based at Winthrop College in Rock Hill, the clubs offered young farm girls from across the state an opportunity to learn about gardening and canning and also to make a little money by selling the fruits of their labors. Here is a Girls' C & P club on the steps of Main Building (now Tillman) at Winthrop c. 1918.

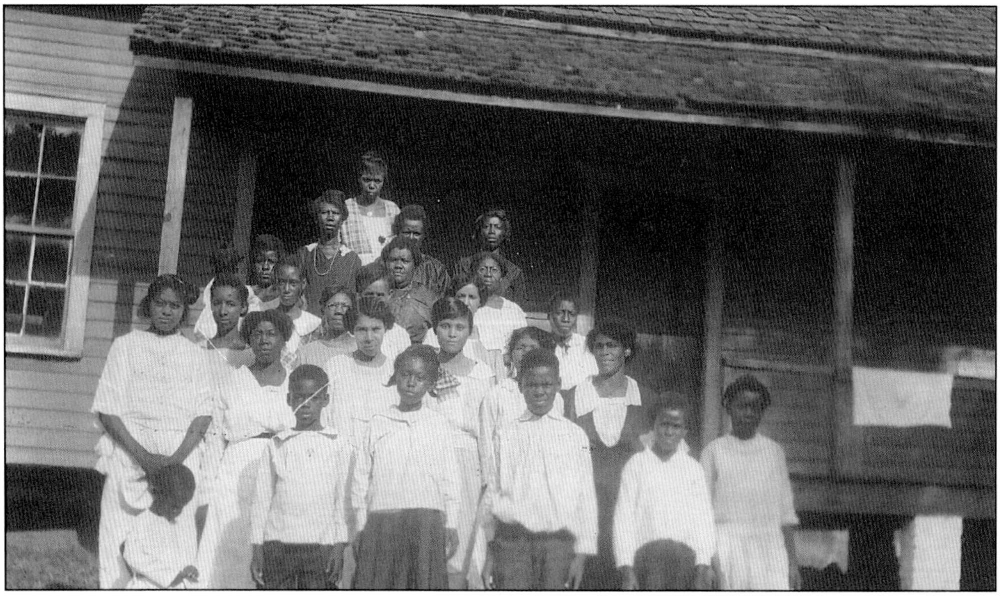

Pictured here is a similar York County club for African Americans in 1921.

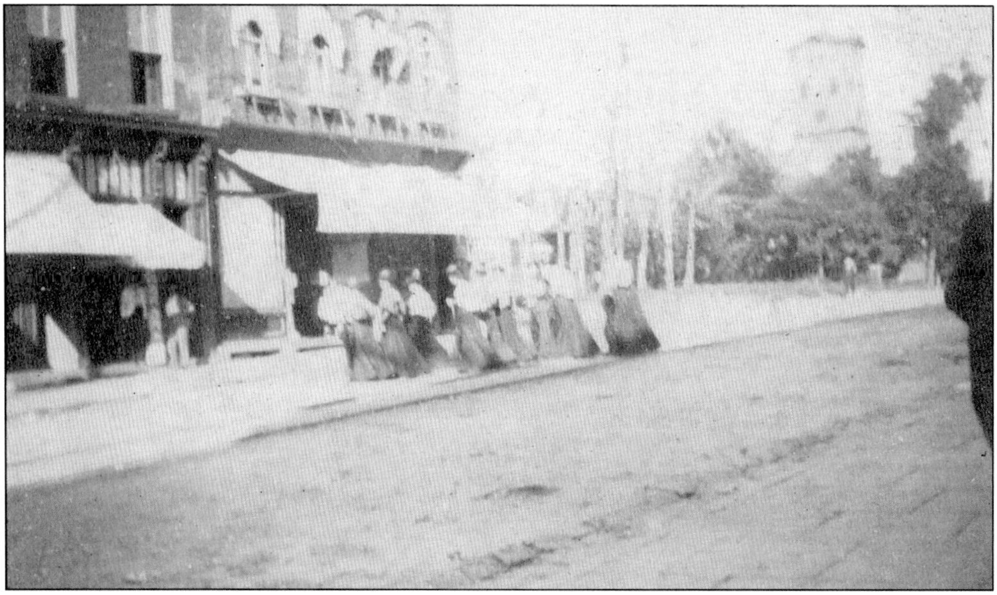

Winthrop Normal and Industrial College (later Winthrop College) students cross a Rock Hill street about 1897. Winthrop girls wore navy uniforms and adhered to strict regulations concerning trips to town.

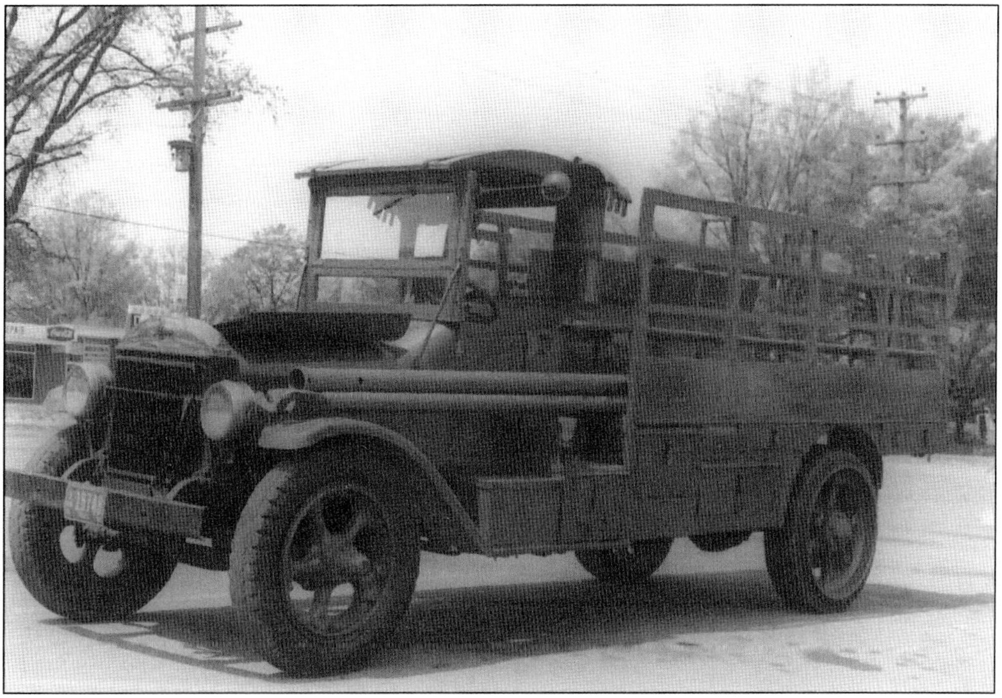

A 1927 Rock Hill Telephone Company truck and its maintenance crew kept home telephones in good repair.

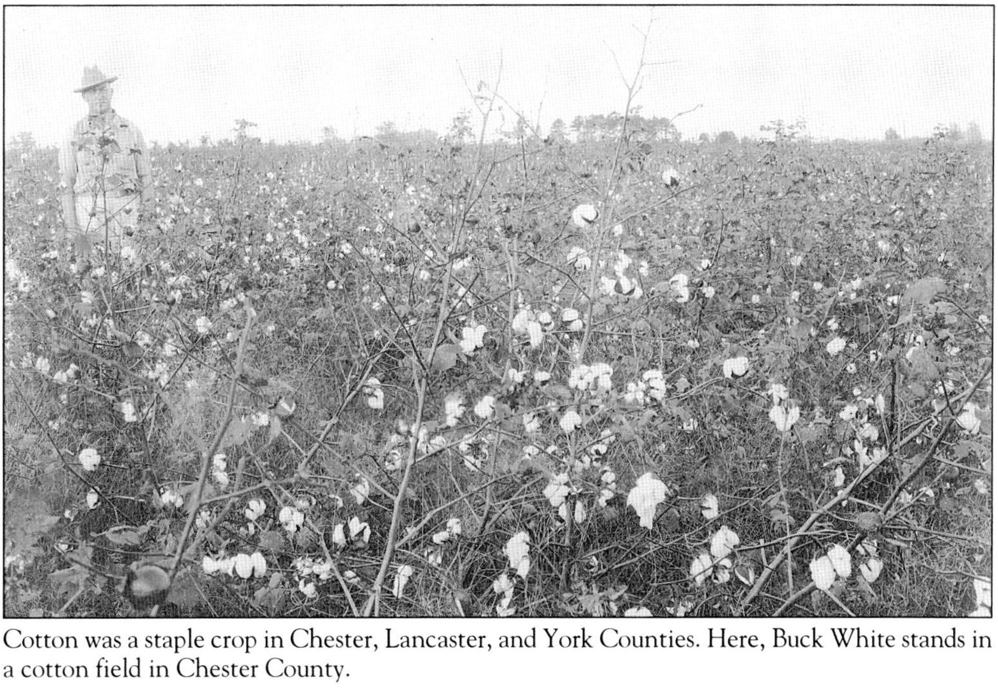

Cotton was a staple crop in Chester, Lancaster, and York Counties. Here, Buck White stands in a cotton field in Chester County.

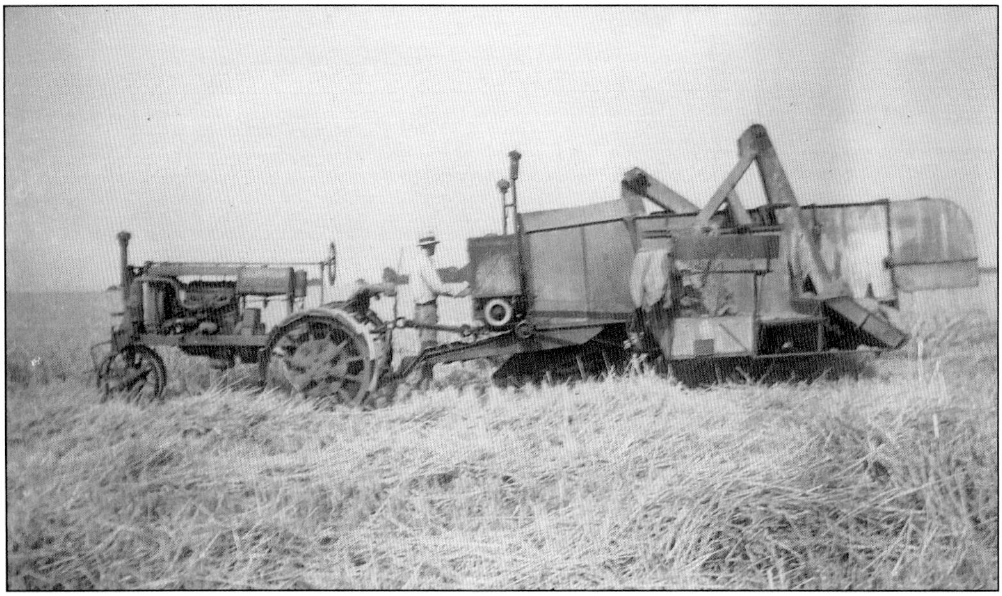

A tractor and combine in York County are pictured here *c.* 1940s.

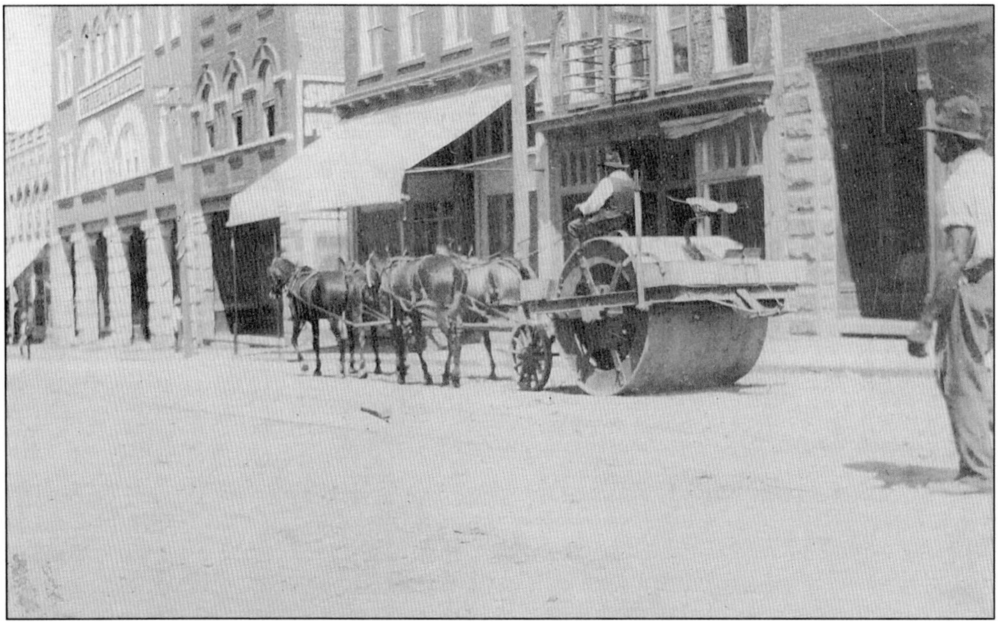

This man is pictured rolling down the streets of Rock Hill *c.* 1897.

An unidentified Catawba Indian family was captured on film *c.* 1930s.

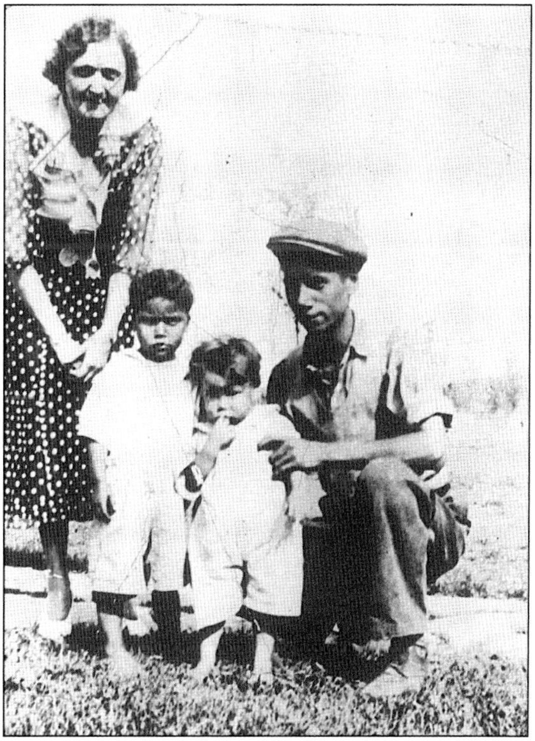

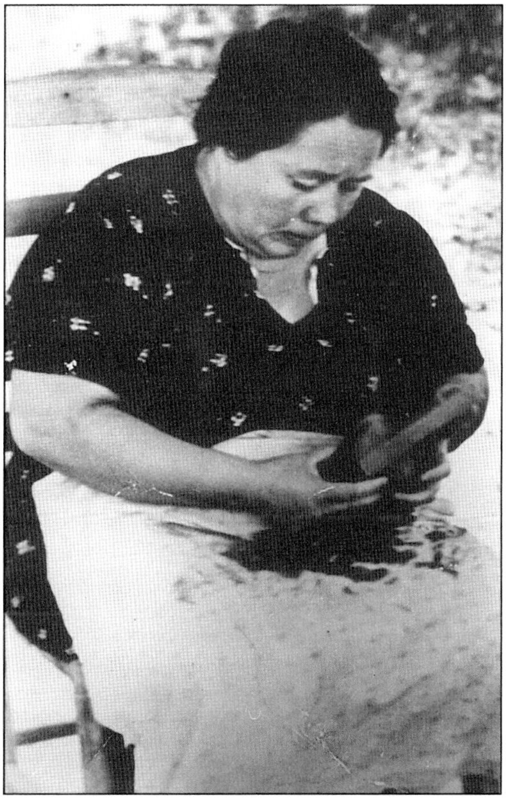

The Catawba Indians are famous for their wonderful pottery made from local clay. Here, an unidentified Catawba woman holds a piece of pottery.

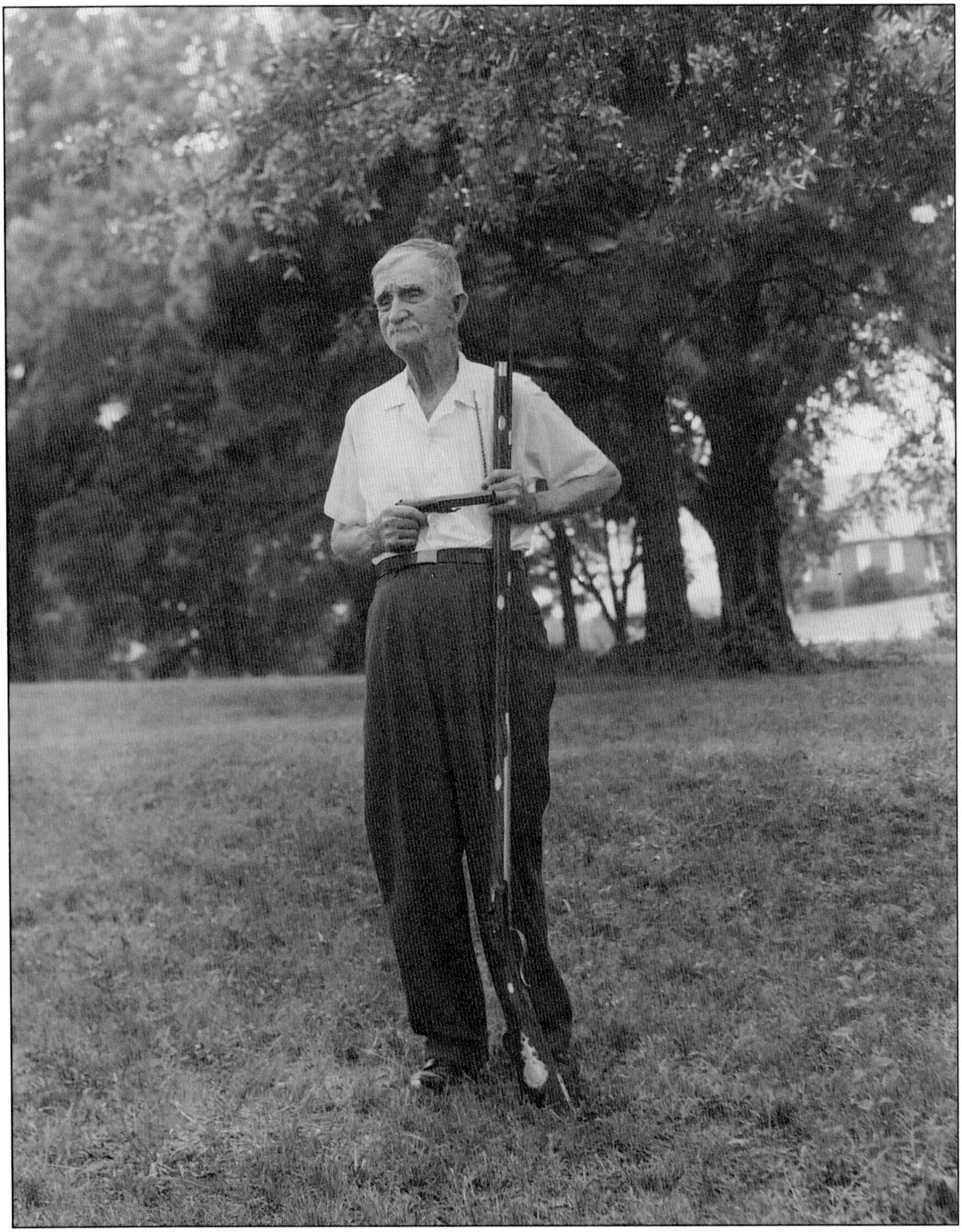

Family history means a great deal to the residents of the Catawba region. Here, W.T. Castles of Chester holds a rifle and pistol made by his grandfather Thomas Bennett (1812–1861), a gunsmith in Chester County.

One means of transportation around Rock Hill in the first part of the 20th century was the streetcar. The "electric railway," as it was called, was not electric at all. It derived its name from the names of the mules that pulled it. They were called "Lec" and "Tric." This unidentified gentleman is a passenger on the streetcar.

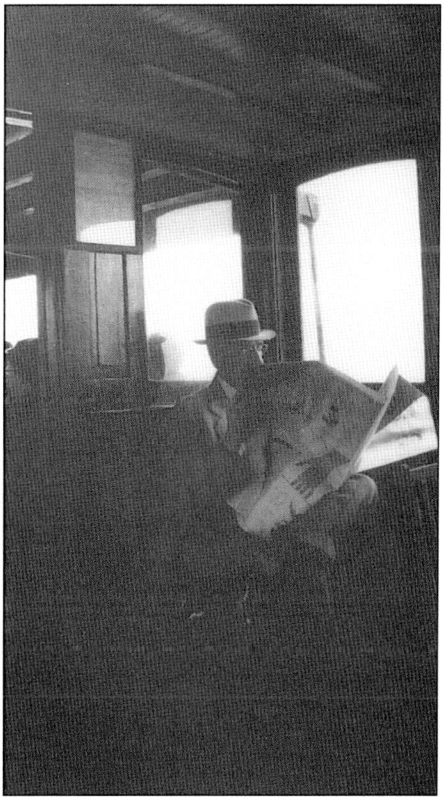

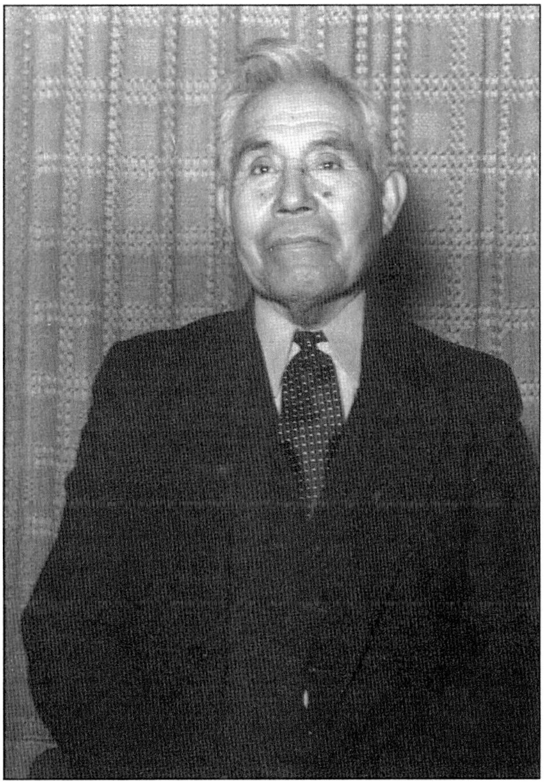

This photograph of Robert Harris, a Catawba chief, was taken in the early 1940s.

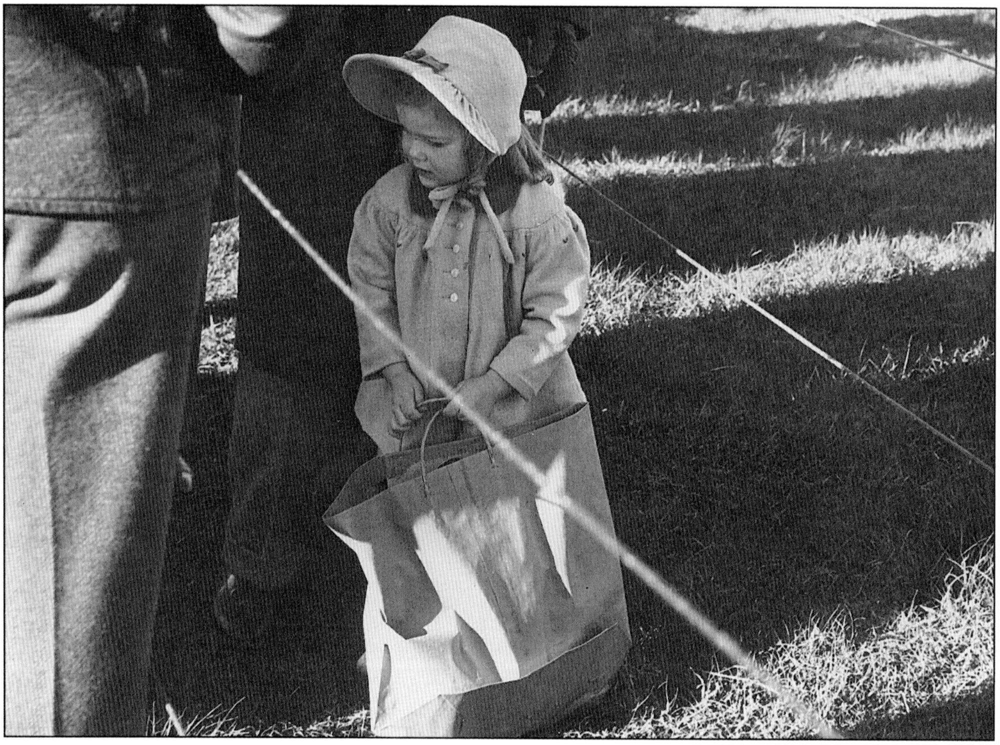

Christmas in the Catawba region has always been a family event. This little girl is attending the Bleachery (Rock Hill Printing and Finishing) Christmas tree party in 1946.

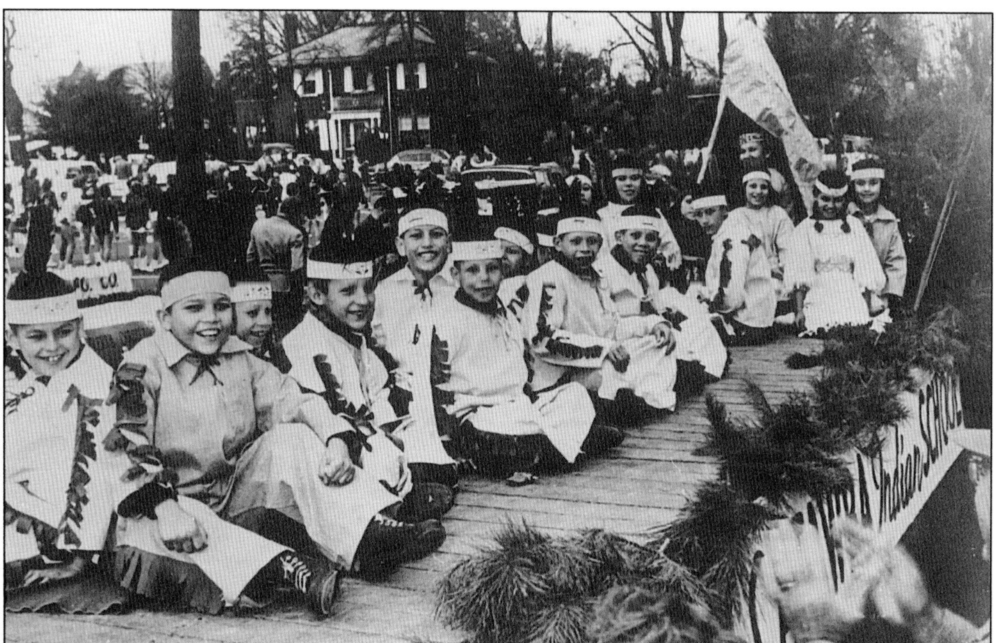

These children from the Catawba Indian School are on a Christmas parade float.

Boating is a favorite pastime along the Catawba River, as these girls found in the early 1940s.

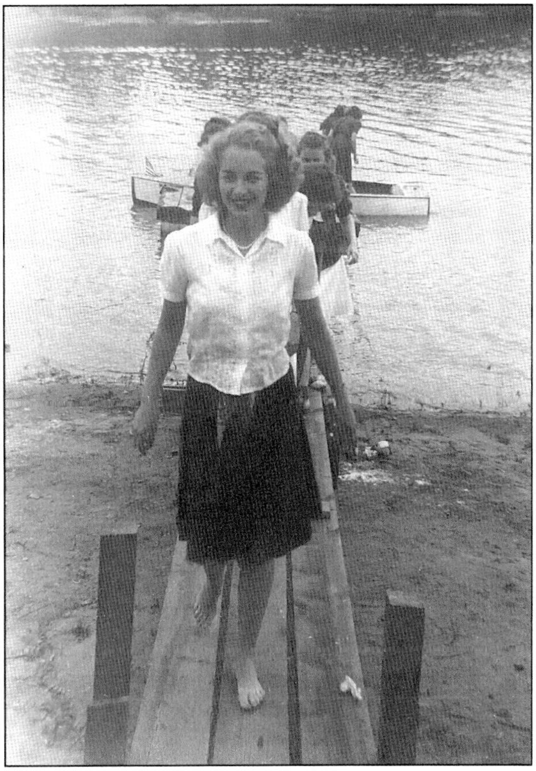

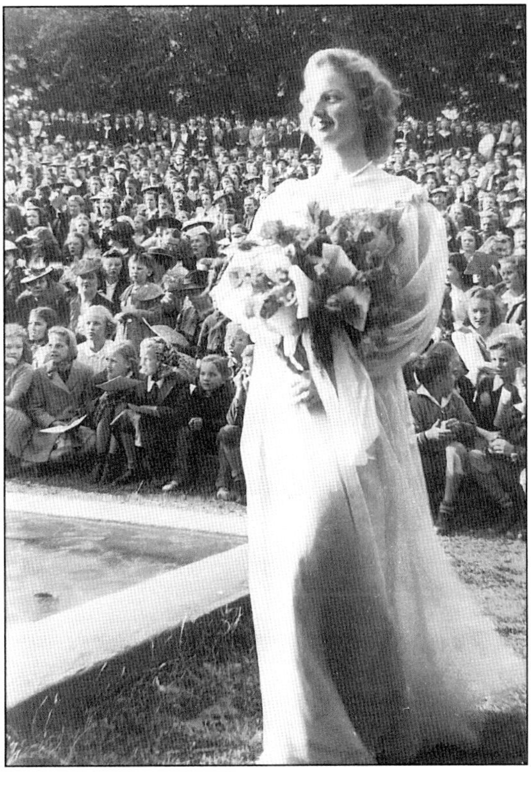

The people in the area surrounding Rock Hill would gather at the amphitheater at Winthrop College on the first Saturday in May to watch the May Day festivities. Here, a member of the May court ascends the stage in the early 1940s.

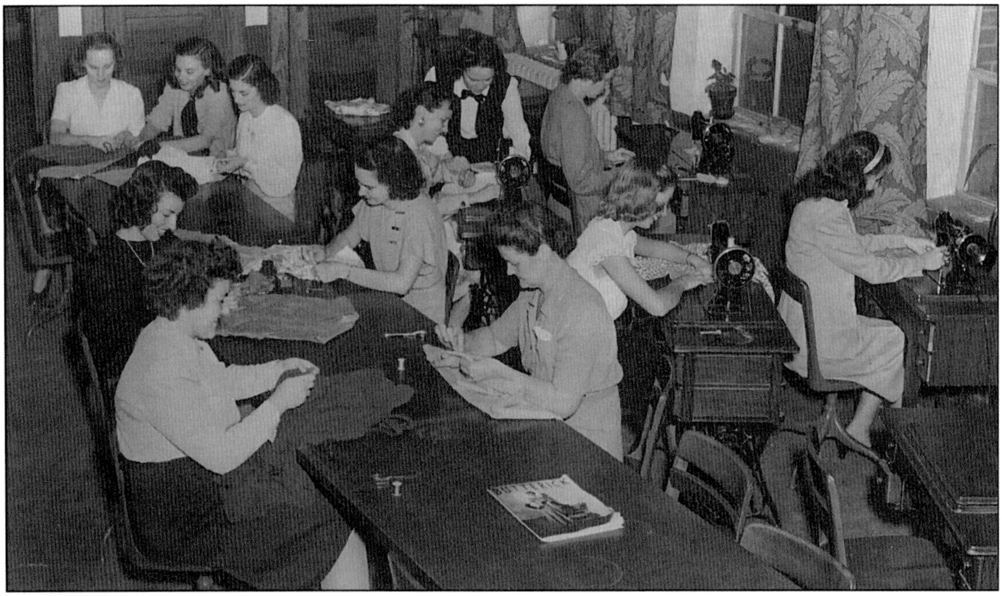

The Lancaster Chapter of Junior Homemakers held a night class in sewing for business girls in the 1940s.

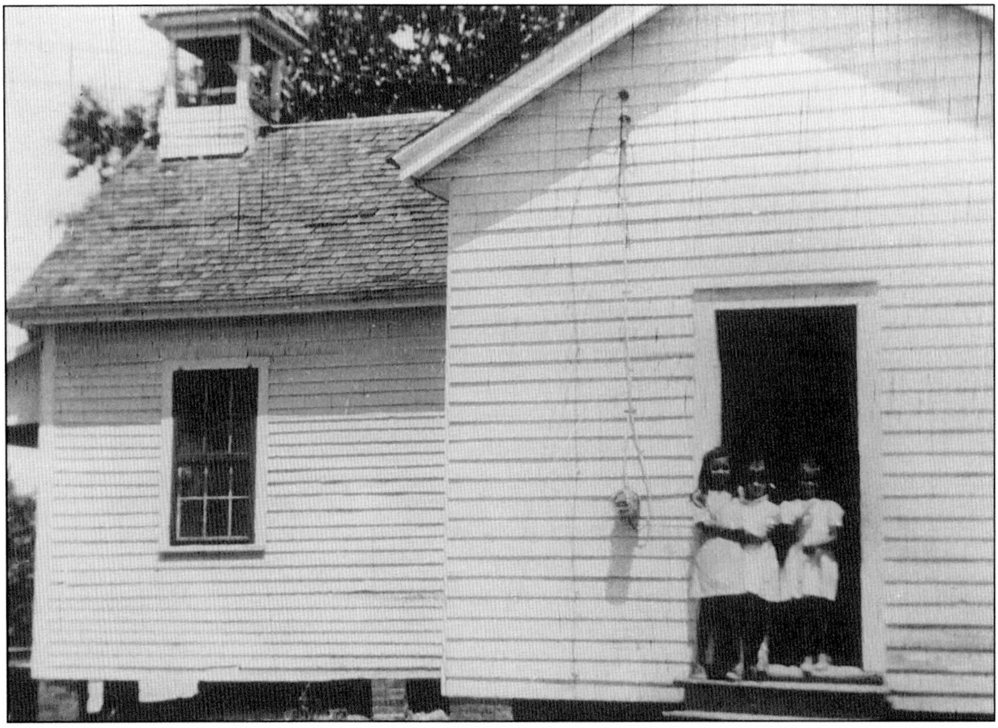

These unidentified Catawba children stand in a doorway on the reservation in the 1940s.

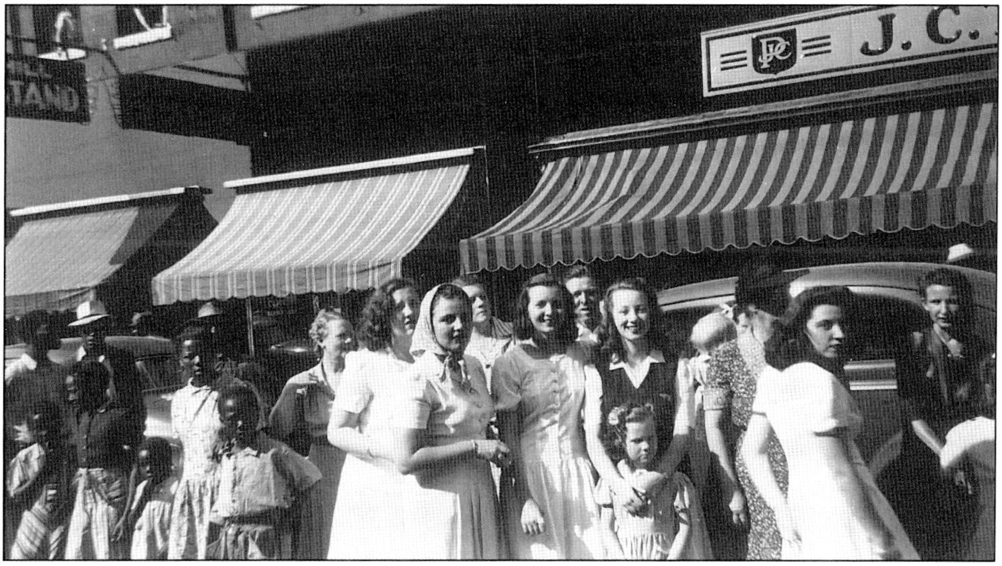

Pictured here are shoppers in downtown Rock Hill in the 1940s.

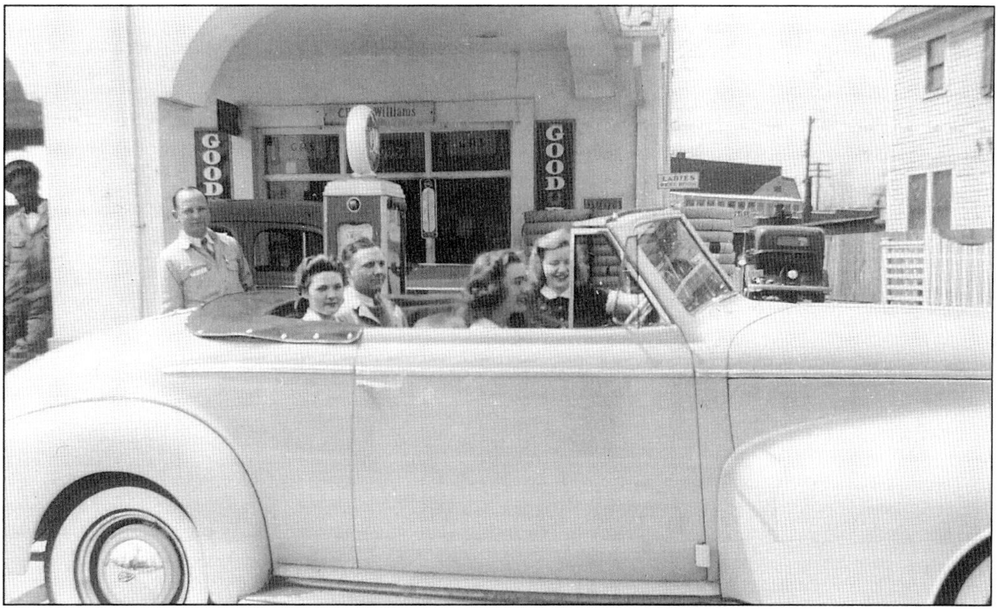

A car full of citizens, enjoying a sunny afternoon, stop by Williams Gulf in Rock Hill to fill up.

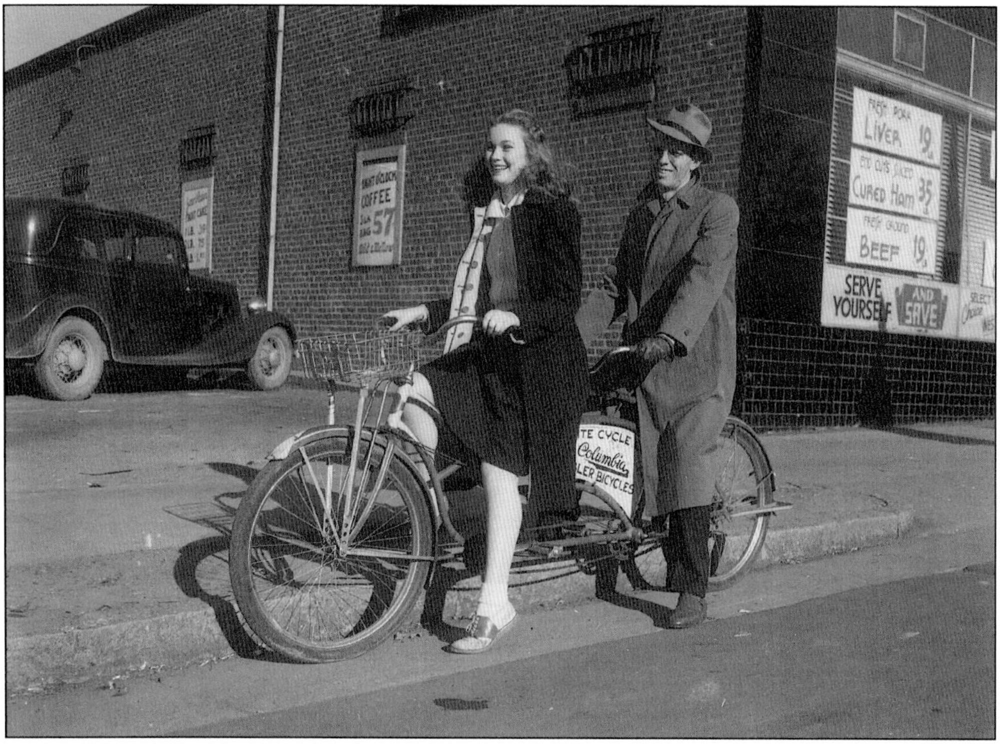

James White Jr. and a friend ride on a Colson tandem in front of the A&P in Rock Hill about 1940.

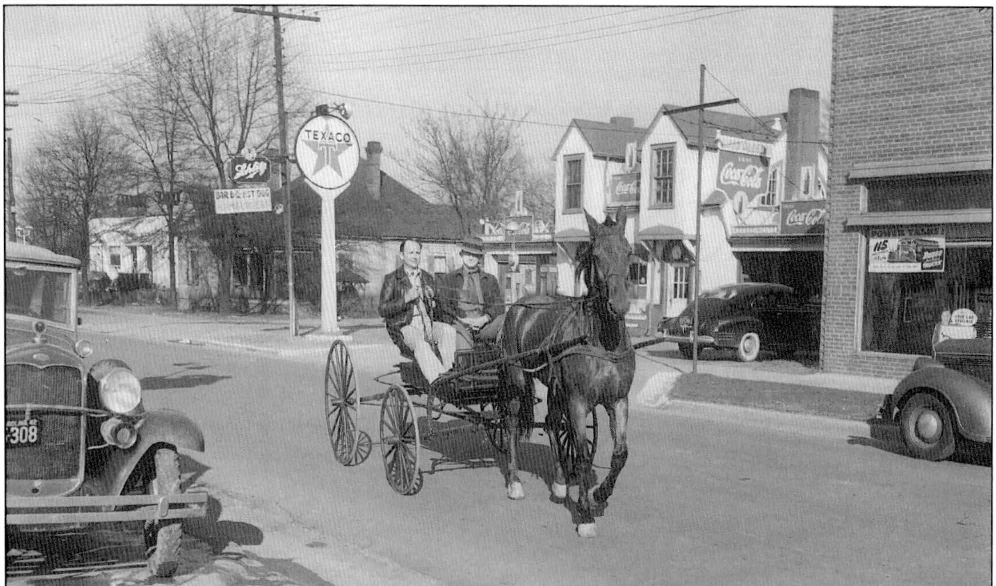

Ed Allen and Harris Williams, who owned gas stations across Oakland Avenue from each other, ride in a horse and buggy in front of their stations in this 1942 image. That is a Model A Ford on the left.

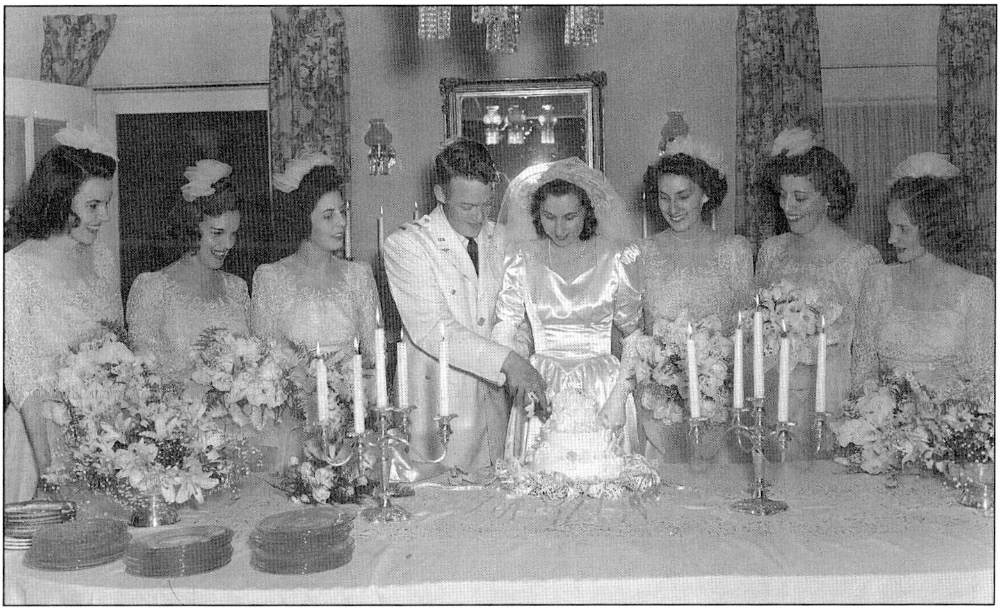

Weddings in the Catawba region are generally an occasion for families to gather. This is the wedding party of Goodwin Thomas and Nancy Craig in 1943.

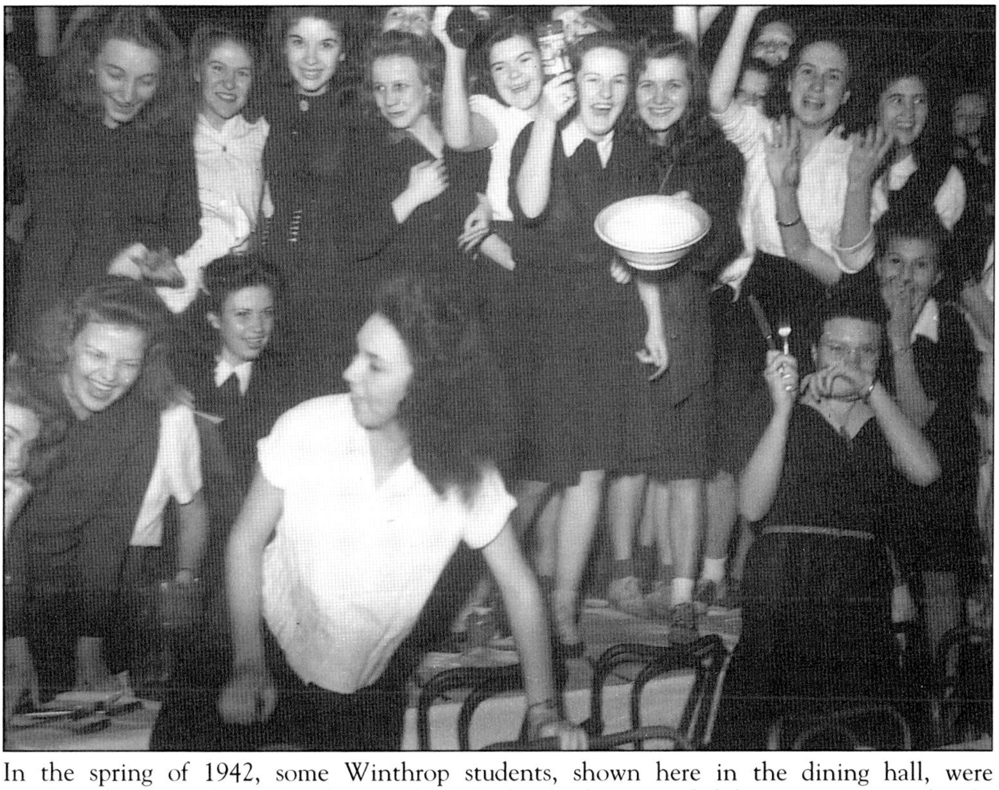

In the spring of 1942, some Winthrop students, shown here in the dining hall, were accidentally skipped over by the people with the food carts and did not receive any lunch. The students jumped up on the tables and pointed to their empty bowls, indicating their lack of sustenance.

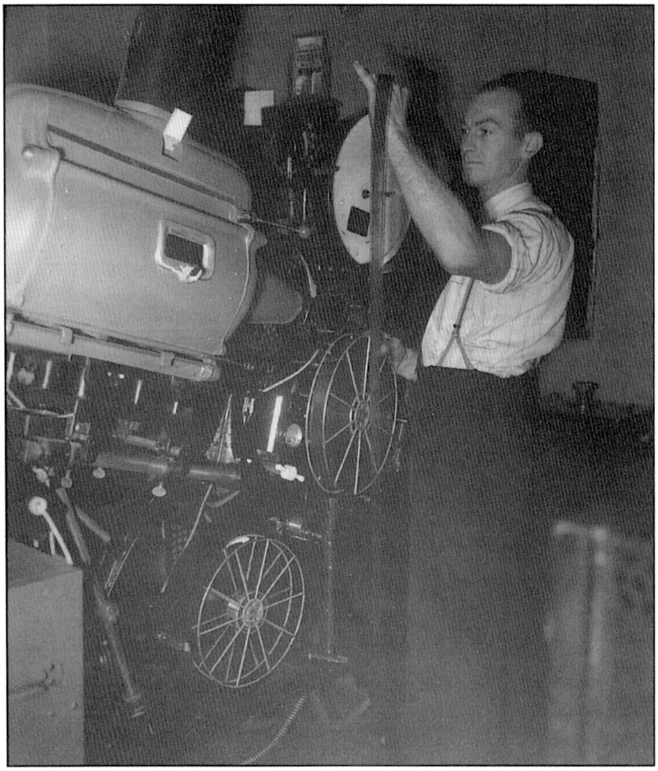

Movies became an integral part of weekend fun during the middle part of the 20th century. Theater assistant manager and projectionist Carroll Hester works on a film in Rock Hill in the late 1930s.

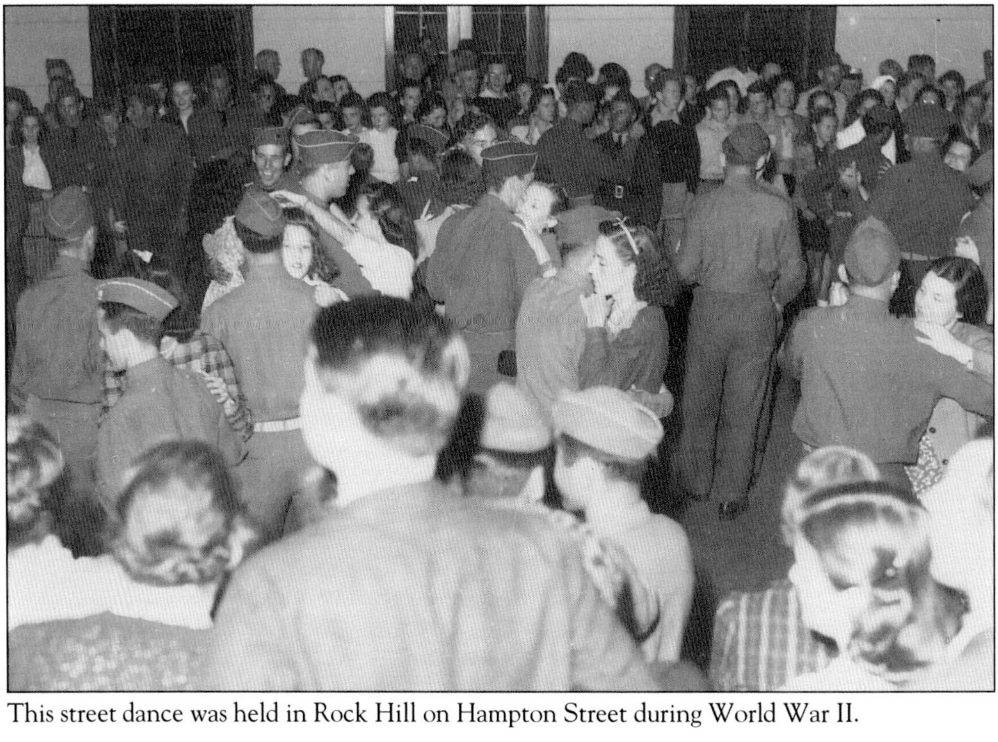

This street dance was held in Rock Hill on Hampton Street during World War II.

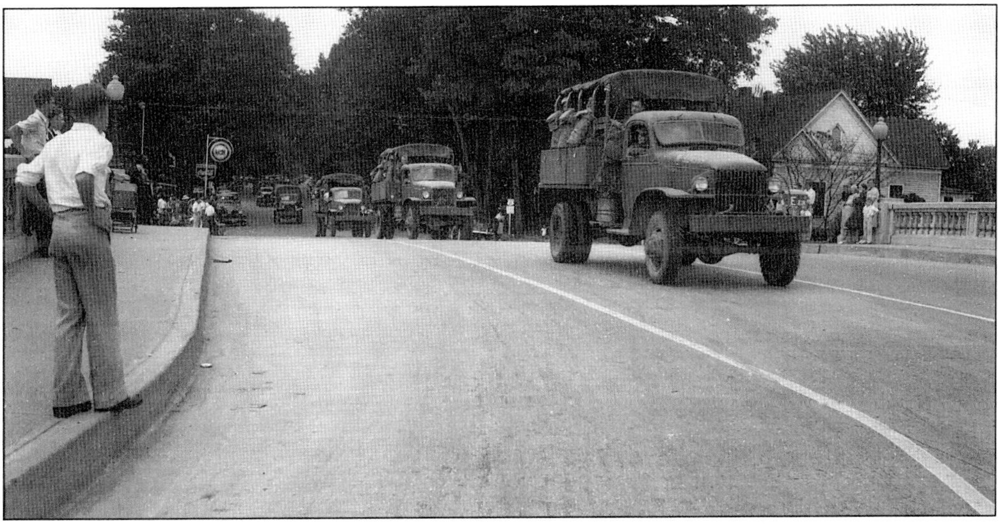

In 1941, the U.S. Army conducted maneuvers in the Catawba region. Above is a convoy going over the bridge on Oakland Avenue in Rock Hill. In the image below, soldiers have built a pontoon bridge across the river.

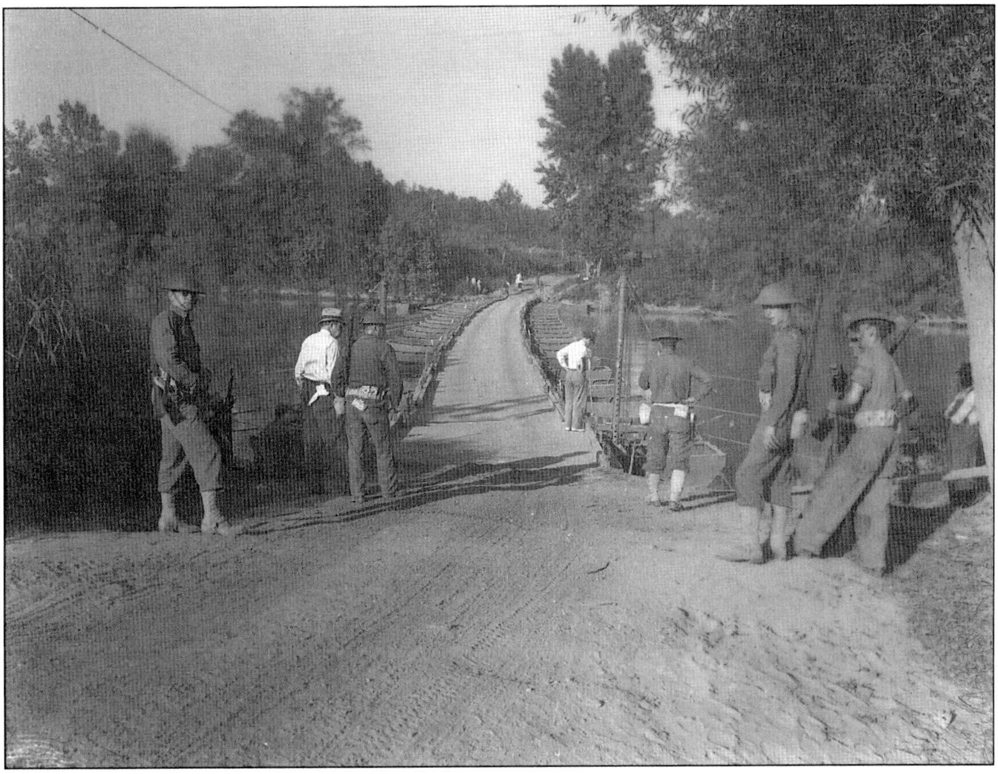

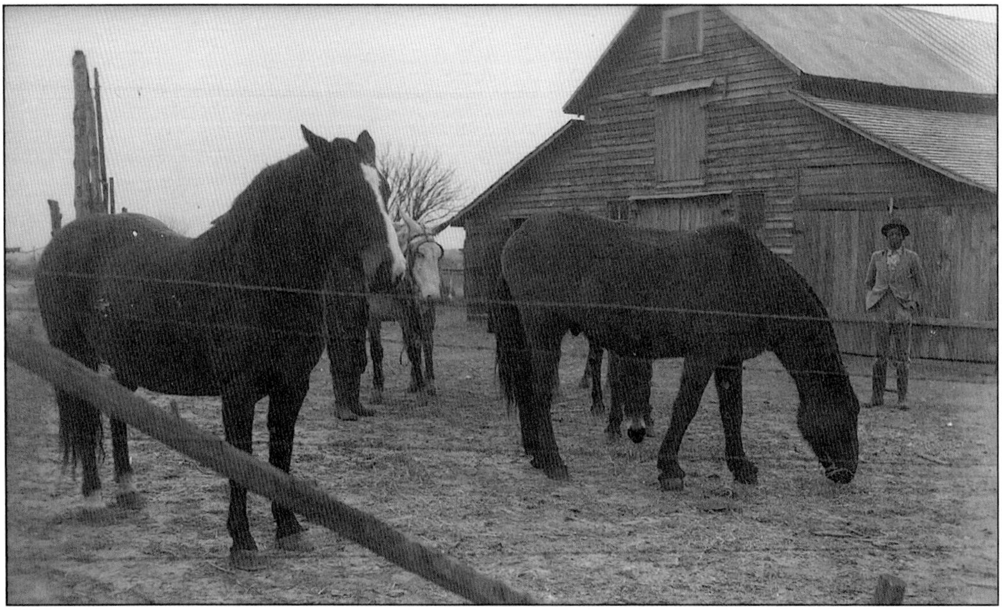

A typical Catawba Region farm is seen here in the 1940s.

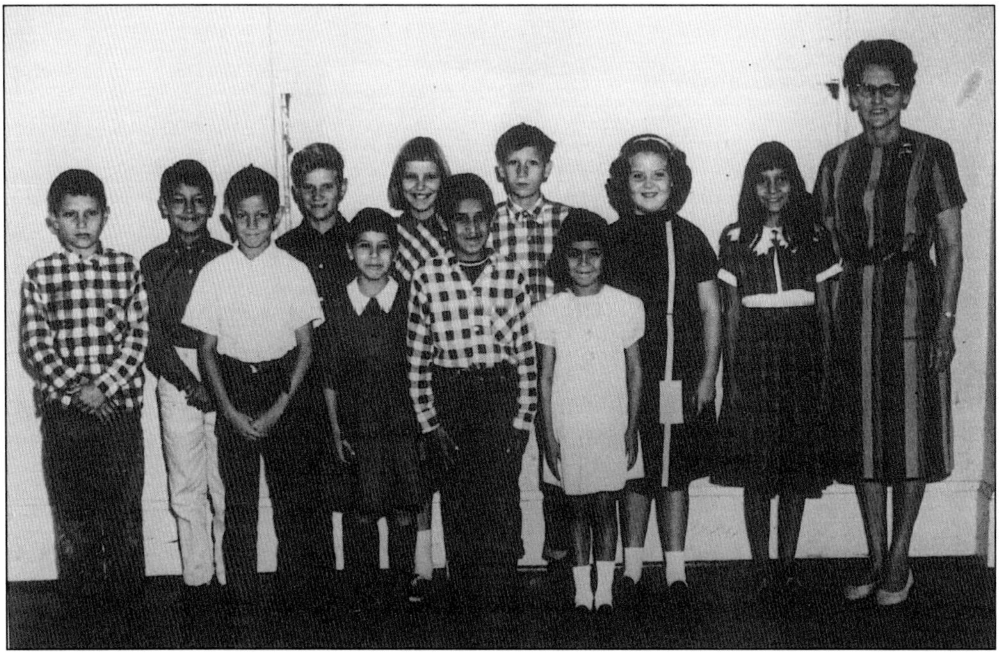

Mrs. Robinson and the third and fourth grade classes at the Catawba Indian Elementary School are pictured here in the 1960s.

Lancaster County put out a brochure extolling the many advantages of living there in the late 1950s.

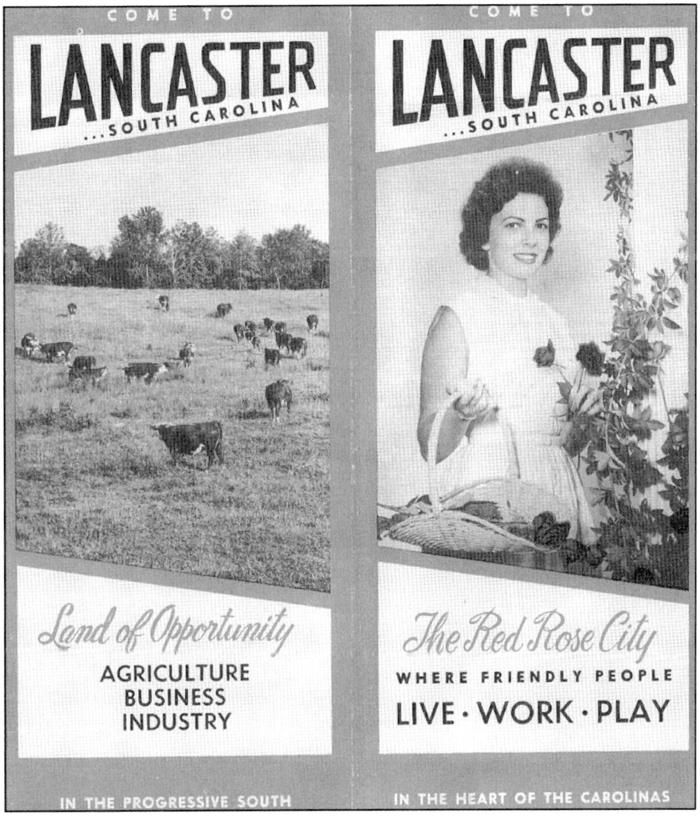

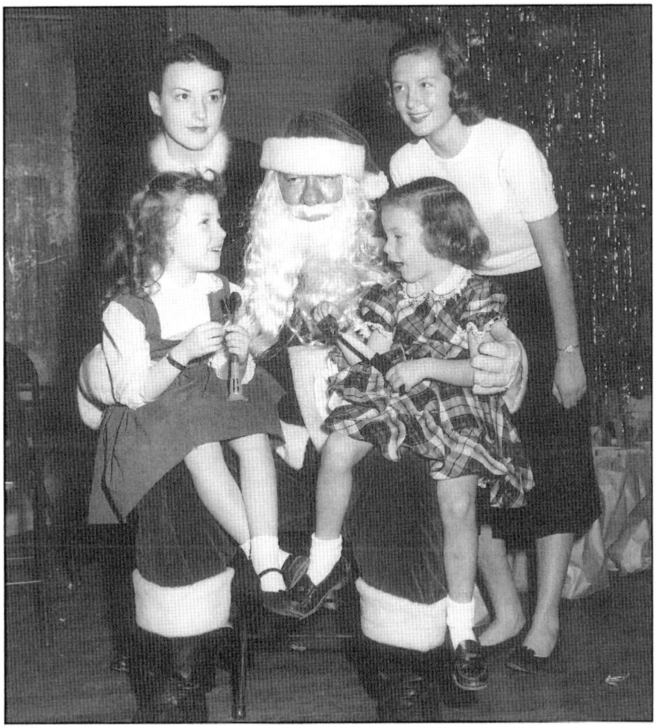

Christmas was a special time for families in the Tri-County area. Pictured here on December 25, 1956, from left to right are Wylene Grant, Vicki Clinard, Frances Moore, and Tracy McDill.

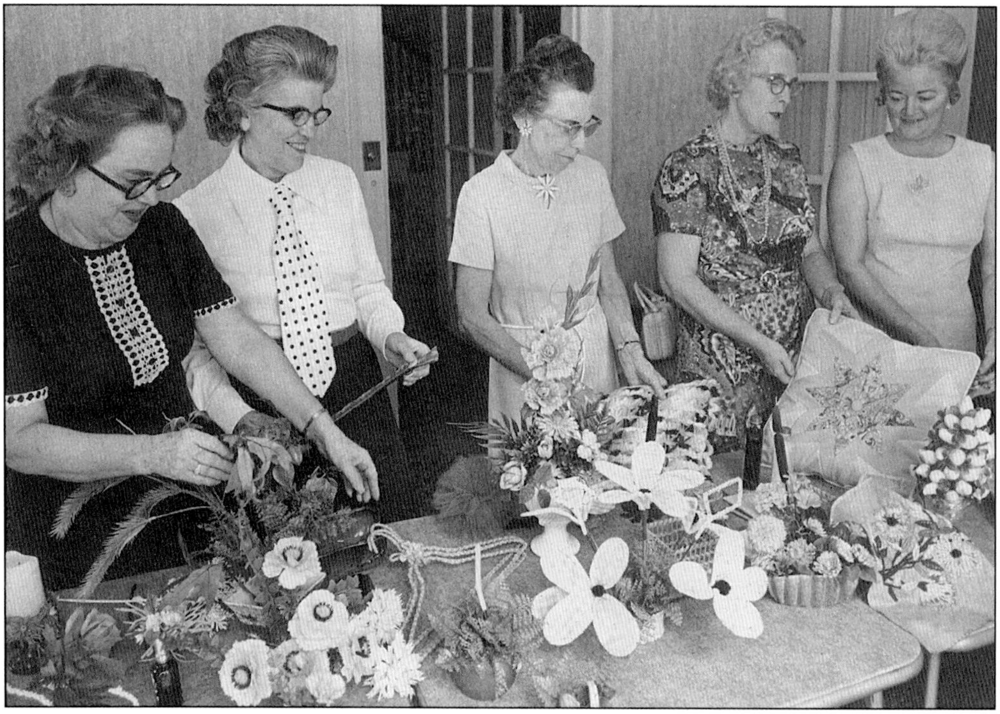

Many Catawba region women throughout the 20th century have belonged to organizations and clubs. Here, the Women's Club of Rock Hill displays some of the items for sale in 1973.

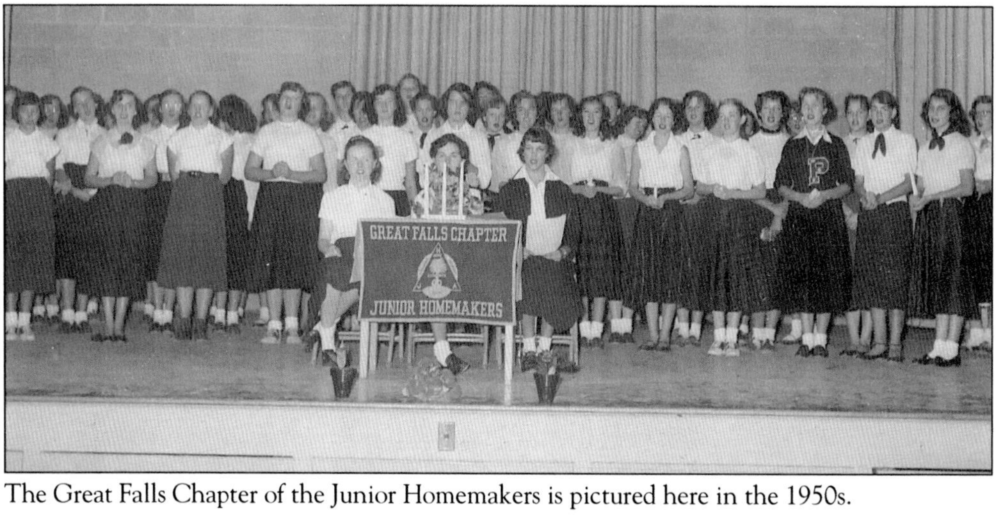

The Great Falls Chapter of the Junior Homemakers is pictured here in the 1950s.

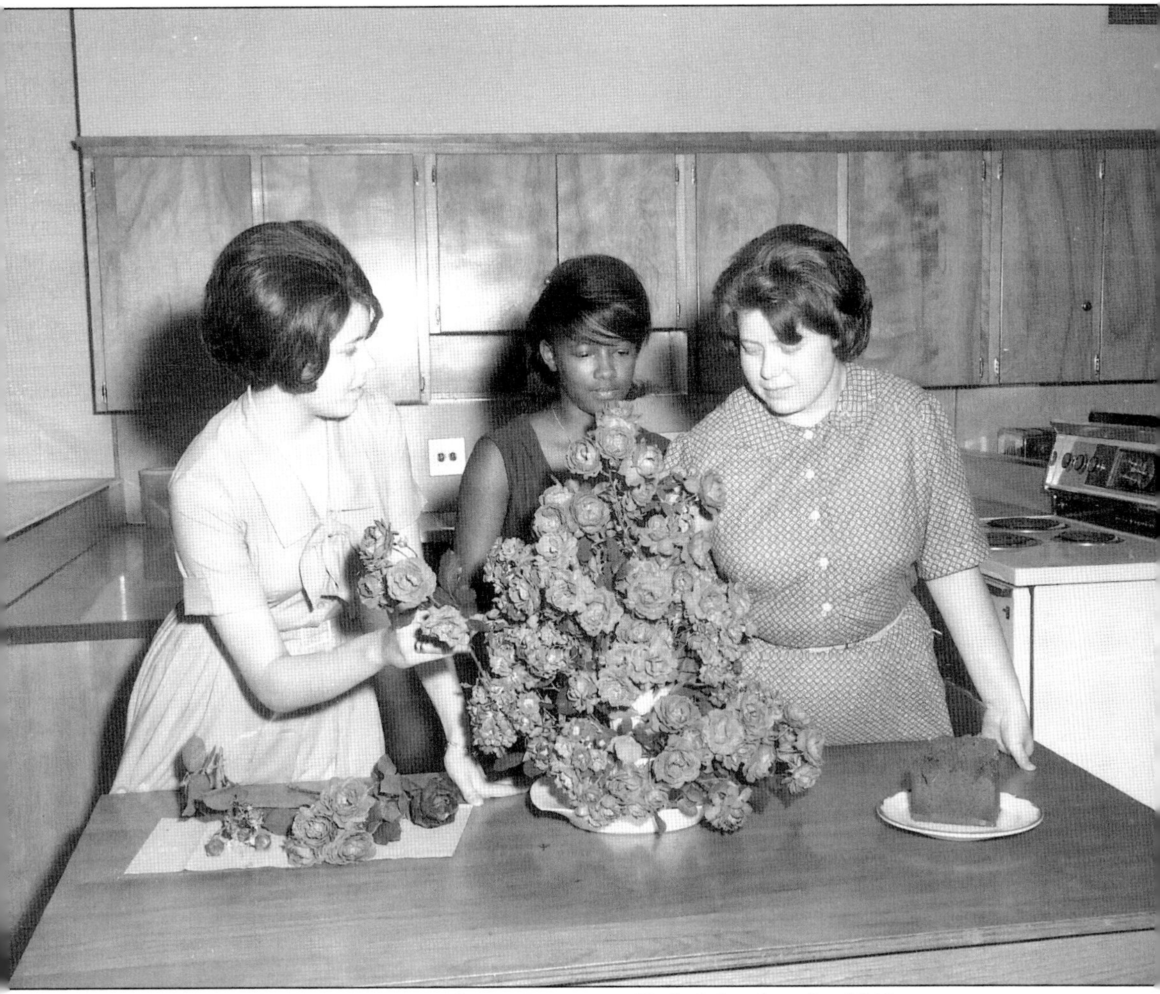

Pictured here is a home economics class at Lancaster High School in the 1960s.

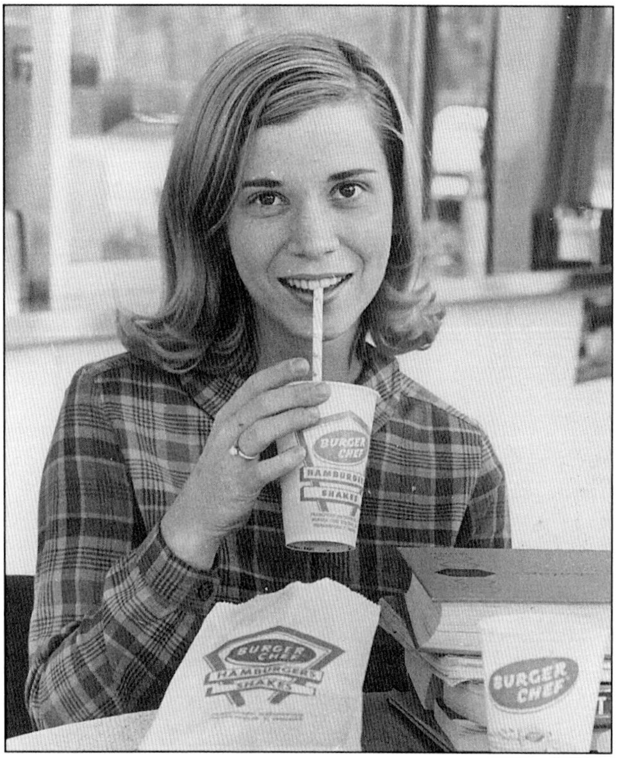

A Winthrop student enjoys the food at the Burger Chef on Cherry Road in Rock Hill in the 1960s.

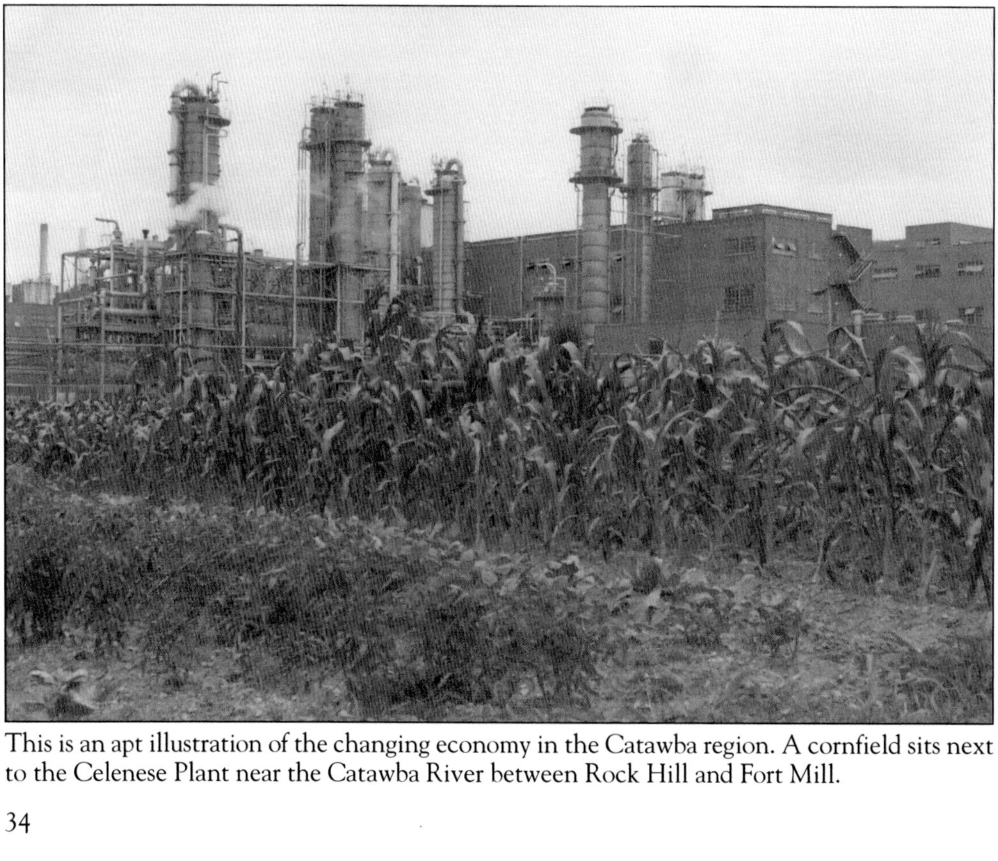

This is an apt illustration of the changing economy in the Catawba region. A cornfield sits next to the Celenese Plant near the Catawba River between Rock Hill and Fort Mill.

Two

EDUCATION

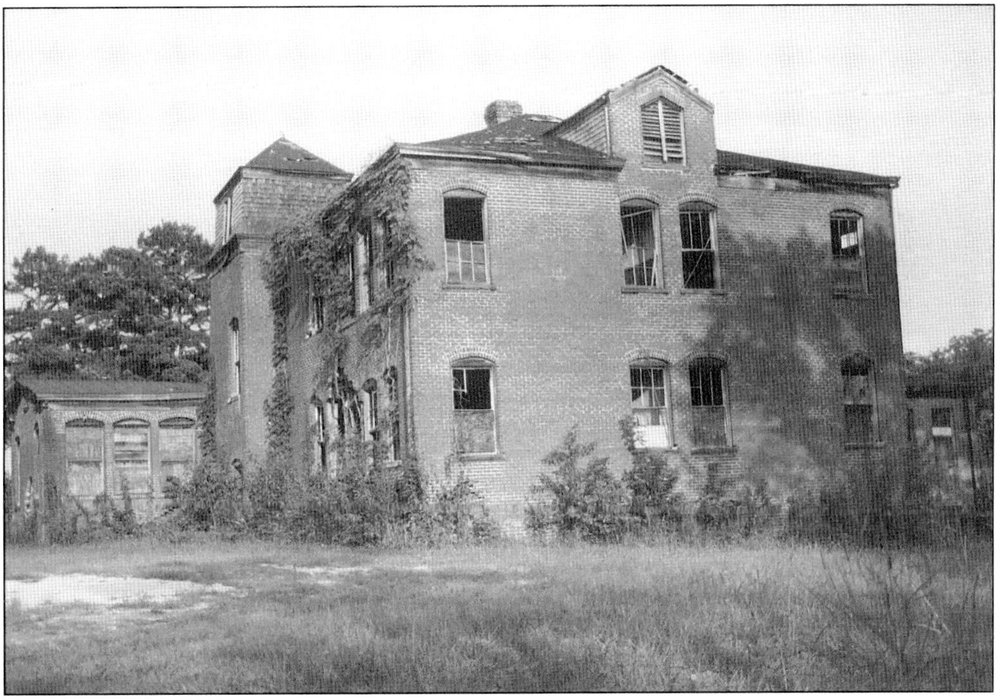

Brainerd Institute, a prominent Chester County landmark, began in 1866 as a Presbyterian-supported school for recently freed African Americans. This building, Tweed Hall, no longer exists.

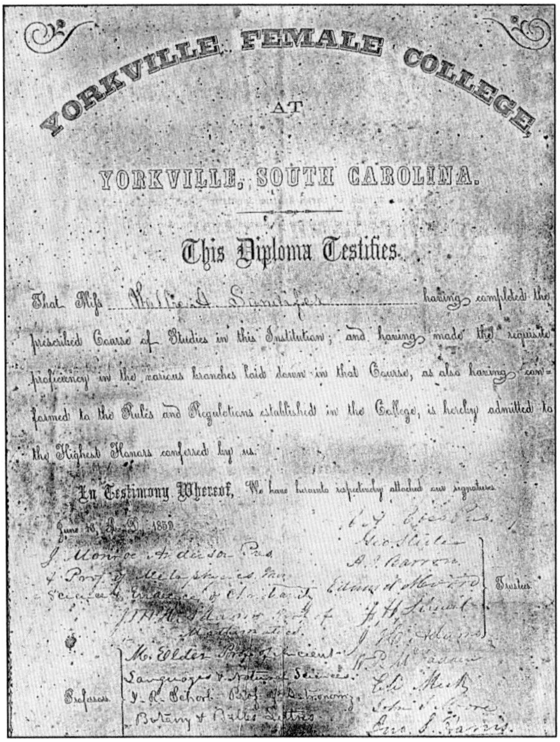

YORKVILLE FEMALE COLLEGE

AT

YORKVILLE, SOUTH CAROLINA.

This Diploma Testifies.

That Miss Sallie A. Sandifer having completed the prescribed Course of Studies in this Institution; and having made the requisite proficiency in the various branches laid down in that Course, as also having conformed to the Rules and Regulations established in the College, is hereby admitted to the Highest Honors conferred by us.

In Testimony Whereof, We have hereunto respectively attached our signatures.

June 10, A.D. 1859.

This faded 1859 diploma is the oldest educational document in the Winthrop Archives. Sallie A. Sandifer was its recipient.

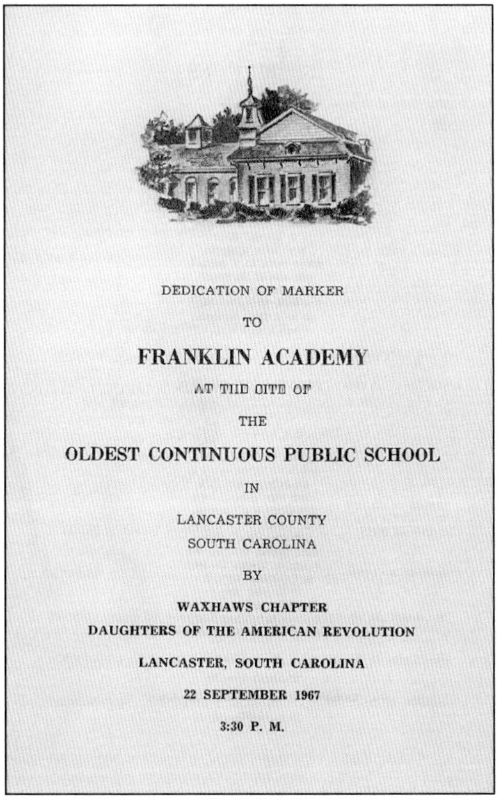

DEDICATION OF MARKER

TO

FRANKLIN ACADEMY

AT THE SITE OF

THE

OLDEST CONTINUOUS PUBLIC SCHOOL

IN

LANCASTER COUNTY

SOUTH CAROLINA

BY

WAXHAWS CHAPTER

DAUGHTERS OF THE AMERICAN REVOLUTION

LANCASTER, SOUTH CAROLINA

22 SEPTEMBER 1967

3:30 P. M.

Organized in 1925 in Lancaster County, the Franklin Academy was the most widely known of the four schools that occupied the site. Henry Connelly was the school's first principal, and J. Marion Sims, who would later achieve fame as a surgeon, was a student there.

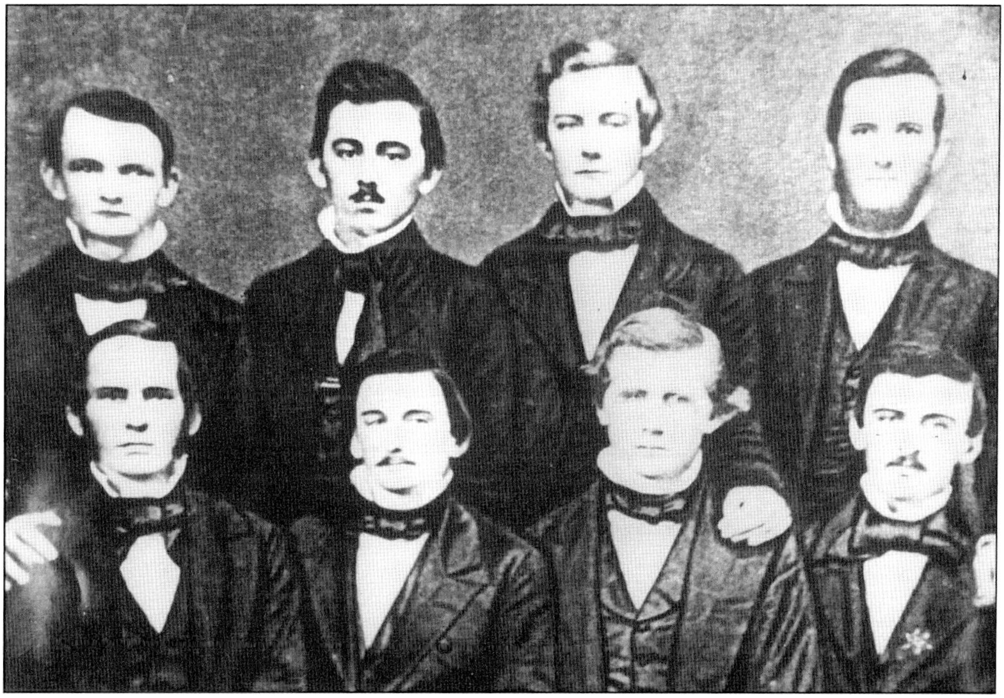

Many of Chester's young people continued their education in Columbia at South Carolina College, now the University of South Carolina. Taken in 1850, this photo shows students who were residents of a tenement known as "Egypt." They are, from left to right, (front row) Sam Melton, Thomas McLure, J. Lucius Gaston, and John Neely; (back row) J.H. Henderson, Harry Hammond, J. Brown Gaston, and David H. Porter.

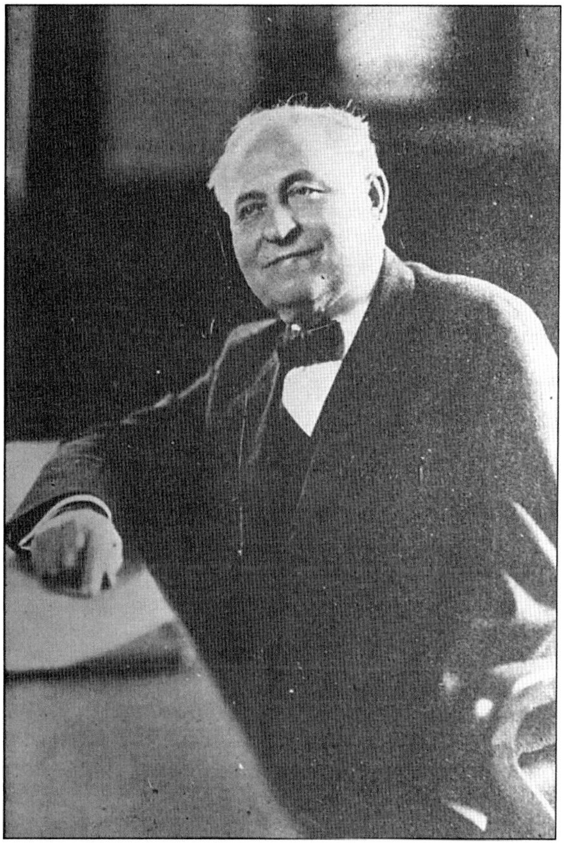

D.B. Johnson (1856–1928) was one of 20th-century South Carolina's greatest educators. He founded Winthrop College in Columbia in 1886, and, after moving the school to Rock Hill in 1895, it grew to be one of the largest women's colleges in the country. Today, Winthrop is fully co-educational and has more than 5,500 students.

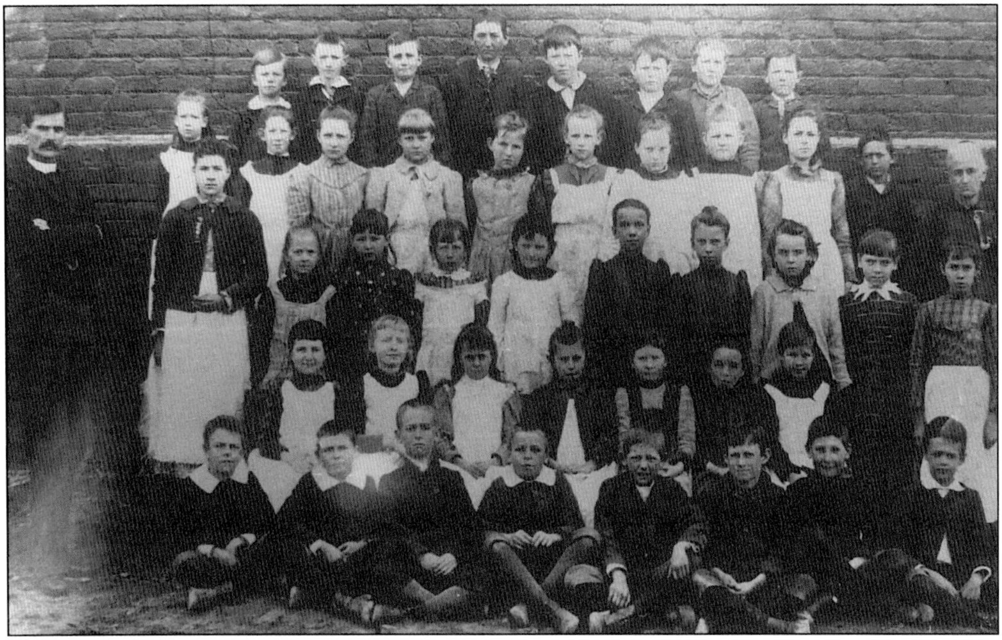

Shown here are the third and fourth graders of Chester's Academy Street School in 1891. The teachers were John C. Douglas and Mrs. Bland. Pictured, from left to right, as best as can be determined, are (front row) Jimmy Daniel, unknown, Cal Ratteree, Raymond Thompson, Ned Graham, Hall Murphy, Nixon Stringfellow, and Frank Spratt; (second row) Sadie Gunhouse, Blanche Gunhouse, Elfreida Nail, Mamie Ferguson, Angie Thompson, Amelia Ratteree, and Ethel Cross; (third row) Mamie Reid, Effie Steinkuhler, ? Allen, Mary McAliley, Edna McLure, Cora Hardin, Lola Hardin, Minnie Timmie, Mary Owen, and ? Young; (fourth row) Kate Mills, Sara Coleman, Annie Belle Morgan, Eugenia Jaggers, Beatrice Walker, Alexa McClure, Belle Simrill, and ? Pritchard; (fifth row) Lucia Mills, George McFadden, Henry White, McFadden Neely, Joe Cloud, Gus Fennell, Pete Fennell, Glenn Carroll, and Albert Steinkuhler.

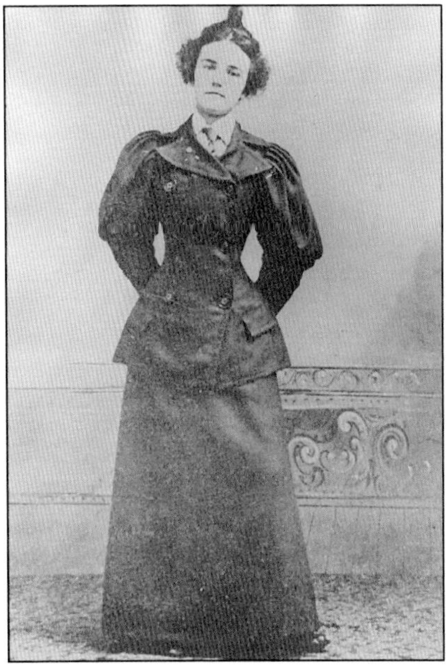

A Winthrop student models the winter uniform for the 1896–1897 school term. Winthrop students were required to wear uniforms until 1954. The rationale for uniforms was that it would break down the distinction between rich and poor students.

Incorporated in 1905, the Lancaster Normal and Industrial Institute on East Barr Street in Lancaster was a school for African-American students. M.D. Lee was the president, and J.G. McIlwain was the chairman of the board. By 1912, the school was offering elementary and advanced education to a number of students.

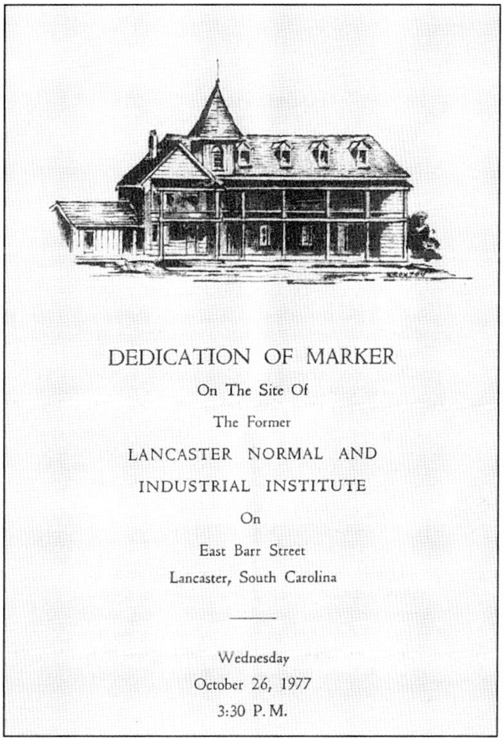

DEDICATION OF MARKER

On The Site Of

The Former

LANCASTER NORMAL AND

INDUSTRIAL INSTITUTE

On

East Barr Street

Lancaster, South Carolina

Wednesday

October 26, 1977

3:30 P.M.

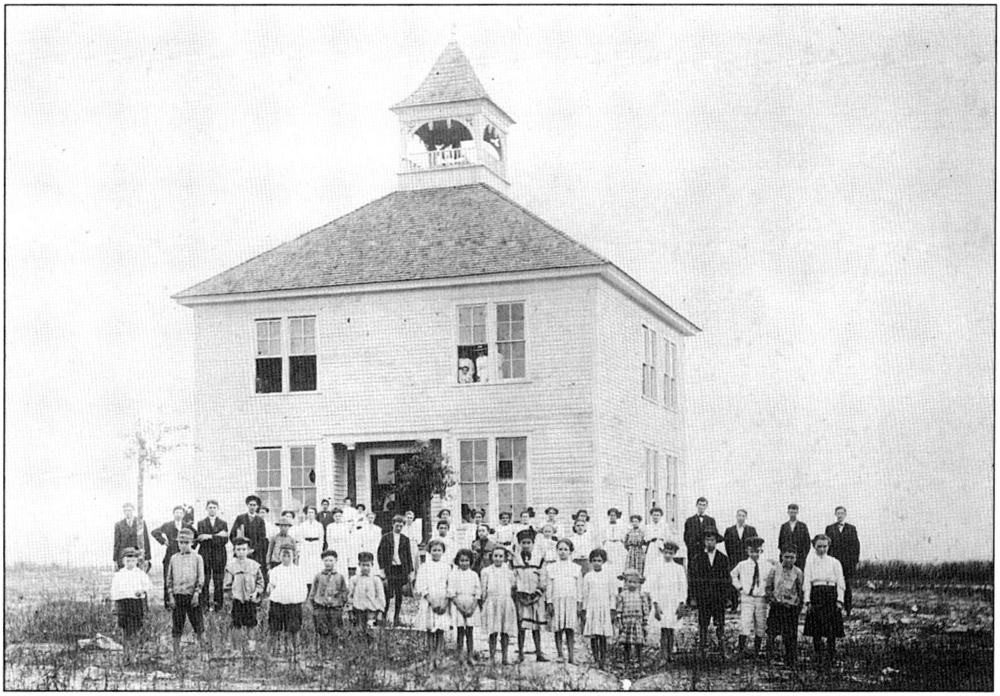

The students of Richburg High School in Chester County pose for a photo in 1911, about a year after their building was constructed. It was torn down in 1950.

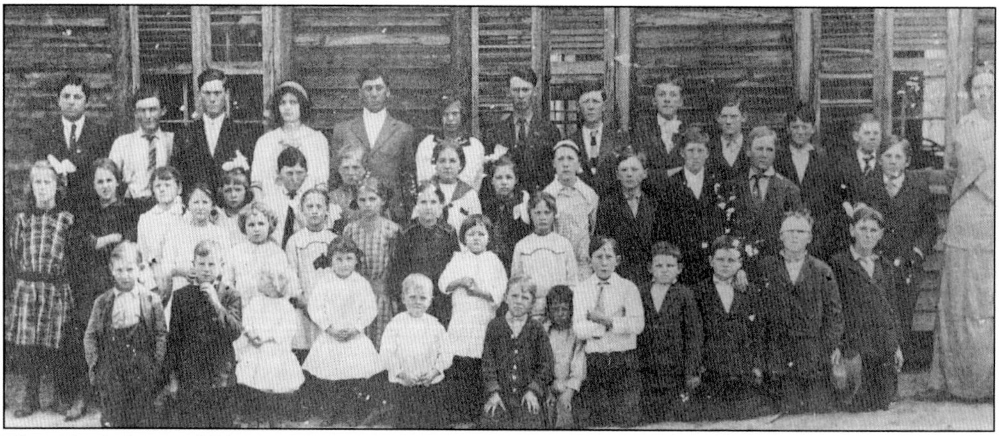

This 1916 photo of Chester County's New Hope School, which is no longer in existence, shows students from grades one to seven standing outside the school building. Pictured, from left to right, are (front row) W.O. Gladden, Ural Thomas, Pearl Dodds, Eula Mae Lipford, Jesse Dodds, Alva Grant, Lindsey Dodds, Tom Lackey, Lander Dodds, Johnny Dodds, Richard Gregory, and T.H. Gladden; (second row beginning behind Ural Thomas) Kate Lackey, Christeen Pressley, Ida Grant, Lois Gladden, Annette Gregory, Mary Edith Pressley, and Iva Grant; (third row) Beth Grant, Louise Pressley, Louise Lipford, Helen Pressley, Rudolph Lipford, Malcolm Thomas, Annie Pressley, Agadale Grant, Annie Lackey, Malva Lipford, White Grant, John Gregory, and Clyde Grant; (back row) teacher Adam Pressley, Alga Grant, Charlton Lipford, Ainsley Grant, Maddie Allen, Sam Grant, Lola Allen, Ezra Lipford, Fred Grant, Leon Pressley, Claude Lipford, Melvin Lipford, Vernon Thomas, and teacher Mrs. Adam Pressley.

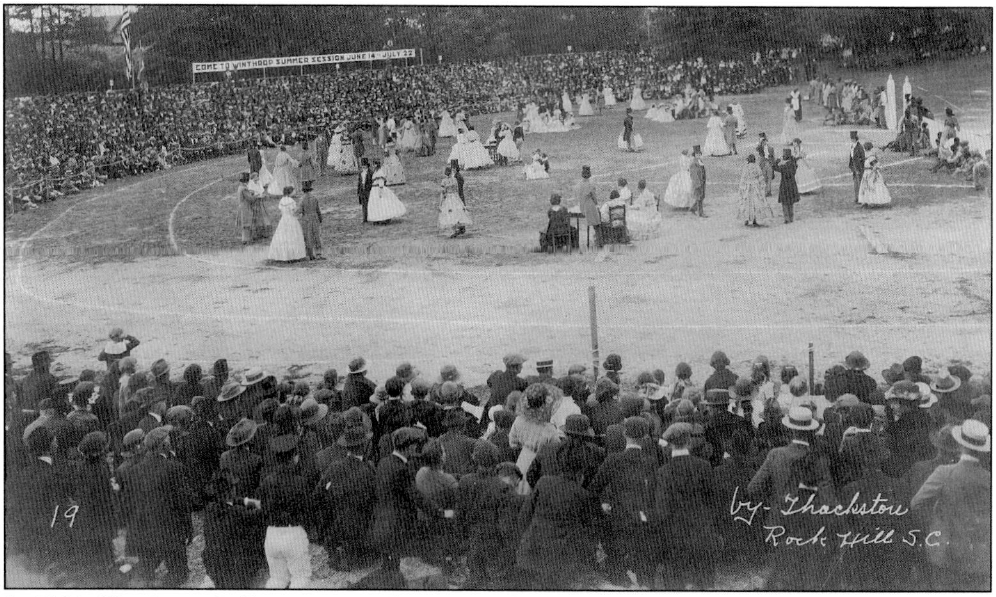

In 1921, Winthrop College sponsored a spectacular historical pageant, which concentrated on the theme of South Carolina history and attracted thousands of people from all over the state.

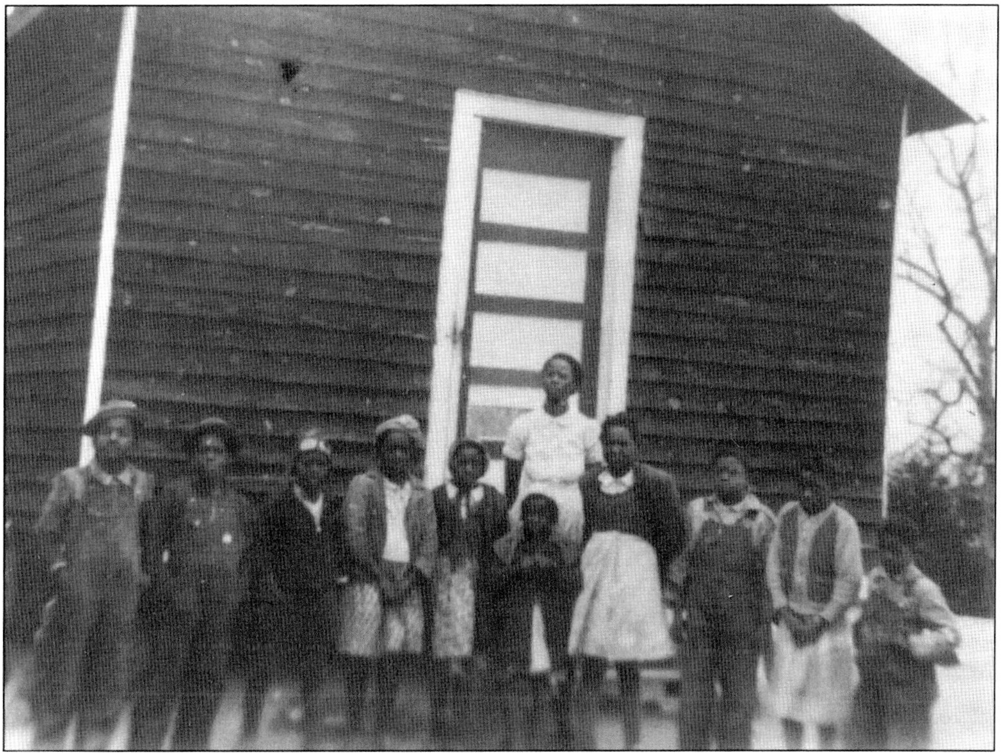

Prior to 1921, public education for African Americans in South Carolina was limited to grades one through six. A school directory for 1919 lists 53 one-teacher African-American schools in Chester County and no schools that had more than three teachers. By 1939, several African-American schools had sufficiently increased their enrollment enough to warrant hiring more than one teacher. However, Roddey School, pictured here, still had only one teacher.

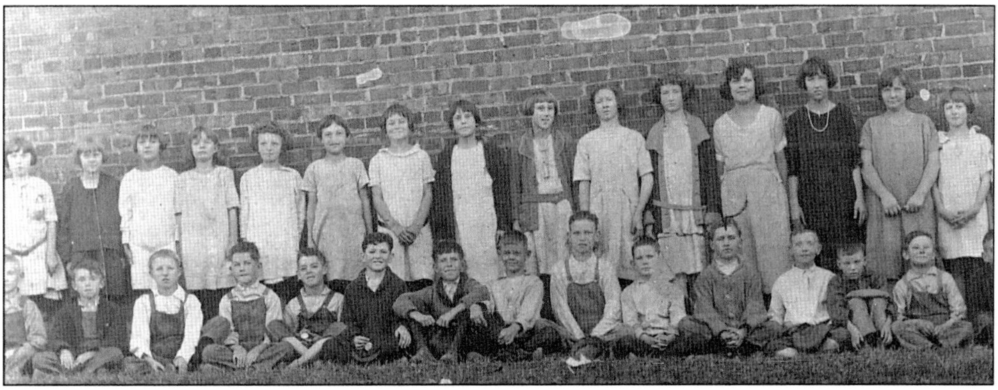

Third and fourth grade students from Lando School in Chester County pose for this photo.

THE CATAWBAN

JOKES

Queen Elizabeth was a very wise, good Queen, and so she never married.

* * *

Mr. Wright: How many wars were waged against Spain?
Joe Robinson: Six, sir.
Mr. W.: Enumerate them.
Joe: One, two, three, four, five, six.

* * *

Mr. W.: What part did the U. S. Navy play in the war?
Banks Good: It played the Star Spangled Banner.

* * *

Mrs. White: What is an abstract noun?
Joe White: An abstract noun is something you can't see when you are looking at it.

* * *

Miss Roddey: Name the parts of speech.
John Lesslie: Lungs and air.

* * *

Mrs. White: What is the future of "he drinks?"
J. T. Givens: "He is drunk."

* * *

Mr. Moseley: Why do you see the smoke from a gun before you hear the report.
Elmer Strait: Because the smoke comes out of the gun before the report.

* * *

Miss Williams: What is a circle?
Roy Purvis: A circle is a line of no depth running around a dot forever.

* * *

Laura O'Neal: Why does cream rise to the top?
Jean Twitty: So people can get it.

Poem by Senior English students:
As I was laying on the green
A small English book I seen
Carlyle's essay on Burns was the edition
So I left it lay in the same position.

* * *

Mr. Hurd: What made the tower of Pisa lean?
Elmer Strait: There was a famine in the land.

* * *

To stop a nosebleed, stand on your head till your heart stops beating.

* * *

A sincere friend is one who says nasty nasty things to your face, instead of saying them behind your back.

* * *

Citizens of the United States may be either male or female upon reaching the age of twenty-one, if of good moral character.

* * *

The form of government in Russia is chaos.

* * *

Forgive us our debts as we forgive our dentists.

* * *

The cold at the North Pole is so great that the towns there are not inhabited.

* * *

Climate is caused by the emotion of the earth around the sun.

* * *

The Puritans found an insane asylum in the wilds of America.

* * *

A well known proverb: "It is a long worm that hath no turning."

1931

Students still had a sense of humor during the Great Depression, as this page from Rock Hill High School's 1931 yearbook, the *Catawban*, shows.

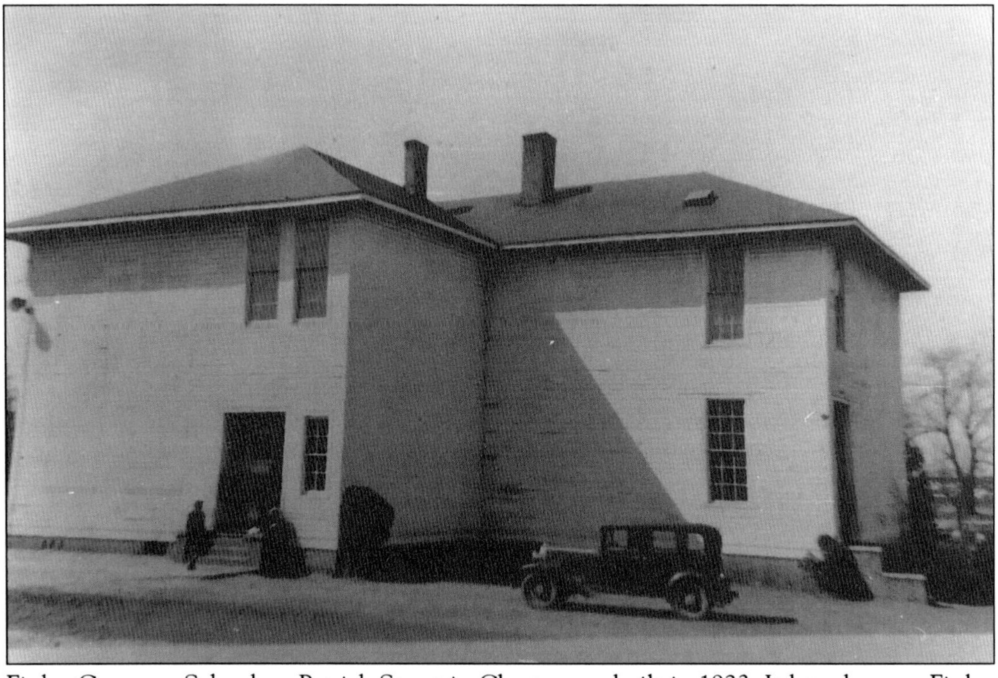

Finley Grammar School on Patrick Street in Chester was built in 1923. It later became Finley Junior High.

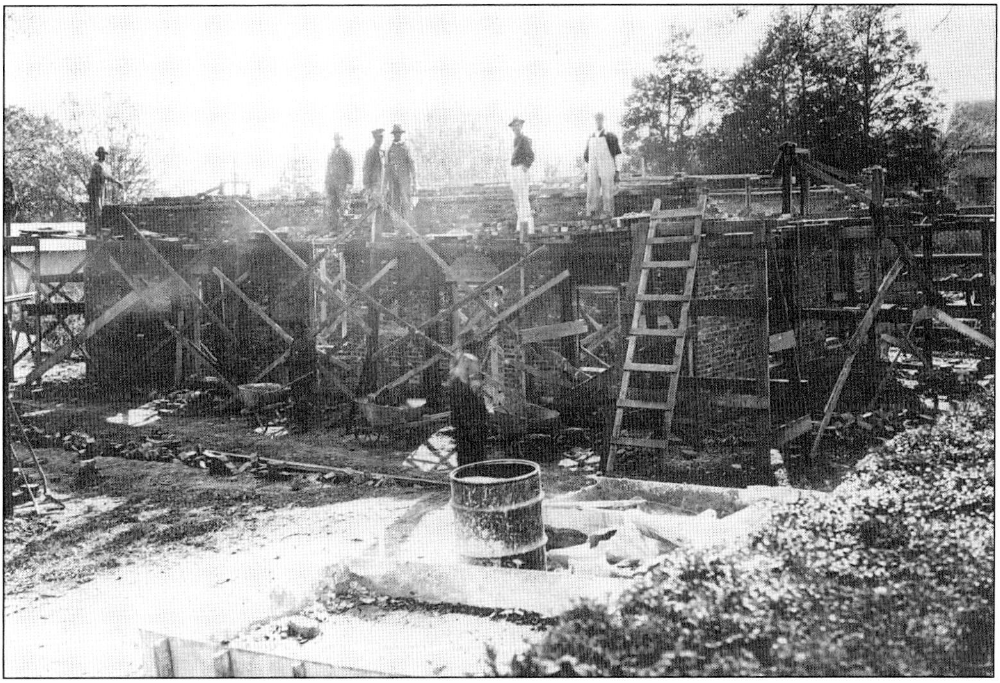

The Little Chapel was the home of Winthrop during its first year of operation (1886–1887) when it was located in Columbia, South Carolina. Officially named the Columbian Seminary Chapel, the Little Chapel was initially built to serve as the stable and carriage house on the grounds of the Ainsley Hall mansion in Columbia about 1823. In 1830, the building was converted into a chapel for the Columbian Theological Seminary, and, in 1936, the building was transported to Rock Hill brick by brick and reconstructed on the Winthrop campus.

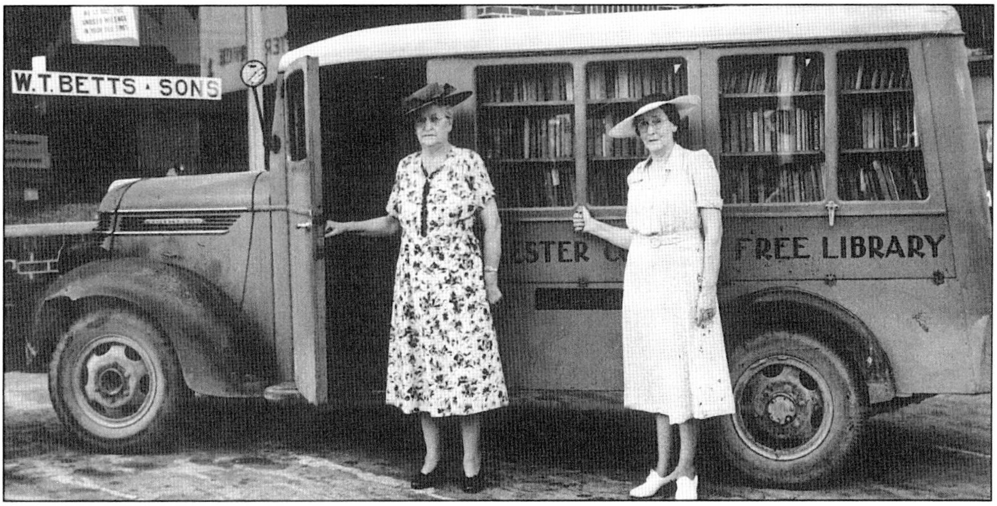

On May 18, 1938, a bright yellow truck was driven up to the back of the Chester County Courthouse and was officially christened the Chester County Free Library. This was the start of regular bookmobile service for Chester County. In 1948, the county took over the responsibility for the service, and the library became known as the Chester County Library. Pictured above are, from left to right, Mrs. Daisy Bonning (driver) and Mrs. Laverne McLane (bookmobile librarian).

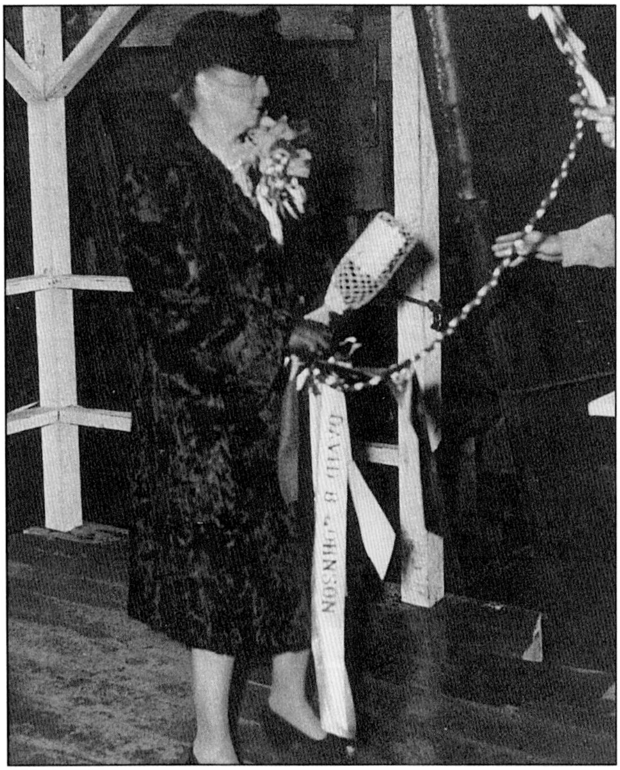

In 1944, Mrs. D.B. Johnson, the wife of Winthrop's late founder David Bancroft Johnson, went to Brunswick, Georgia, to christen the liberty ship, the S.S. *David B. Johnson.* Liberty ships were special cargo ships named for outstanding Americans and delivered badly needed supplies to the allies during World War II.

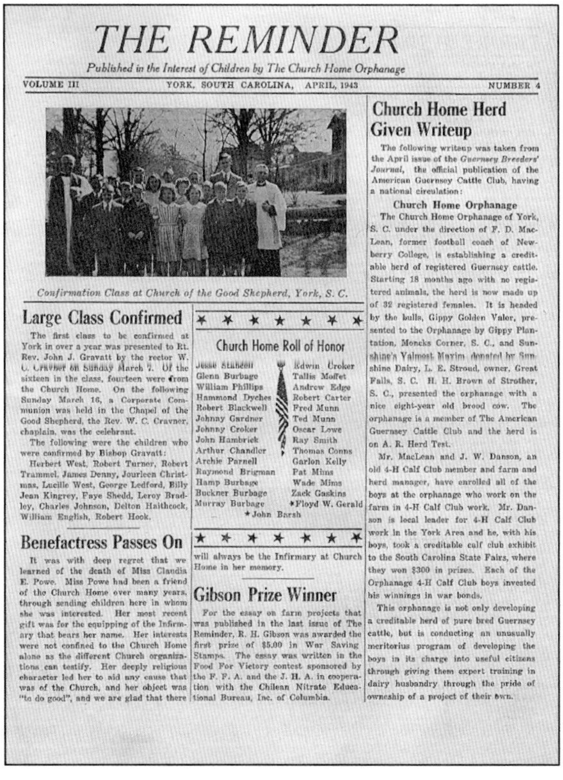

THE REMINDER

Published in the Interest of Children by The Church Home Orphanage

VOLUME III — YORK, SOUTH CAROLINA, APRIL, 1943 — NUMBER 4

Confirmation Class at Church of the Good Shepherd, York, S. C.

Large Class Confirmed

The first class to be confirmed at York in over a year was presented to Rt. Rev. John J. Gravatt by the rector W. C. Cravner on Sunday March 7. Of the sixteen in the class, fourteen were from the Church Home. On the following Sunday March 16, a Corporate Communion was held in the Chapel of the Good Shepherd, the Rev. W. C. Cravner, chaplain, was the celebrant.

The following were the children who were confirmed by Bishop Gravatt:

Herbert West, Robert Turner, Robert Trammel, James Denny, Jourleen Christmas, Lucille West, George Ledford, Billy Jean Kingrey, Faye Shedd, Leroy Bradley, Charles Johnson, Delton Haithcock, William English, Robert Hook.

Benefactress Passes On

It was with deep regret that we learned of the death of Miss Claudia E. Powe. Miss Powe had been a friend of the Church Home over many years, through sending children here in whom she was interested. Her most recent gift was for the equipping of the Infirmary that bears her name. Her interests were not confined to the Church Home alone as the different Church organizations can testify. Her deeply religious character led her to aid any cause that was of the Church, and her object was "to do good", and we are glad that there will always be the Infirmary at Church Home in her memory.

★ ★ ★ ★ ★ ★ ★

Church Home Roll of Honor

Jesse [illegible] — Edwin Croker
Glenn Burbage — Tallis Moffet
William Phillips — Andrew Edge
Hammond Dyches — Robert Carter
Robert Blackwell — Fred Munn
Johnny Gardner — Ted Munn
Johnny Croker — Oscar Lowe
John Hambrick — Ray Smith
Arthur Chandler — Thomas Conns
Archie Parnell — Garlon Kelly
Raymond Brigman — Pat Mims
Hamp Burbage — Wade Mims
Buckner Burbage — Zack Gaskins
Murray Burbage — ★Floyd W. Gerald
★John Barsh

★ ★ ★ ★ ★ ★ ★

Gibson Prize Winner

For the essay on farm projects that was published in the last issue of The Reminder, R. H. Gibson was awarded the first prize of $5.00 in War Saving Stamps. The essay was written in the Food For Victory contest sponsored by the F. F. A. and the J. H. A. in cooperation with the Chilean Nitrate Educational Bureau, Inc. of Columbia.

Church Home Herd Given Writeup

The following writeup was taken from the April issue of the *Guernsey Breeders' Journal*, the official publication of the American Guernsey Cattle Club, having a national circulation:

Church Home Orphanage

The Church Home Orphanage of York, S. C. under the direction of F. D. MacLean, former football coach of Newberry College, is establishing a creditable herd of registered Guernsey cattle. Starting 18 months ago with no registered animals, the herd is now made up of 32 registered females. It is headed by the bulls, Gippy Golden Valor, presented to the Orphanage by Gippy Plantation, Moncks Corner, S. C., and Sunshine's Valmost Maxim, donated by Sunshine Dairy, L. E. Stroud, owner, Great Falls, S. C. H. H. Brown of Strother, S. C., presented the orphanage with a nice eight-year old brood cow. The orphanage is a member of The American Guernsey Cattle Club and the herd is on A. R. Herd Test.

Mr. MacLean and J. W. Danson, an old 4-H Calf Club member and farm and herd manager, have enrolled all of the boys at the orphanage who work on the farm in 4-H Calf Club work. Mr. Danson is local leader for 4-H Calf Club work in the York Area and he, with his boys, took a creditable calf club exhibit to the South Carolina State Fairs, where they won $300 in prizes. Each of the Orphanage 4-H Calf Club boys invested his winnings in war bonds.

This orphanage is not only developing a creditable herd of pure bred Guernsey cattle, but is conducting an unusually meritorius program of developing the boys in its charge into useful citizens through giving them expert training in dairy husbandry through the pride of ownership of a project of their own.

This is the cover page of the April 1943 issue of *The Reminder*, the newspaper of the Episcopal Church Home for Children, which was later known as York Place. Founded as a church home orphanage in Charleston in 1850, the institution was moved to York (then known as Yorkville) in 1909.

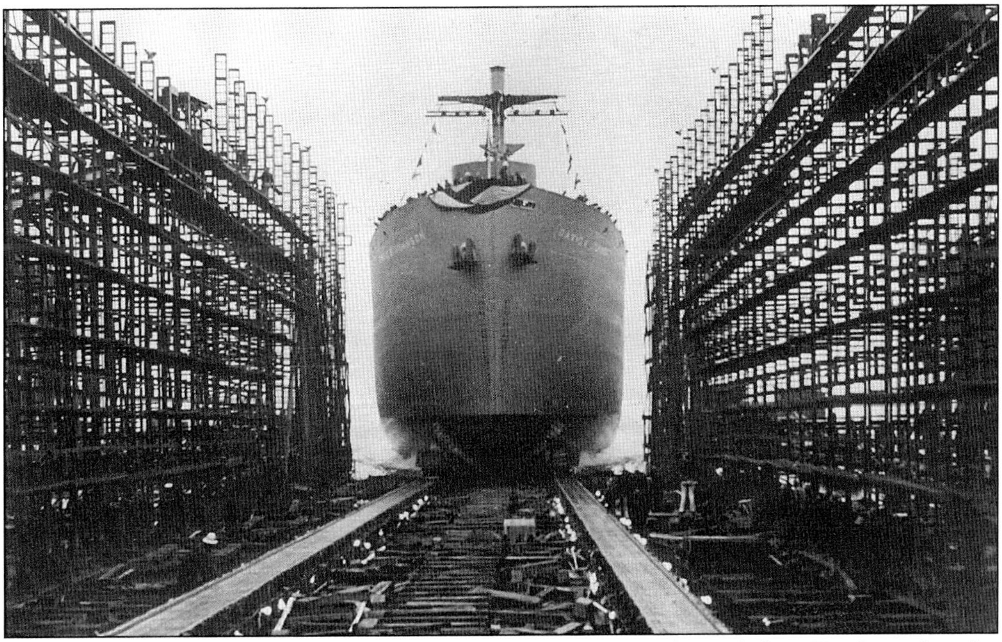

This 1944 photo shows a liberty ship named the S.S. *D.B. Johnson* (after Winthrop founder David Bancroft Johnson). Liberty ships were used to haul supplies across the Atlantic Ocean to Allied troops.

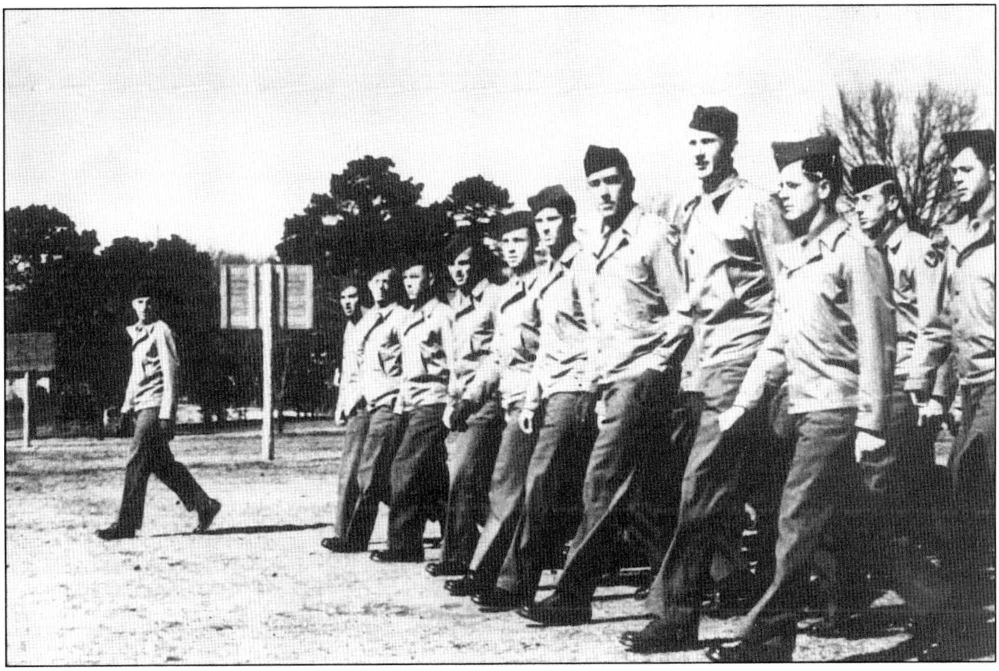

Here, cadets who were a part of the Army Air Corps Cadets program practice drills on the Winthrop campus during World War II. The program ran from 1942 to 1944 and was designed to prepare cadets both physically and mentally for pre-flight and flight school training in other parts of the country.

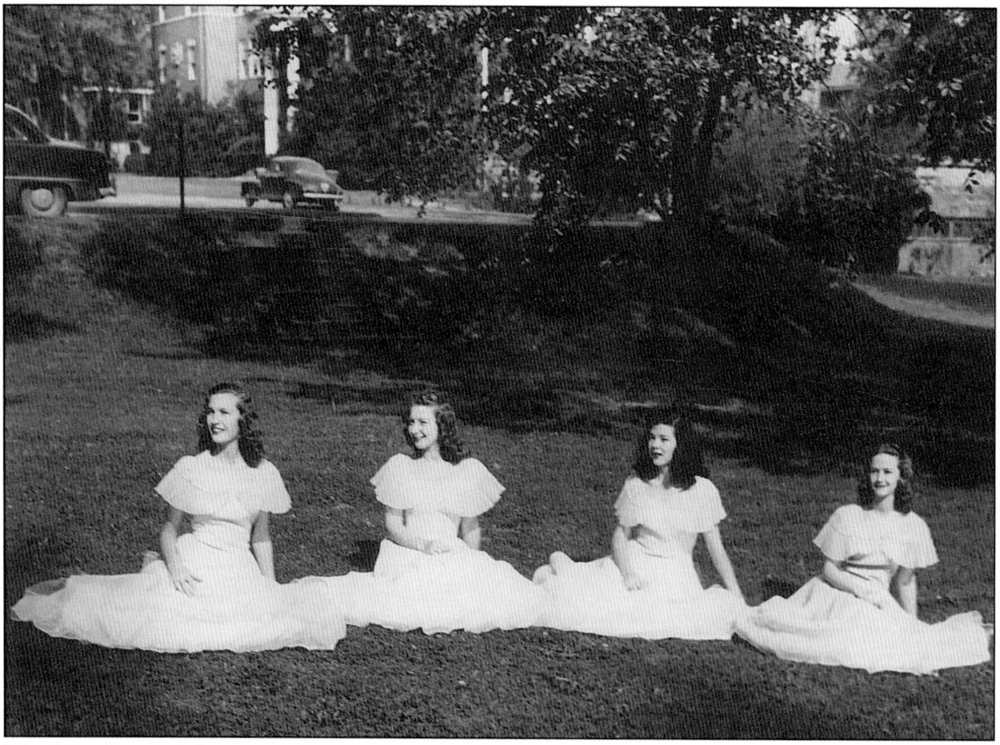

The May Day celebration, this one in 1949, was a Winthrop tradition that began in 1925. On the first Sunday in May, hundreds of parents, alumni, students, and townspeople filled the brick tiers of the amphitheater. The May court consisted of 16 handmaidens, four from each class.

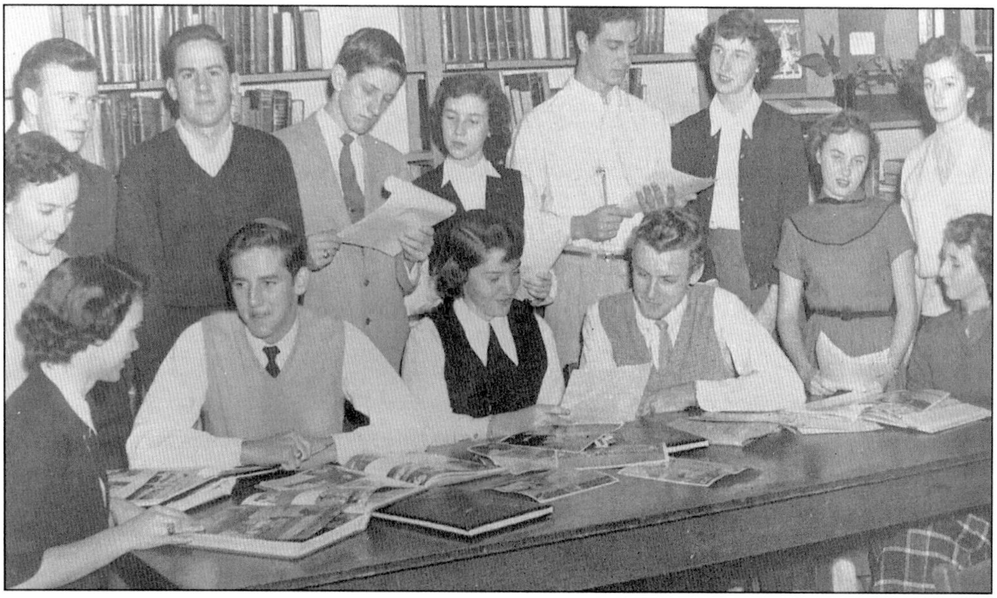

This was the staff of Chester High School's yearbook, the *Cestrian*, in 1953. Pictured, from left to right, are (front row) Wenona Eberhardt, Don Nunnery, Charlotte Plyer, Vincent Wright, and Joan Lutz; (back row) Gloria Roddey, Jimmy Still, Pick Collins, Don Crosby, Lib Joseph, Clarence Stone, Pat Bigham, Peggy Mattox, and Rose Lewis.

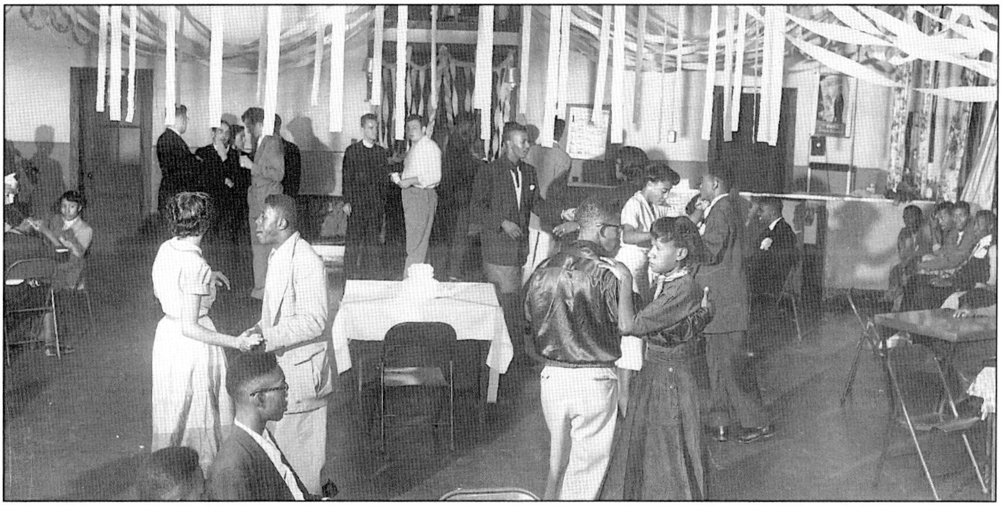

This party was held at St. Mary's Catholic Church in Rock Hill in the early 1950s.

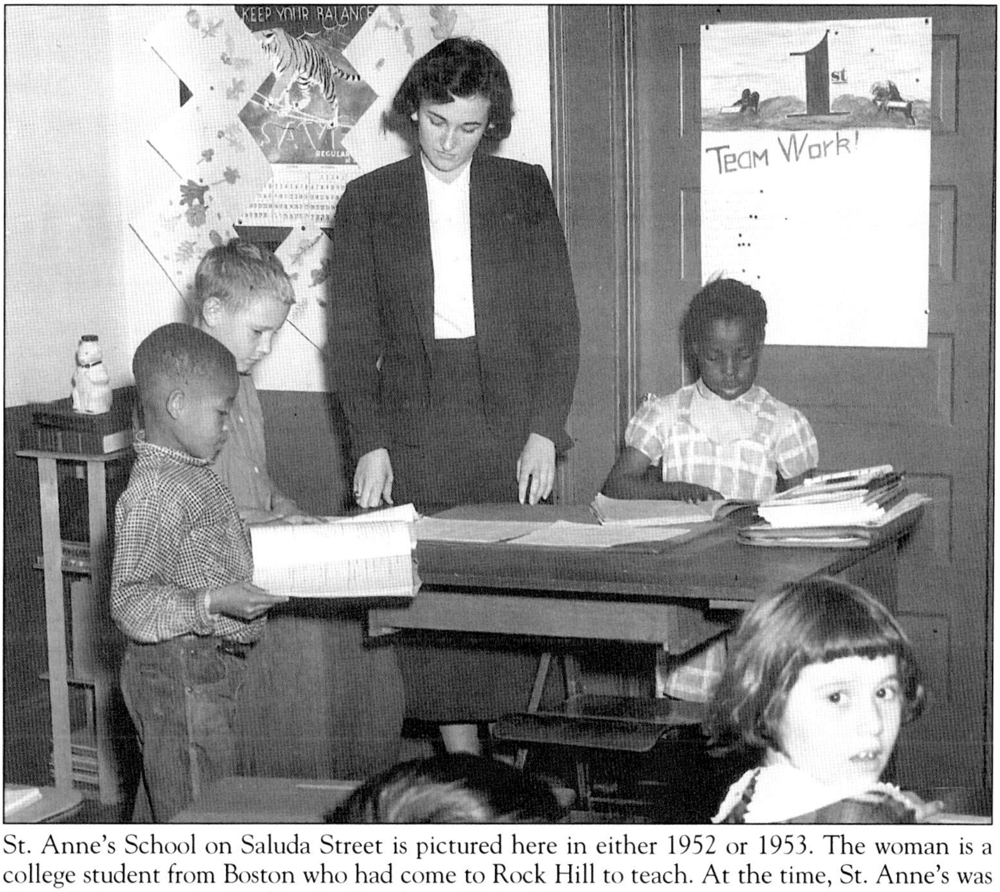

St. Anne's School on Saluda Street is pictured here in either 1952 or 1953. The woman is a college student from Boston who had come to Rock Hill to teach. At the time, St. Anne's was the only integrated school in the Southeast United States.

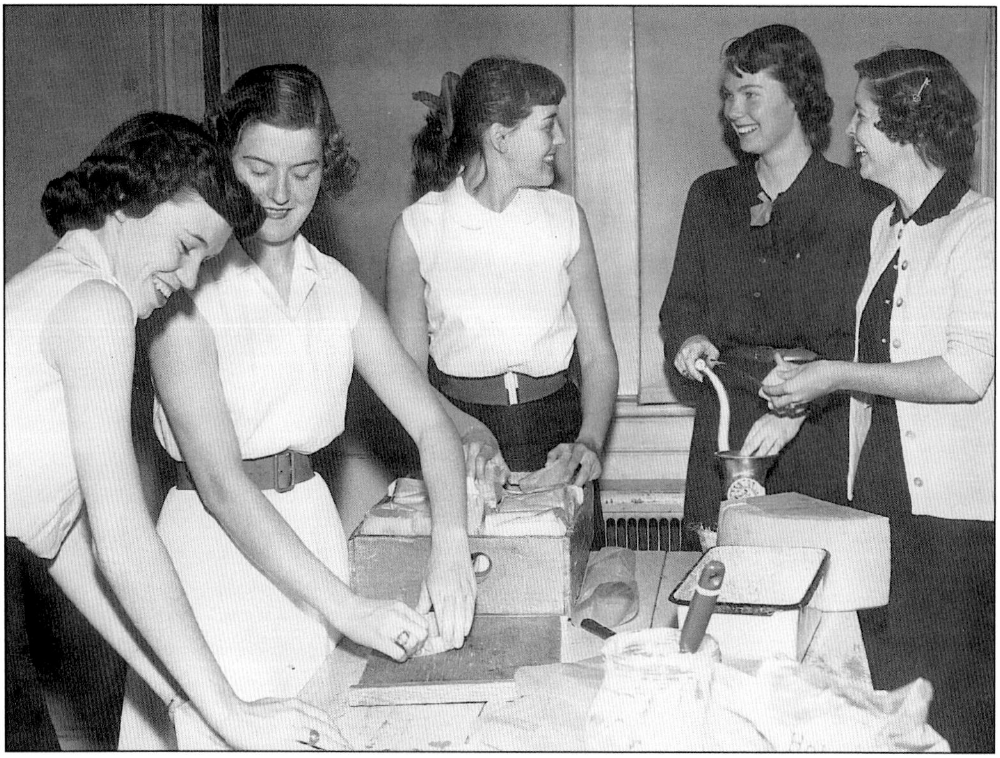

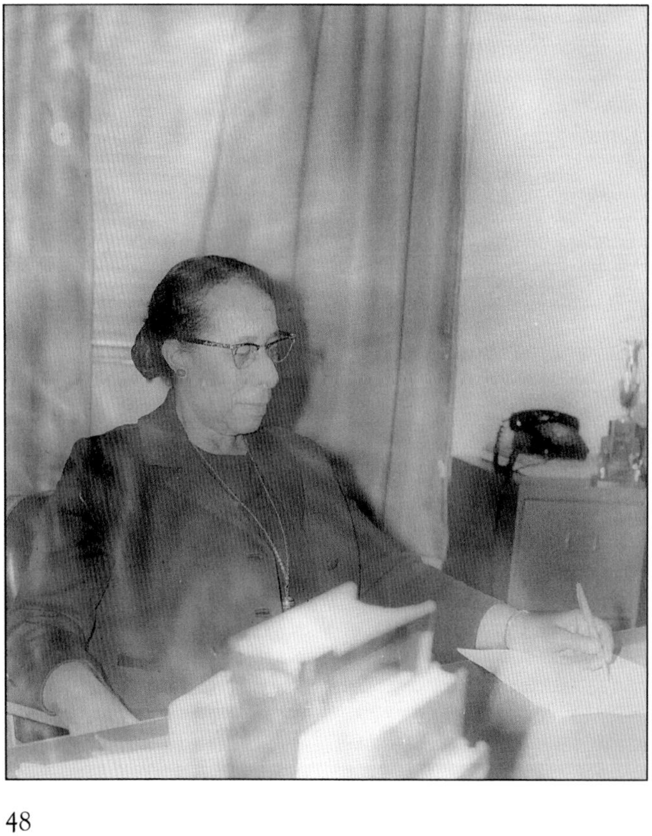

An Association of Childhood Education meeting was held at Winthrop in 1953. From left to right are Virginia Reynolds of Chesnee; Nancy Inabinet of Bowman; Mildred Rea of Sumter; Jackie Hembree of Anderson; and Shirley Beeson of Marion.

Dr. S.V. Moreland, Clinton College president, works in her office. Dr. Moreland served as Clinton's president from 1946 to 1994.

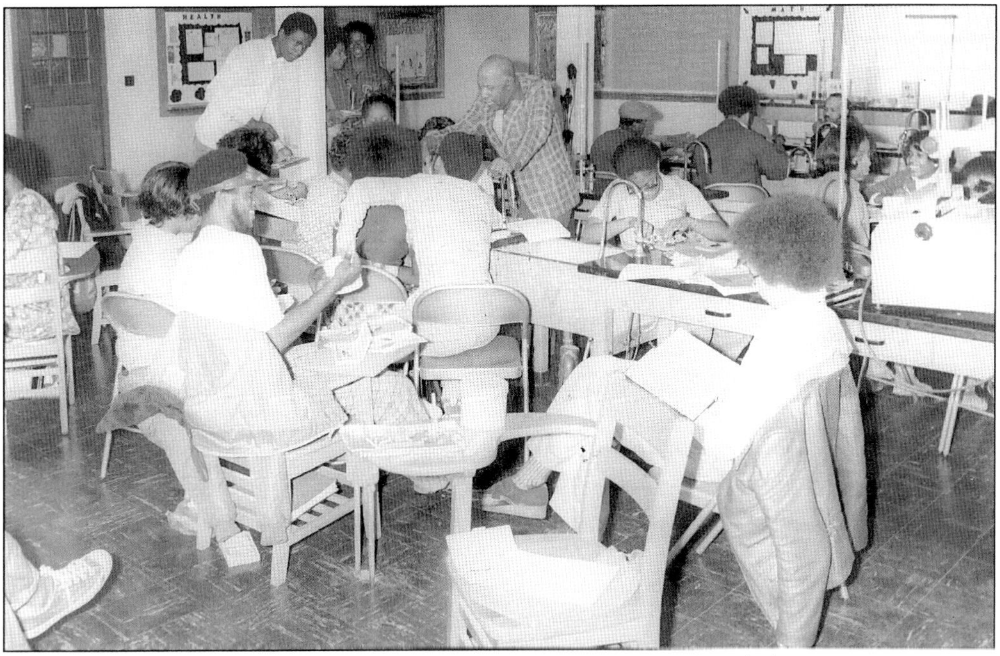

This 1950s scene is from Rock Hill's Clinton College, which was founded in 1894.

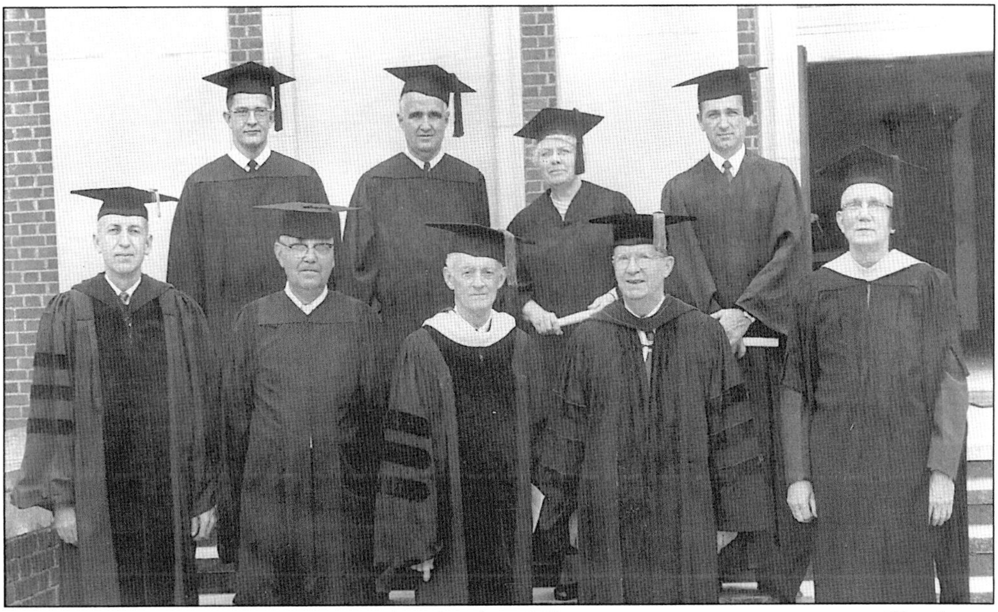

A group of distinguished citizens gather for the 1957 commencement ceremony at Winthrop. Pictured, from left to right, are S.J. McCoy, Winthrop dean; William H. Grier, trustee; Hon. David E. Finley, former director of the National Gallery of Art in Washington, D.C.; Henry R. Sims, Winthrop president; and John G. Kelly, registrar; (back row) Rev. Everette Lineberger; John T. Roddey, trustee; Mrs. J.E. Boatright, trustee; and Rev. Henry Pope Mobley.

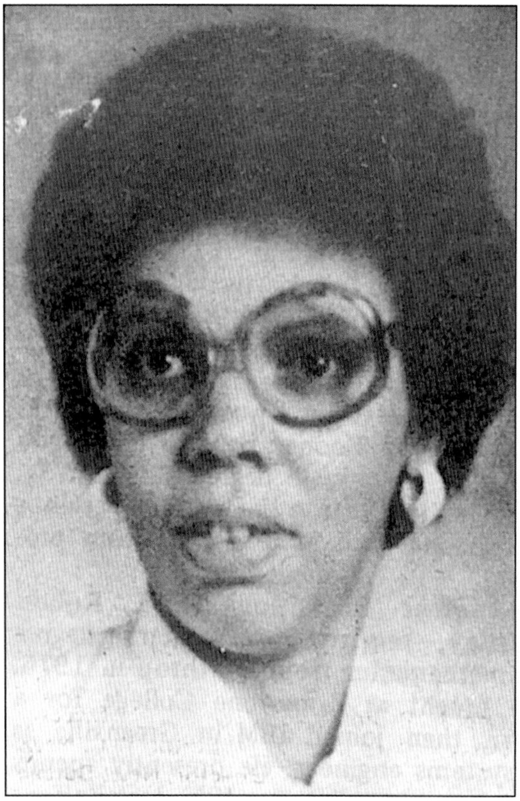

In 1964, Cynthia Plair Roddey became the first black student to enroll at Winthrop College.

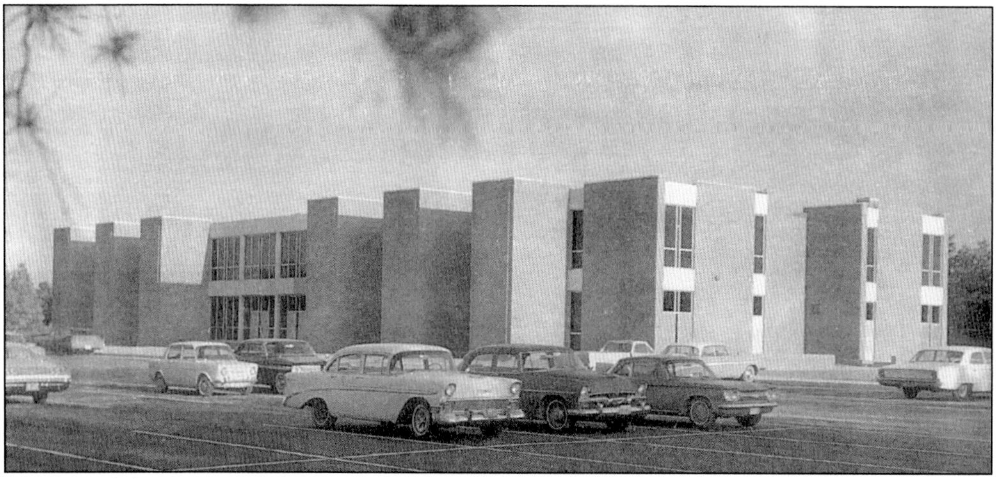

As part of the University of South Carolina's expansion program, a regional campus of the university was established in Lancaster in the mid-1960s.

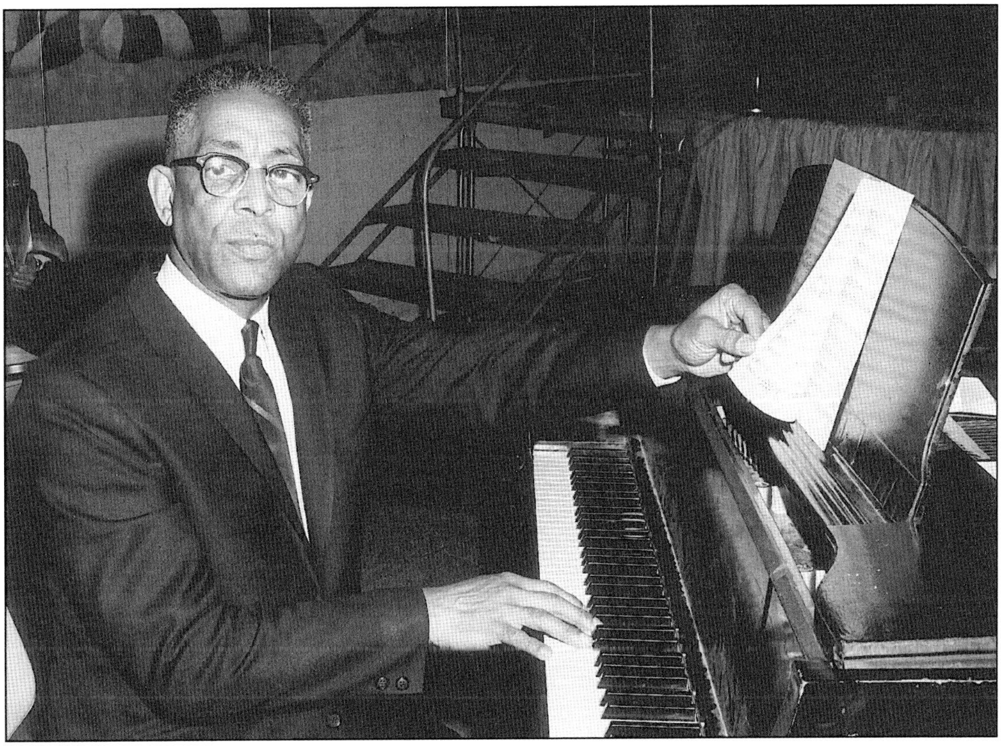

Samuel Louis Finley was the distinguished Chester citizen for whom Finley High School in Chester was subsequently named.

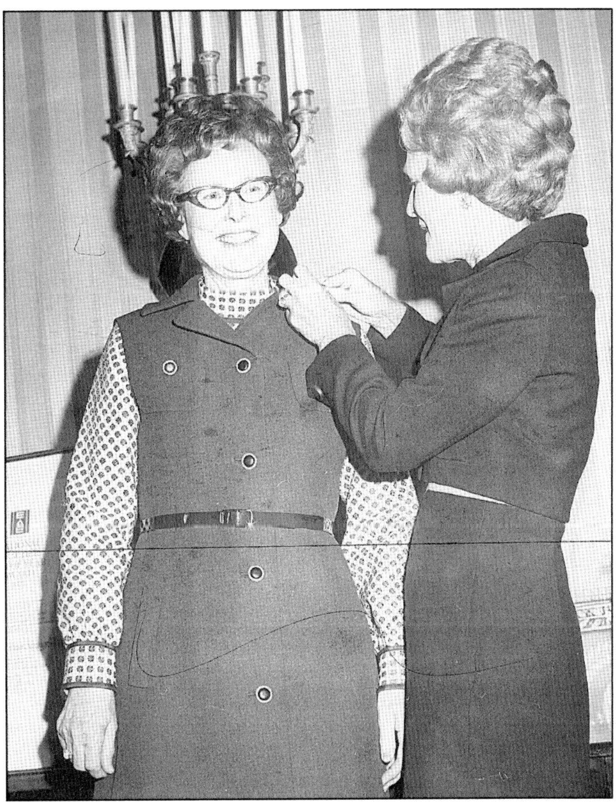

Chester native Martha Marian Stringfellow was named National Teacher of the Year in 1971. Here, she is shown with First Lady Pat Nixon.

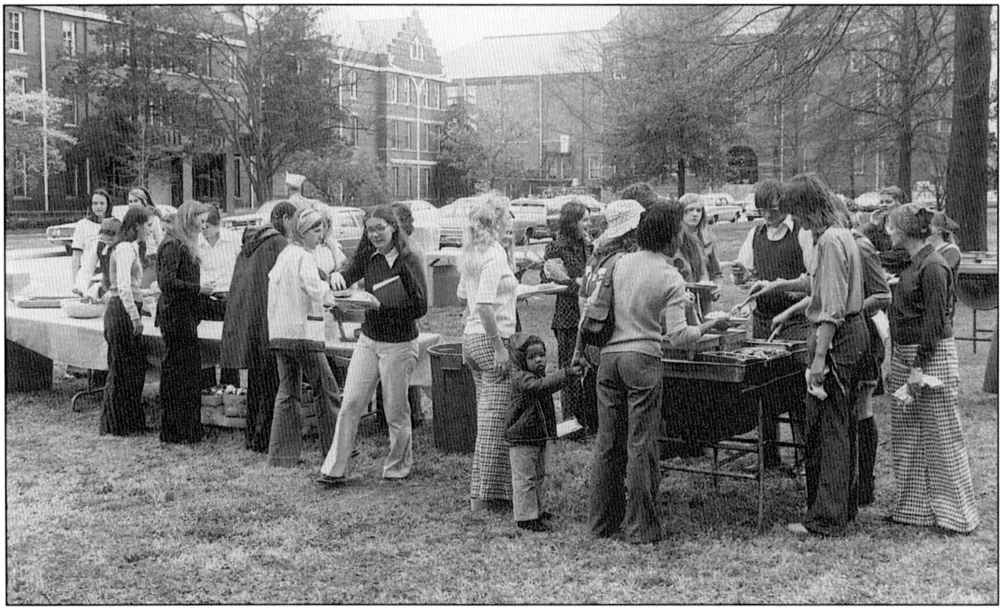

South Carolina governor John C. West signed the co-education bill into law in 1974, paving the way for the admittance of males to Winthrop without restriction. Here, Winthrop College students celebrate a "victory picnic."

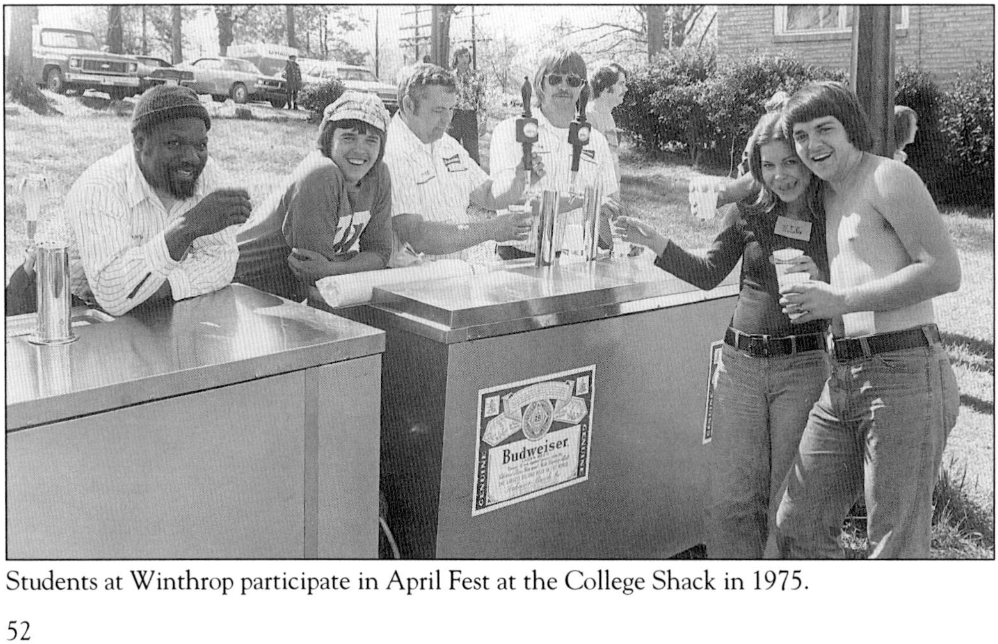

Students at Winthrop participate in April Fest at the College Shack in 1975.

Pictured here is one of Winthrop's most distinguished professors in the school's history—Dr. Ruth Hovermale. Dr. Hovermale (b. 1928-d. 1978) was Winthrop's first dean of the School of Home Economics when the department became a professional school in 1966.

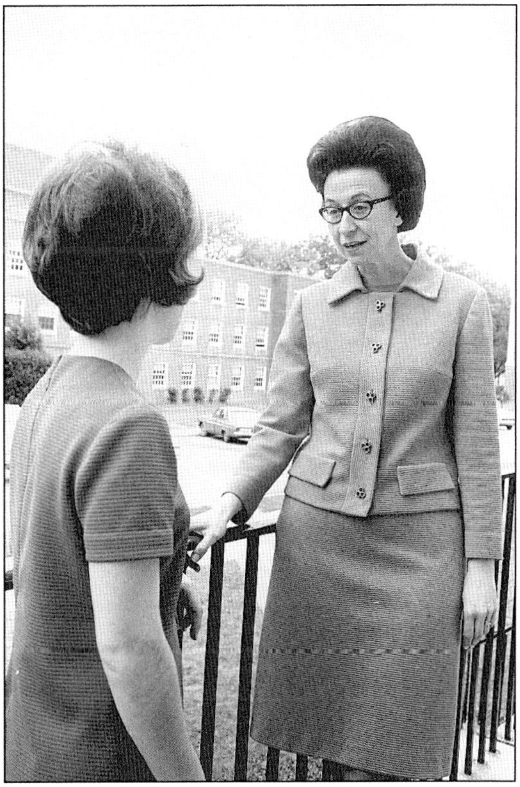

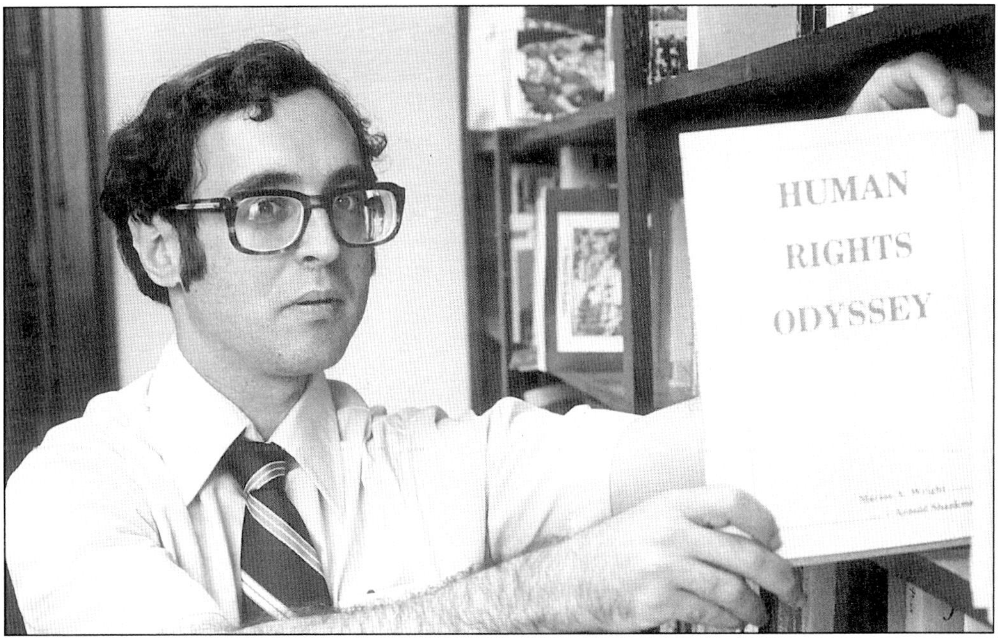

Dr. Shankman (b. 1946-d. 1983), a Winthrop professor of history from 1975 to 1983, was a prolific scholar and award-winning teacher who played a seminal role in the early development of the Winthrop University Archives.

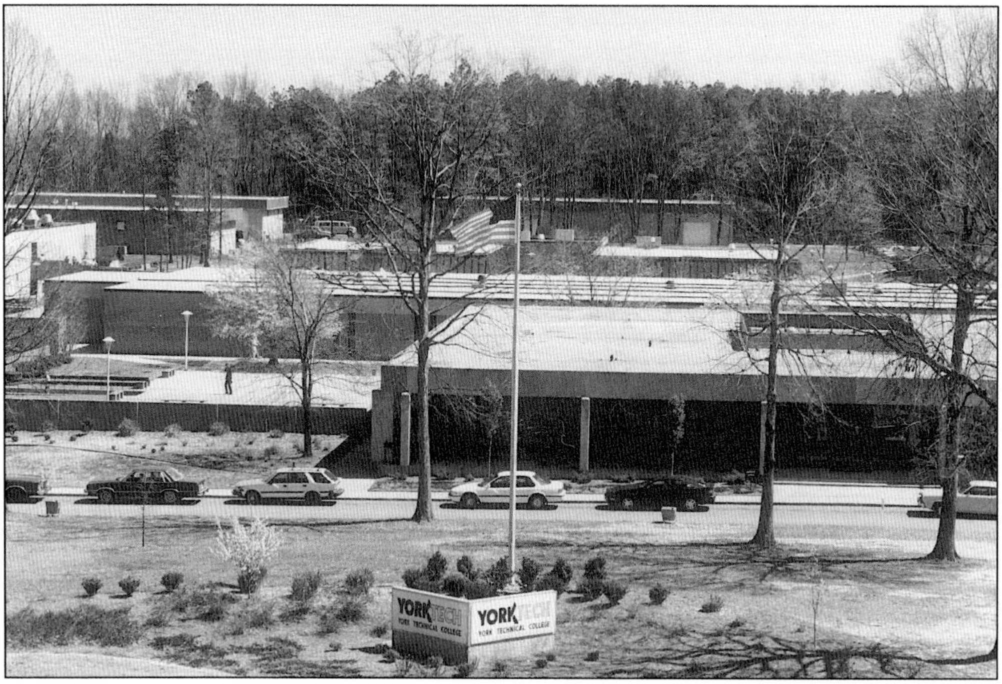

York Technical College is a pubic community-based, two-year institution that promotes marketable skills and economic development in the Catawba region.

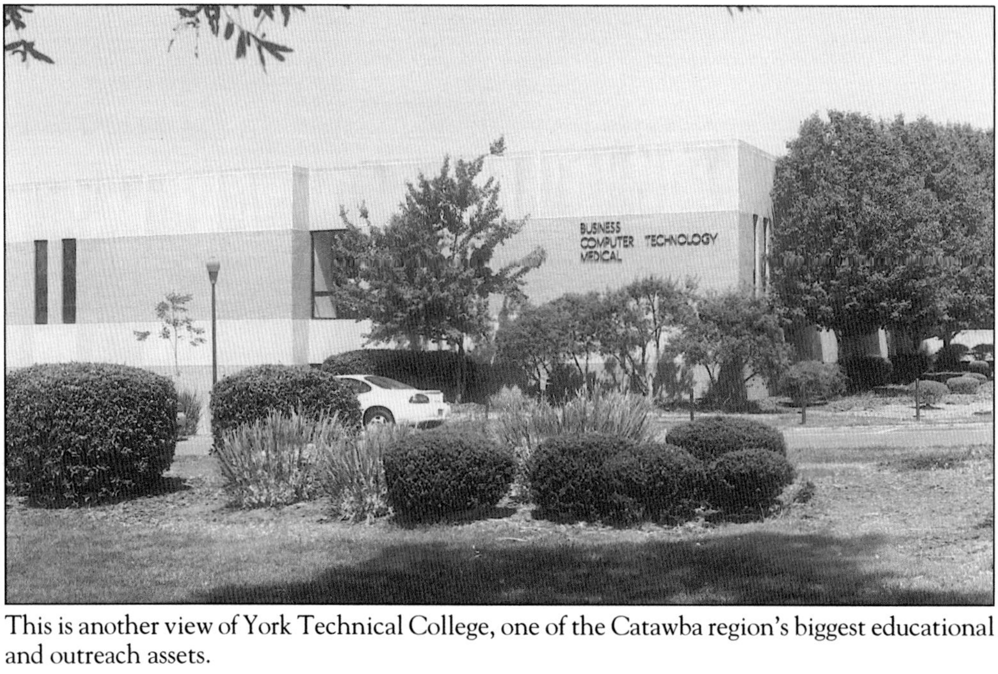

This is another view of York Technical College, one of the Catawba region's biggest educational and outreach assets.

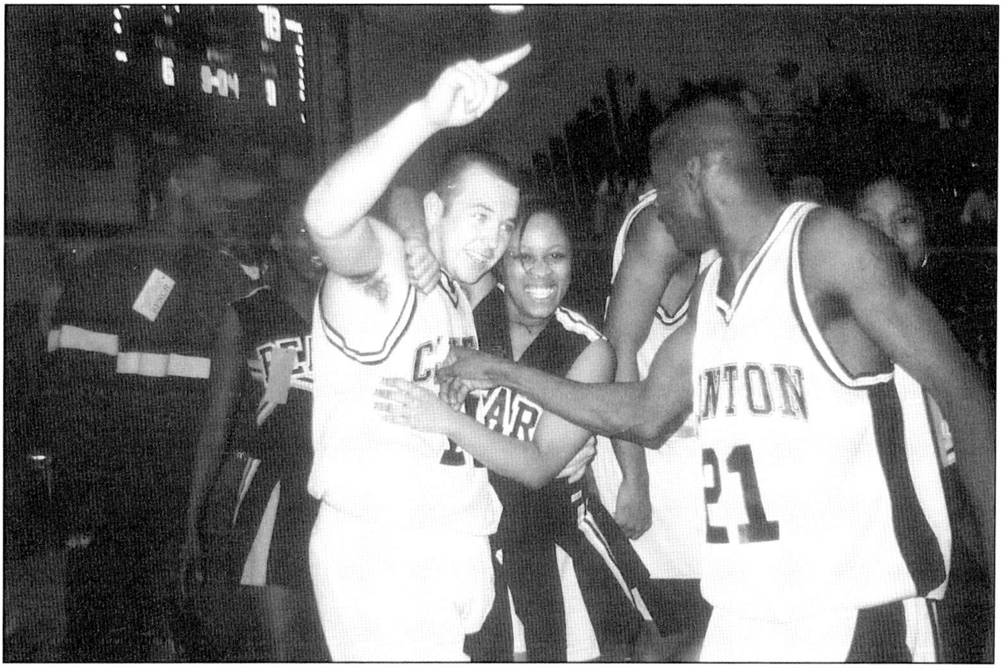

Basketball is still played at Clinton College in 1999. Pictured above, from left to right, are Brian Branham, Tameka Worthy, and Stanley Bailey. Below, these Clinton women's basketball team members are, from left to right, Danielle Parks, Monica Davis, and Conchetta Jones.

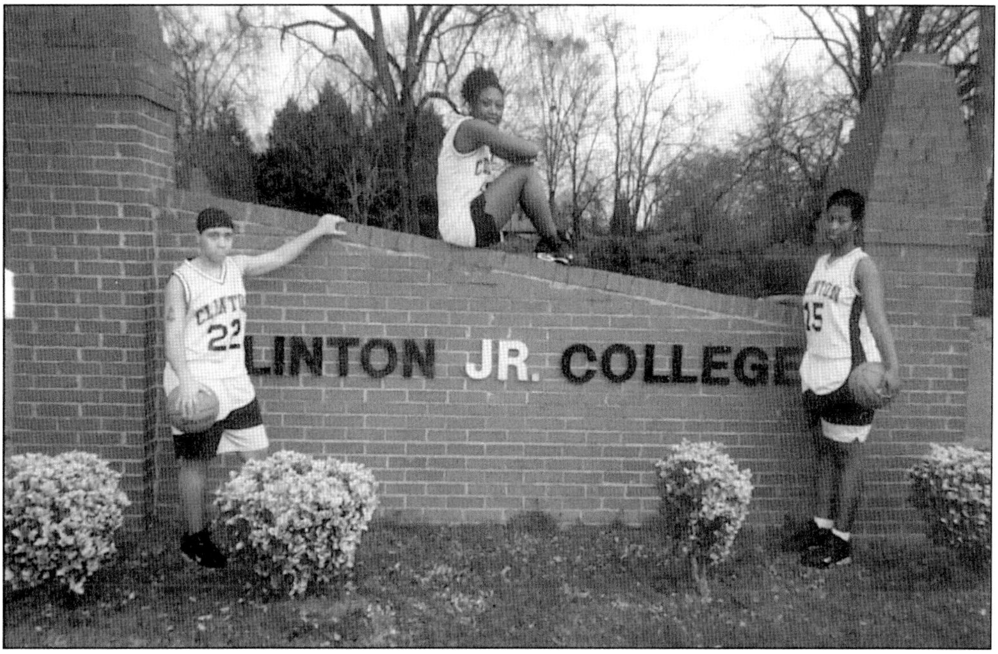

With an average enrollment of 100 students, Clinton College offers two-year associate degrees in business administration and the liberal arts. Clinton College is a private two-year, co-educational institution of higher learning sponsored by the A.M.E. Zion Church and located in Rock Hill.

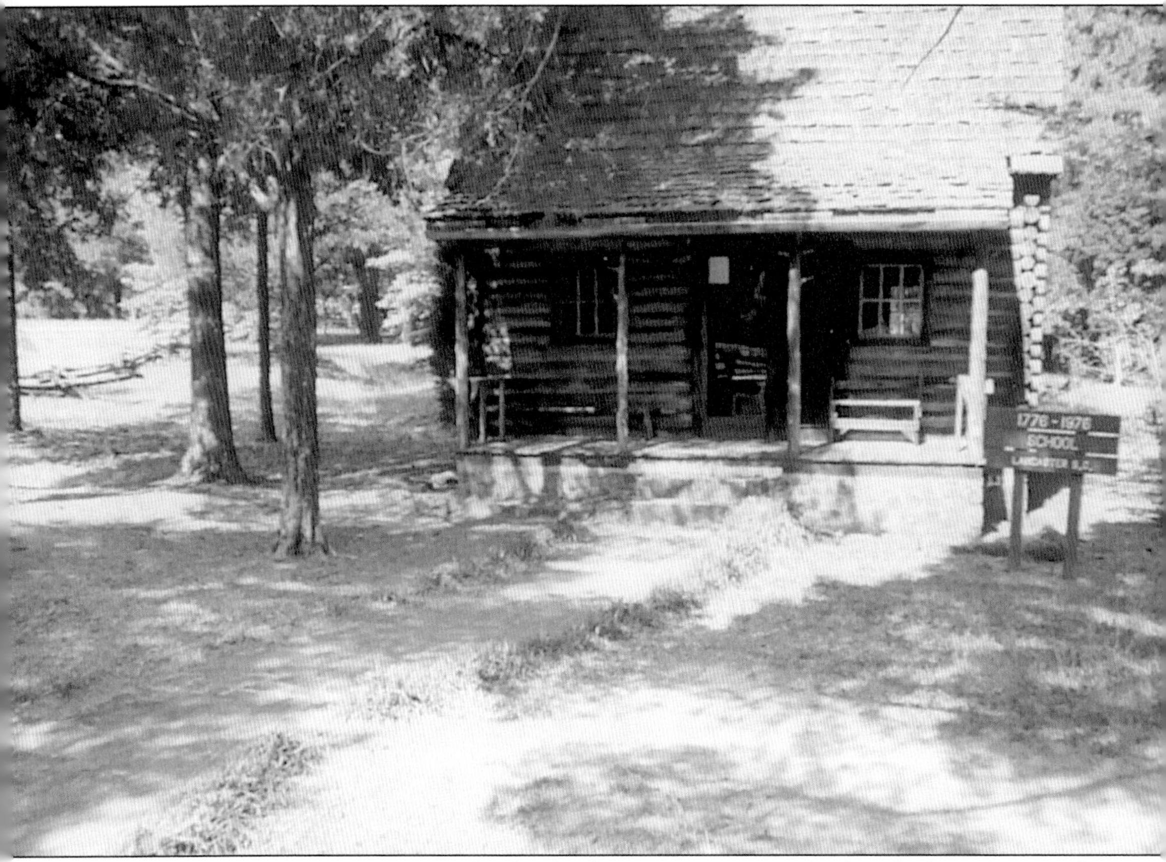

The Lancaster County Bicentennial School, a historic structure in Andrew Jackson State Park, is staffed by volunteers of the Lancaster County Retired Teachers Association.

Three

Historical Sites

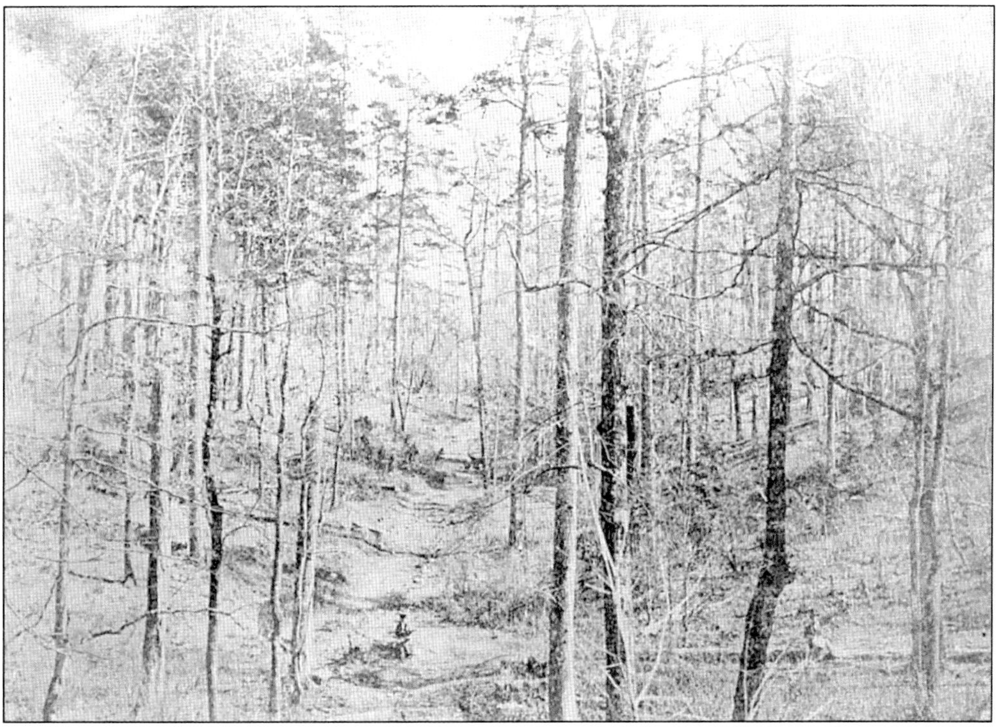

Yorkville photographer John R. Schorb took this photograph of the Kings Mountain Battleground c. 1860. The Revolutionary War battle took place in northern York County in 1780.

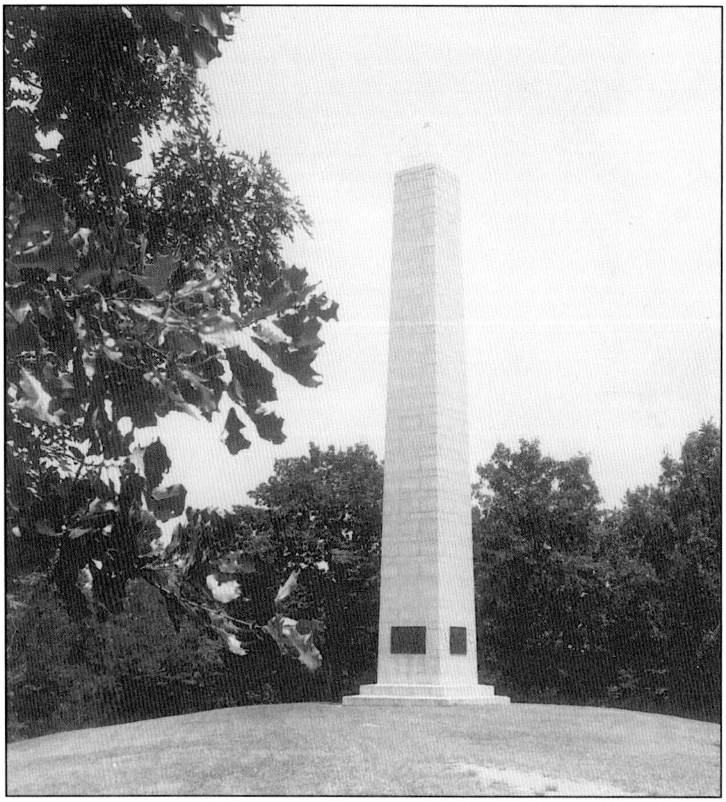

This obelisk was erected by the U.S. government at the Kings Mountain Battleground in 1909.

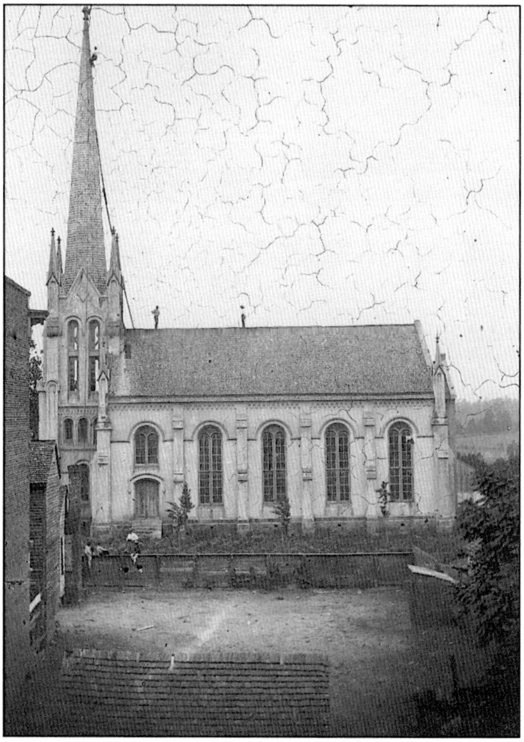

The First Presbyterian Church in York was organized in 1842. Located on West Liberty Street, the sanctuary was built in 1860–1861. This photograph was taken about the time the building was completed.

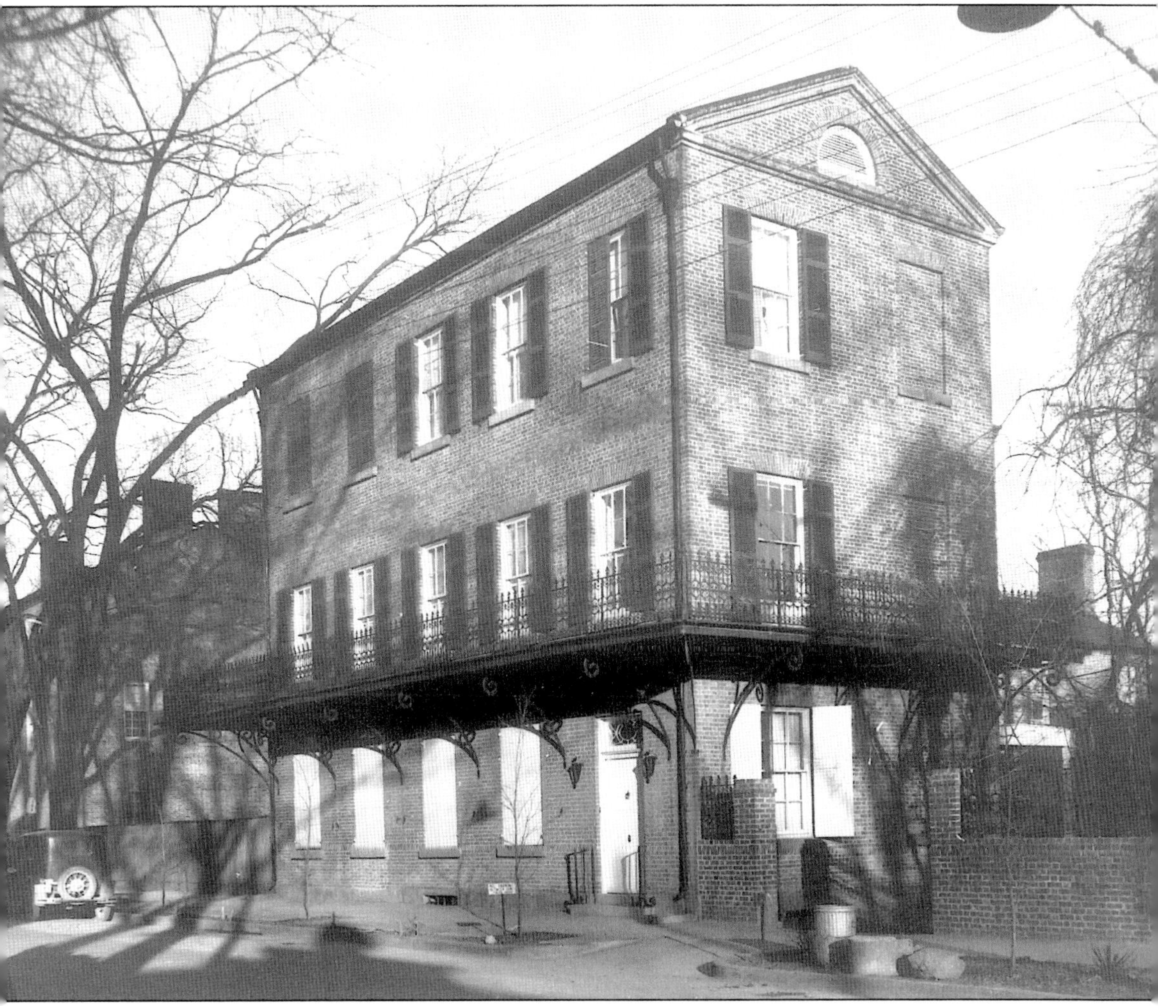

The Latta House in York was built by merchant Robert Latta in 1827 as a dry goods store and home. This photograph was taken in the 1930s.

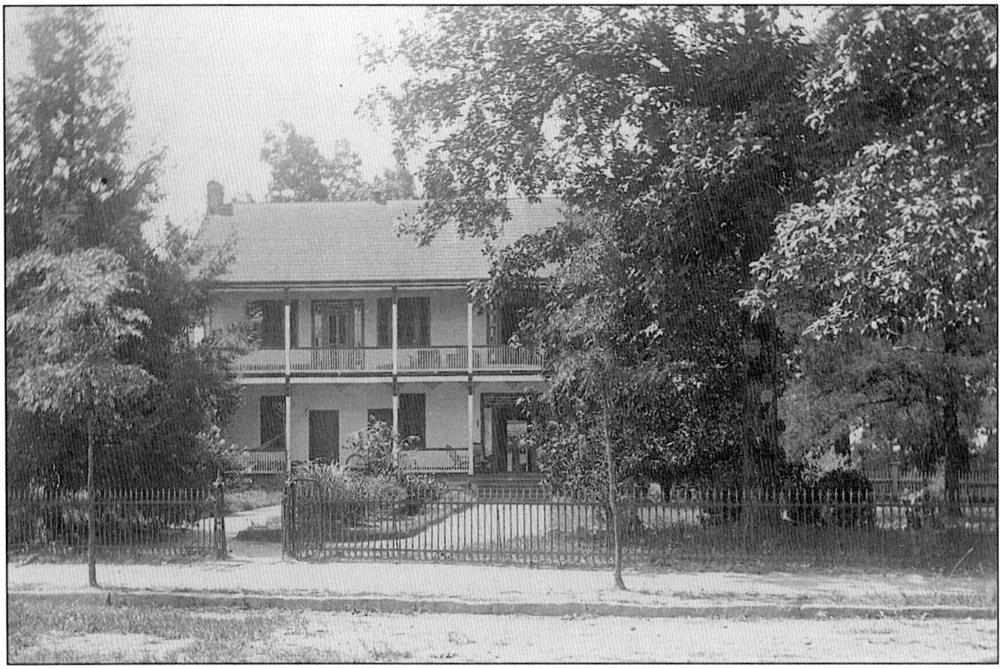

Said to be the oldest house in Rock Hill, the White House is located at the corner of East White Street and Elizabeth Lane. It was built in the 1830s by George P. and Ann Hutchison White and is still occupied by their descendants. This photograph was taken in 1897.

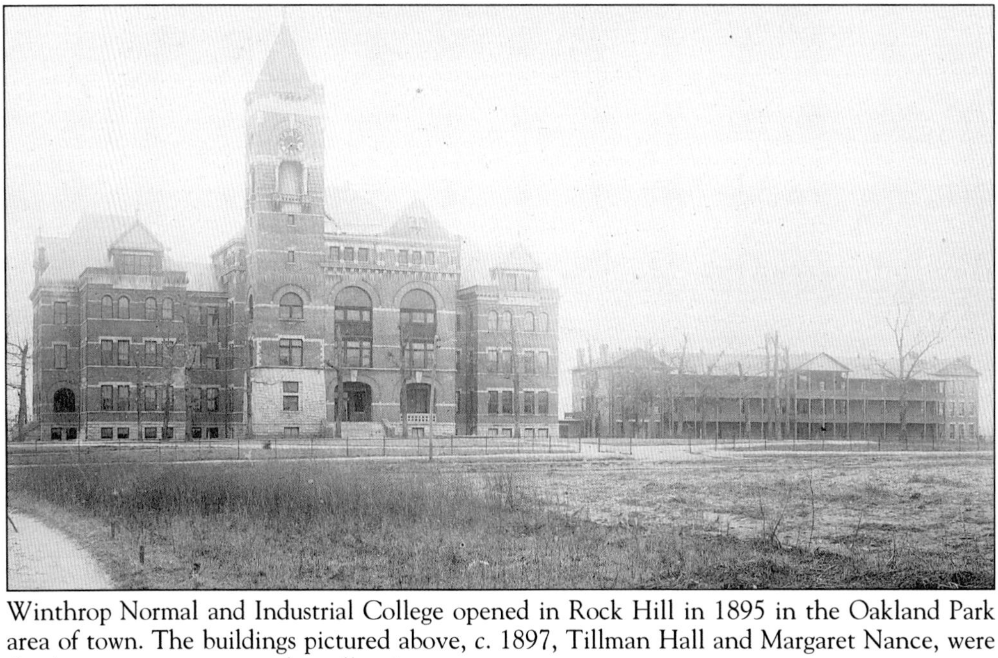

Winthrop Normal and Industrial College opened in Rock Hill in 1895 in the Oakland Park area of town. The buildings pictured above, c. 1897, Tillman Hall and Margaret Nance, were the first two structures on the college's campus.

The First Baptist Church in Lancaster was organized in 1874. This is the old sanctuary at the corner of South White Street and East Arch Street.

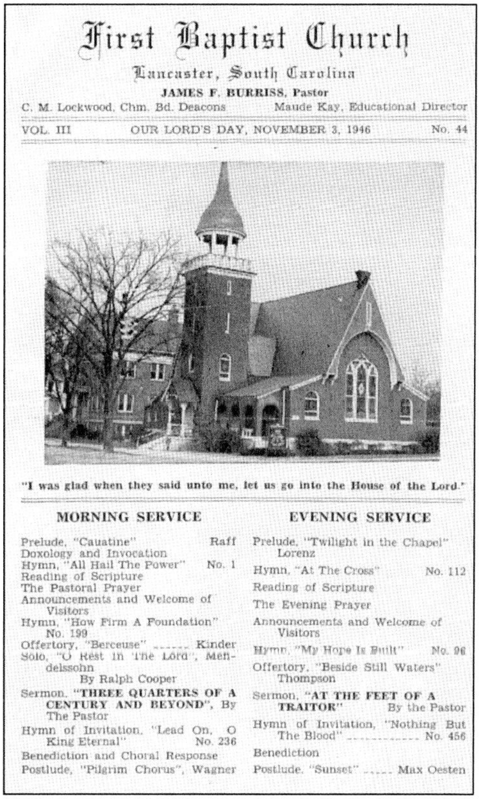

First Baptist Church

Lancaster, South Carolina

JAMES F. BURRISS, Pastor

C. M. Lockwood, Chm. Bd. Deacons — Maude Kay, Educational Director

VOL. III — OUR LORD'S DAY, NOVEMBER 3, 1946 — No. 44

"I was glad when they said unto me, let us go into the House of the Lord."

MORNING SERVICE

Prelude, "Cauatine" Raff
Doxology and Invocation
Hymn, "All Hail The Power" No. 1
Reading of Scripture
The Pastoral Prayer
Announcements and Welcome of Visitors
Hymn, "How Firm A Foundation" No. 199
Offertory, "Berceuse" ...... Kinder
Solo, "O Rest in The Lord", Mendelssohn
By Ralph Cooper
Sermon, **"THREE QUARTERS OF A CENTURY AND BEYOND"**, By The Pastor
Hymn of Invitation, "Lead On, O King Eternal" No. 236
Benediction and Choral Response
Postlude, "Pilgrim Chorus", Wagner

EVENING SERVICE

Prelude, "Twilight in the Chapel" Lorenz
Hymn, "At The Cross" No. 112
Reading of Scripture
The Evening Prayer
Announcements and Welcome of Visitors
Hymn, "My Hope Is Built" No. 96
Offertory, "Beside Still Waters" Thompson
Sermon, **"AT THE FEET OF A TRAITOR"** By the Pastor
Hymn of Invitation, "Nothing But The Blood" .... No. 456
Benediction
Postlude, "Sunset" ..... Max Oesten

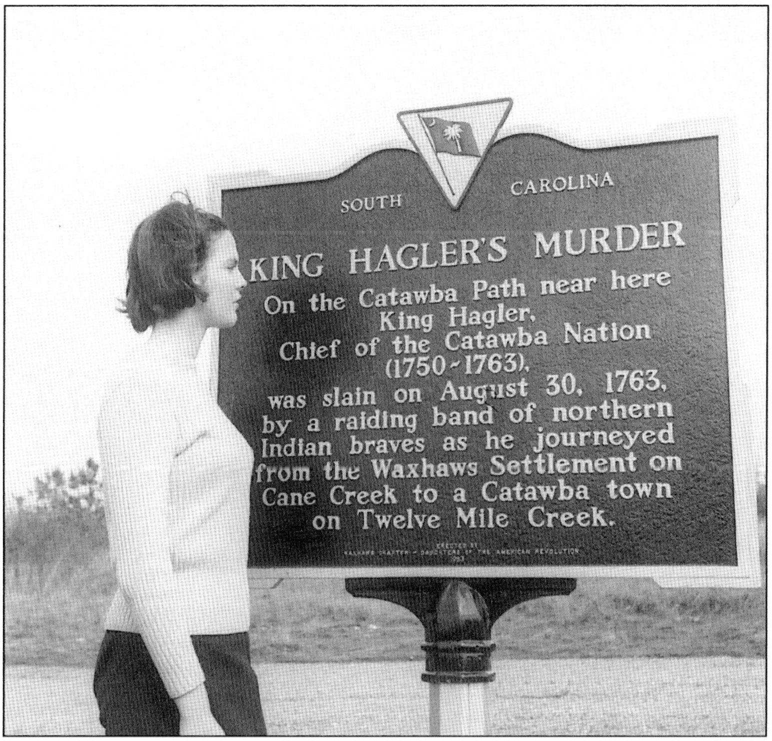

This historical marker in Lancaster County commemorates King Hagler's death in 1763. Hagler was the chief of the Catawba Nation from 1750 until his death.

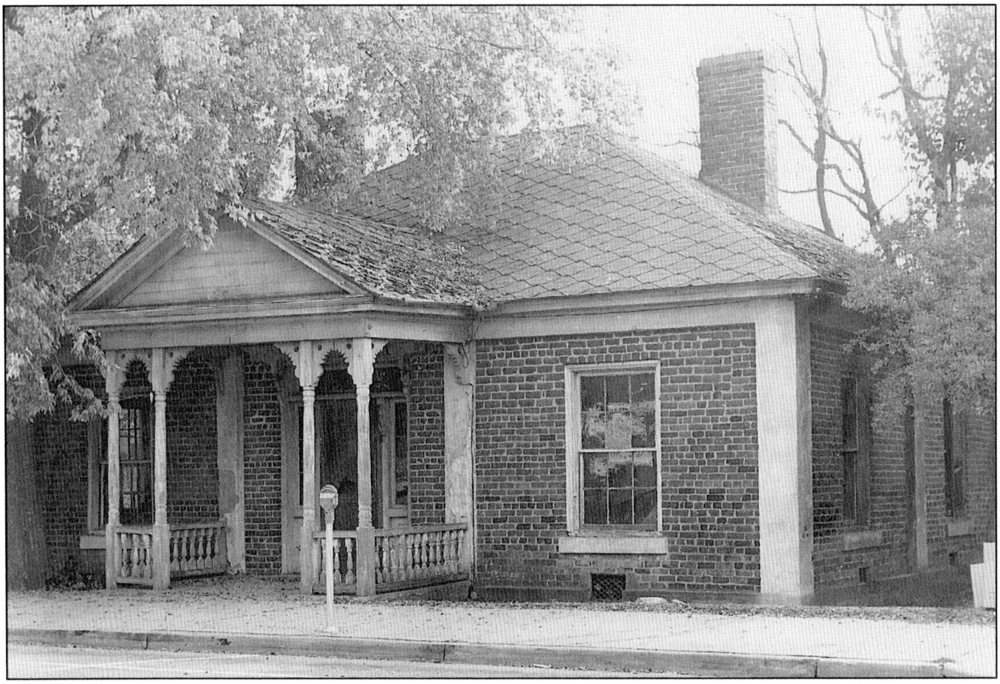

The McCosh House on East Black Street in Rock Hill was built by Capt. and Mrs. Reid. H. McCosh in 1872. It is currently used as a law office.

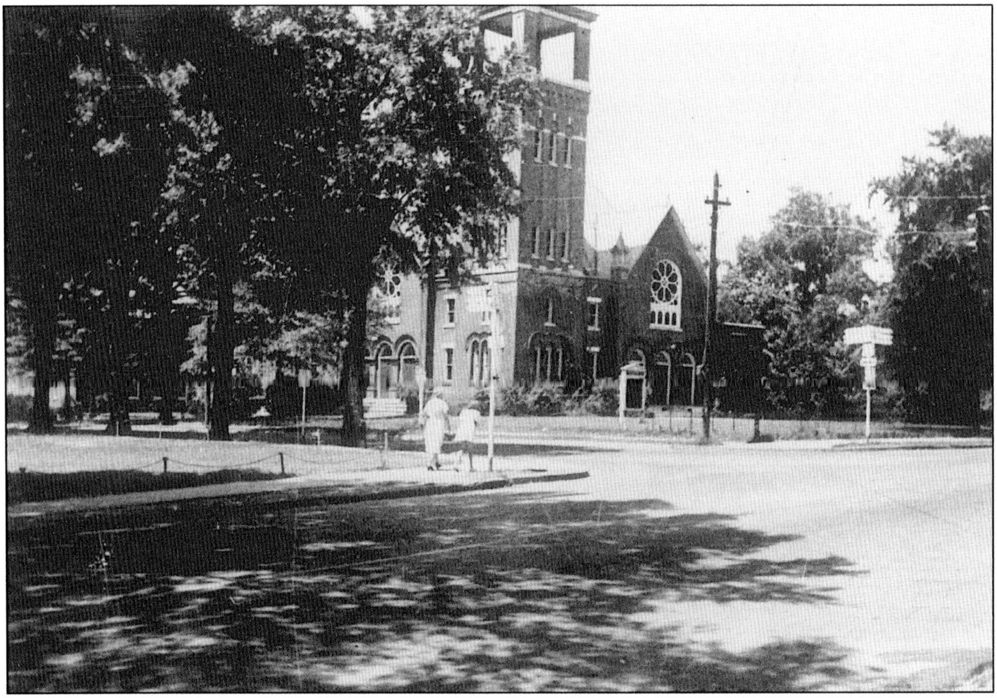

The First Presbyterian Church in Rock Hill was chartered in 1869. This building was constructed in 1895 and is located on the corner of Main and Saluda Streets. This photograph was taken in the 1940s.

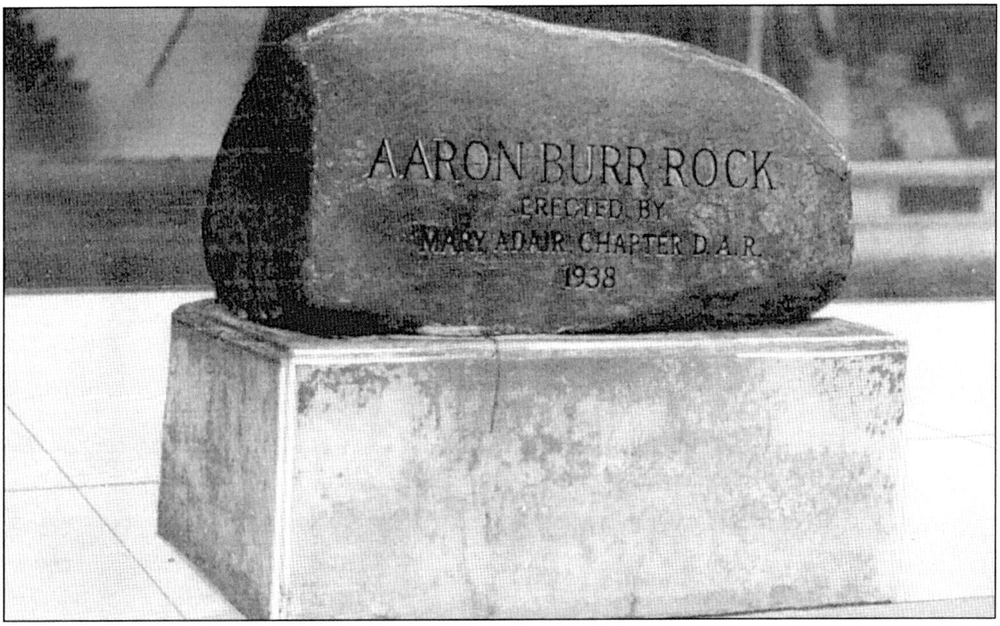

This postcard of Main Street in Chester shows the rock upon which Aaron Burr, the third U.S. vice president (1801–1805), dismounted in the spring of 1807 and appealed to the citizens of Chester for protection. Burr had been arrested for treason and was being taken to Richmond, Virginia, for trial.

DEDICATION OF MARKER

— AT —

Hanging Rock Battle Ground

Under the Sponsorship of the

Waxhaws Chapter Daughters Of The American Revolution

JUNE 8, 1947

4:00 P. M.

Mrs. Ben C. Hough, Jr., Regent, Presiding

Call To Order .... SpringMaid Band
Invocation .... Rev. H. L. Kingman, President Lancaster Ministerial Association
Salute to the Flag .... Led by the Boy Scouts and Girl Scouts
The National Anthem .... SpringMaid Band
Presentation of Guests .... Mrs. J. R. Kelsey, First Vice Regent
Introduction of Speaker .... Senator W. Bruce Williams
Address .... Mr. A. S. Salley, Jr., State Historian, Historical Commission of South Carolina
Unveiling of Marker .... By Children of Lancaster County who are direct descendants of Soldiers who participated in the Battle of Hanging Rock
Music .... SpringMaid Band
Benediction .... Rev. H. L. Kingman

INSCRIPTION ON MARKER

Here was fought the battle of the Hanging Rock
August 6, 1780
About 600 militia of the Carolinas under
Colonel Thomas Sumter
Destroyed the British Camp and killed and wounded
over 200 of the British troops
Under Major John Carden With a loss of 40 killed
and a few wounded

A marker was dedicated in commemoration of the Battle of Hanging Rock in 1947 by the Waxhaw chapter of the Daughters of the American Revolution (DAR). The Lancaster County Revolutionary War battle was fought on August 6, 1780.

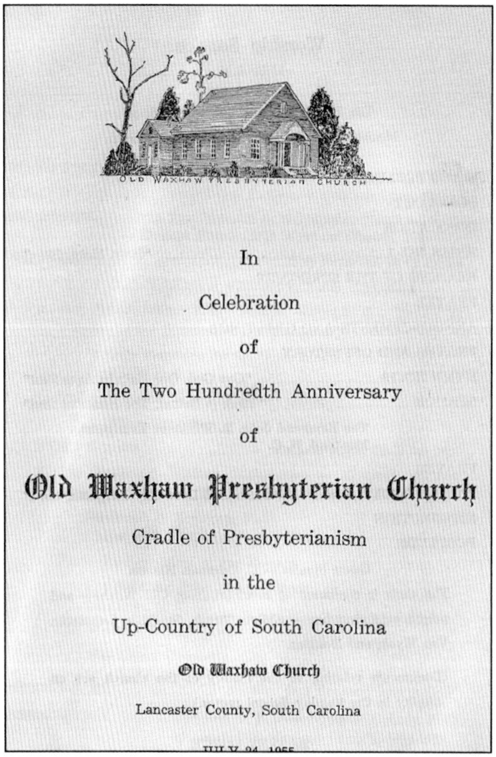

OLD WAXHAW PRESBYTERIAN CHURCH

In

Celebration

of

The Two Hundredth Anniversary

of

Old Waxhaw Presbyterian Church

Cradle of Presbyterianism

in the

Up-Country of South Carolina

Old Waxhaw Church

Lancaster County, South Carolina

The Old Waxhaw Presbyterian Church in Lancaster County celebrated its 200th anniversary in 1955.

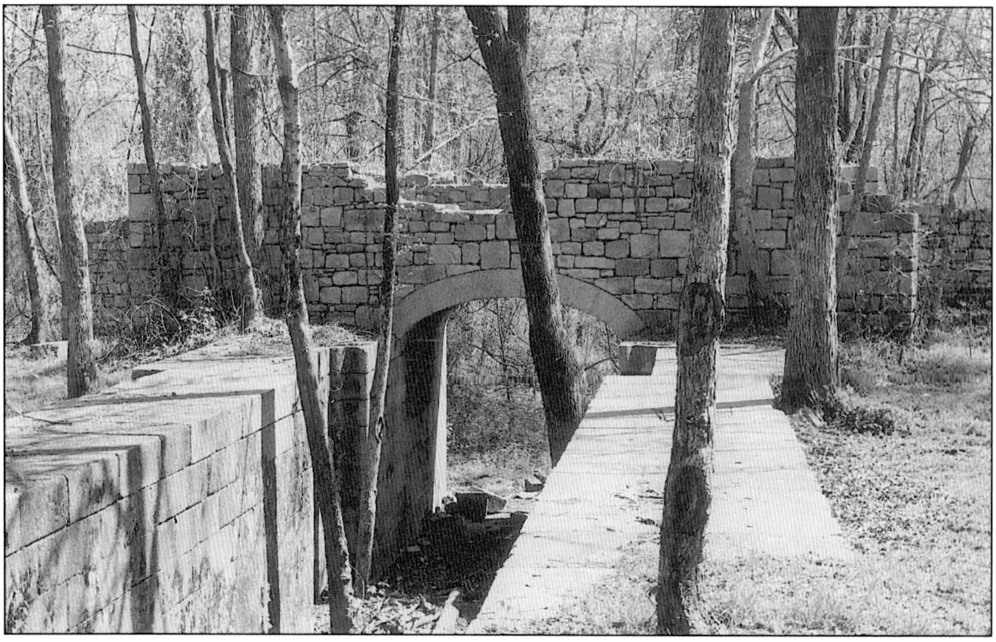

Landsford Canal, along the Catawba River in northeastern Chester County, was built in 1823 under the direction of Joel Poinsett, chairman of the South Carolina Board of Public Works, and Robert Mills, state engineer and architect. The canal was part of a plan to facilitate trade between the Upstate and Charleston and eventually link Charleston with the Mississippi River and the Ohio River Valley. With the coming of railroads, canals became obsolete.

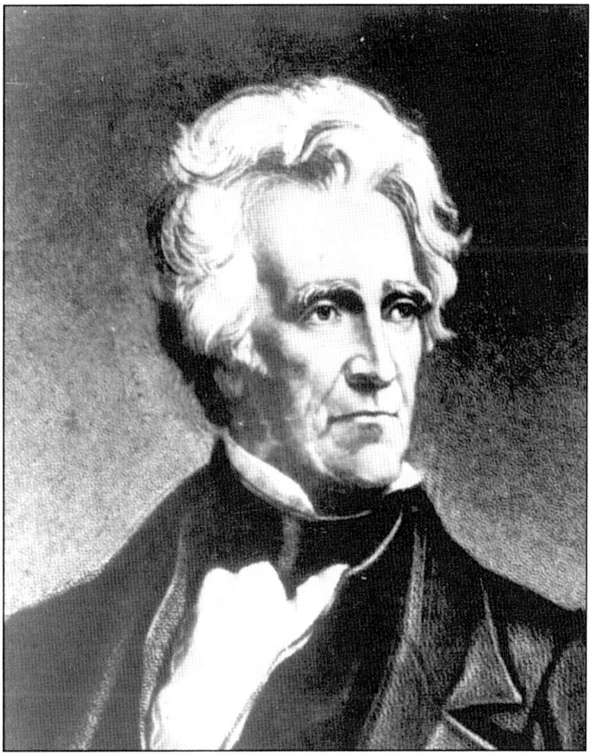

Was Andrew Jackson (1767–1845) born in South Carolina? The long-standing controversy would seem to be put to rest by Jackson's own admission seen below on a monument at Andrew Jackson State Park in Lancaster County. Jackson's portrait is on the right.

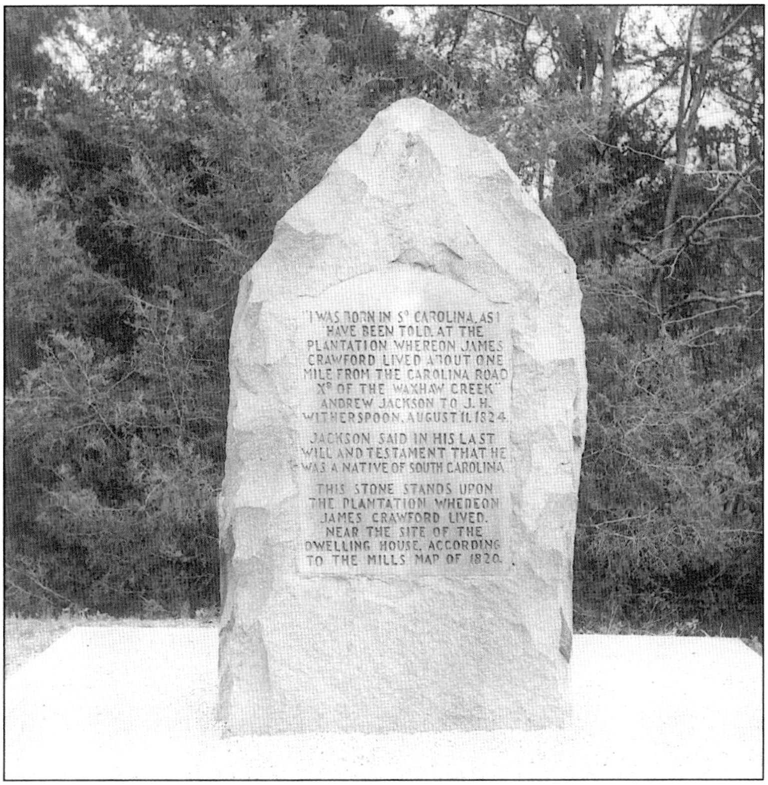

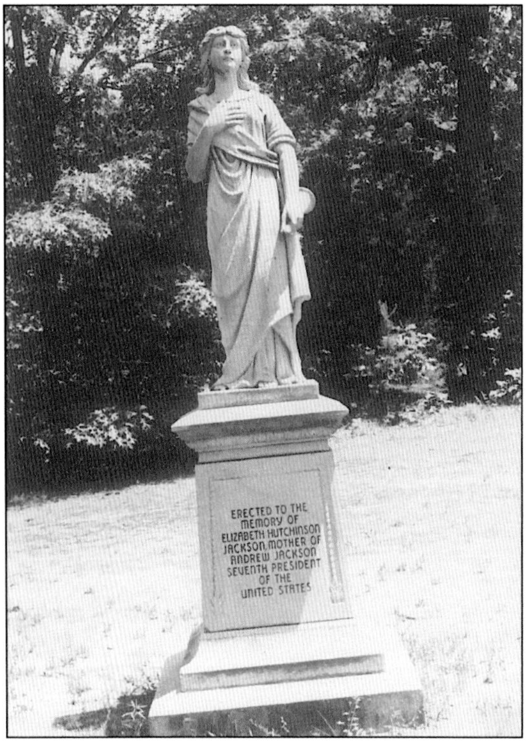

These are two statues at the Andrew Jackson State Park. On the left is a monument to Elizabeth Hutchinson Jackson, Andrew's mother, and pictured below is a statue of Andrew Jackson as a young man by sculptor Anna Hyatt Huntington and given by her as a gift to the children of South Carolina.

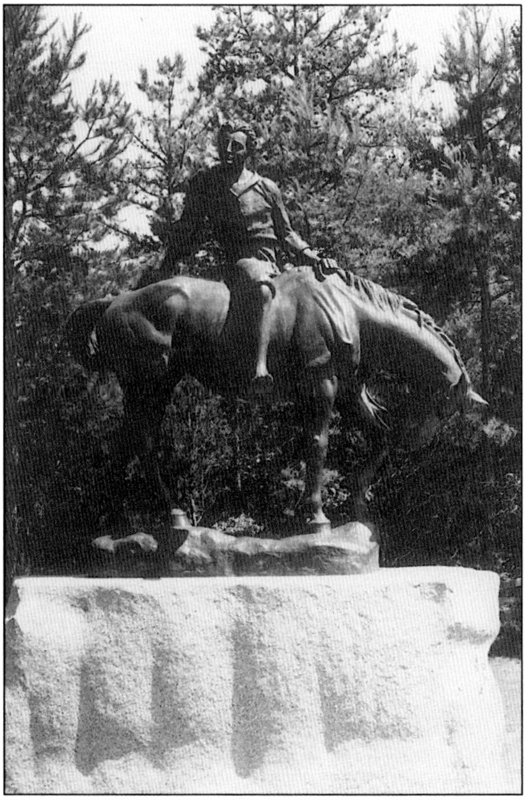

In 1955, the Waxhaw chapter of the DAR erected a marker to commemorate the Buford battleground in Lancaster County. At right is the inscription on the marker.

Inscription on Marker

BUFORD BATTLE GROUND

ERECTED TO THE MEMORY AND IN HONOR OF
THE BRAVE AND PATRIOTIC AMERICAN SOLDIERS
WHO FELL IN THE BATTLE WHICH OCCURRED
AT THIS PLACE ON THE 29th of MAY, 1780
BETWEEN COL. ABRAHAM BUFORD
WHO COMMANDED A REGIMENT OF 350 VIRGINIANS
AND COL. TARLETON OF THE BRITISH ARMY
WITH 350 CAVALRY AND A LIKE NUMBER OF INFANTRY

NEARLY THE ENTIRE COMMAND OF COL. BUFORD
WERE EITHER KILLED OR WOUNDED.
GALLANT SOLDIERS ARE BURIED IN THIS GRAVE,
THAT LEFT THEIR HOMES
FOR THE RELIEF OF CHARLESTON,

HEARING AT CAMDEN OF THE SURRENDER
OF THAT CITY WERE RETURNING.
HERE THEIR LIVES WERE ENDED
IN THE SERVICE OF THEIR COUNTRY.

THE CRUELTY AND BARBAROUS MASSACRE
COMMITTED ON THIS OCCASION
BY TARLETON AND HIS COMMAND
AFTER THE SURRENDER OF COL. BUFORD
AND HIS REGIMENT ORIGINATED THE WAR CRY
"REMEMBER TARLETON'S QUARTERS"
A BRITISH HISTORIAN CONFESSES
AT THIS BATTLE
THE VIRTUE OF HUMANITY WAS TOTALLY FORGOT.

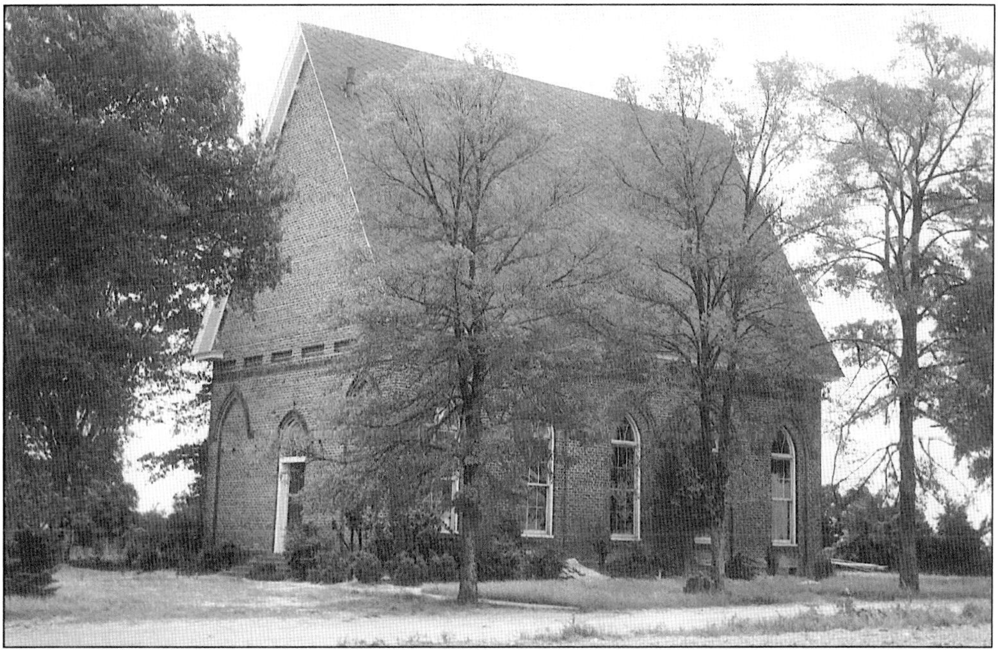

Olivet Presbyterian Church at McConnells in York County was organized in 1842. This building was constructed in 1886 and is still in use today.

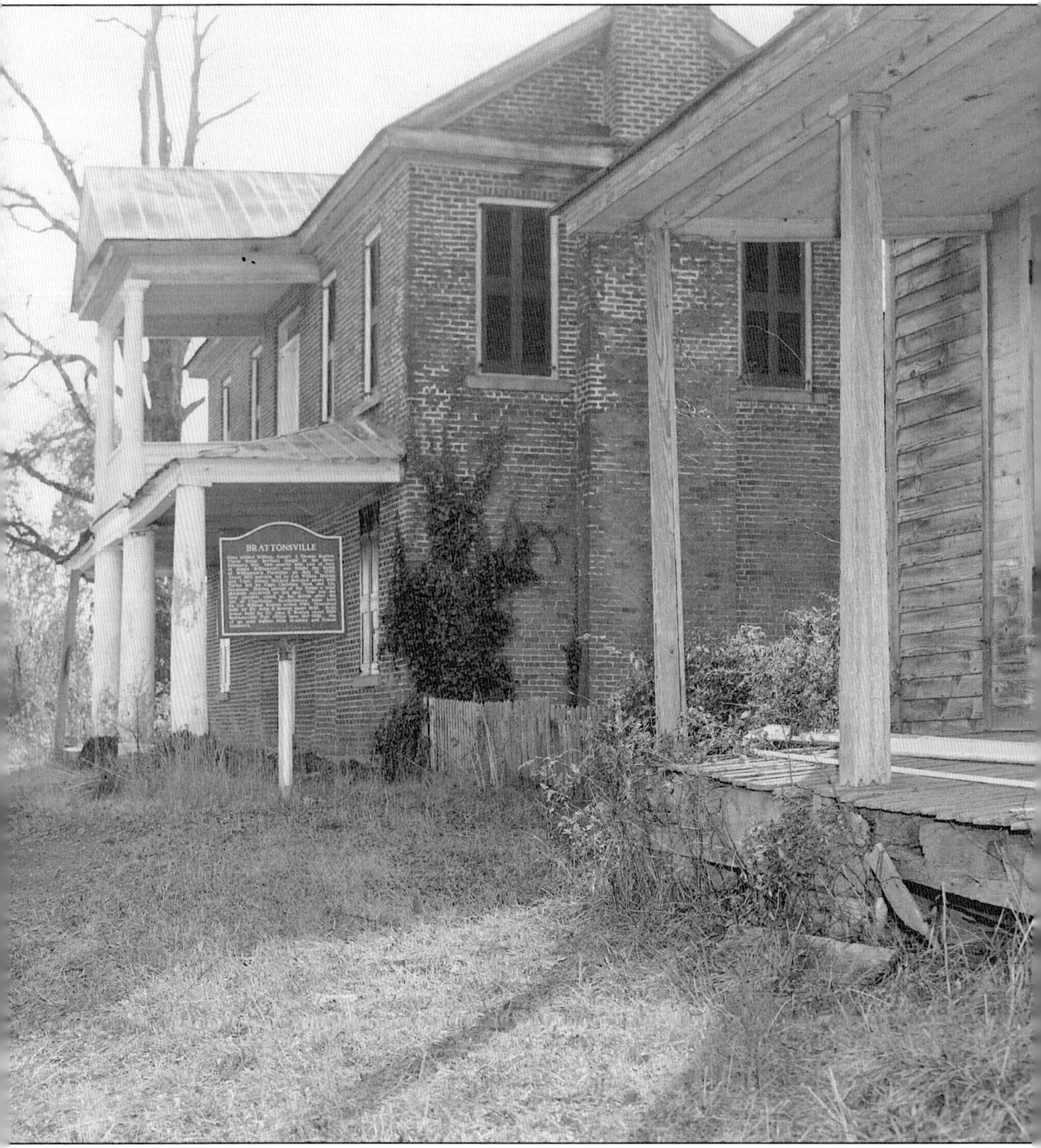

Brattonsville in York County has a remarkable amount of fine examples of antebellum architecture. This 1843 brick house was used as a female academy prior to the War Between the States.

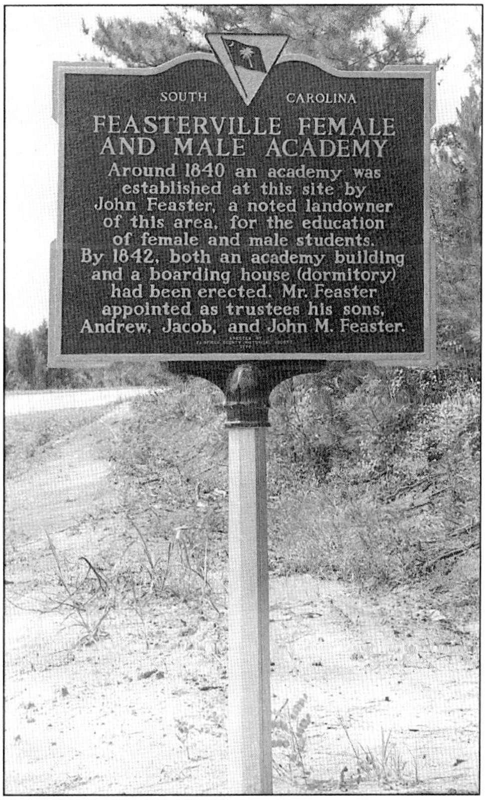

Pictured here is the Feasterville Academy historical marker and dormitory in Chester County.

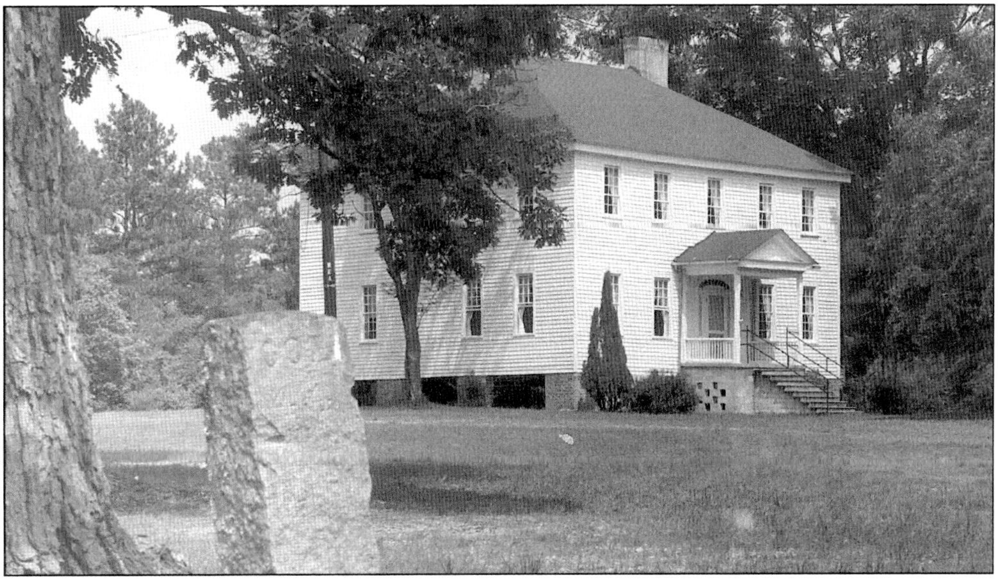

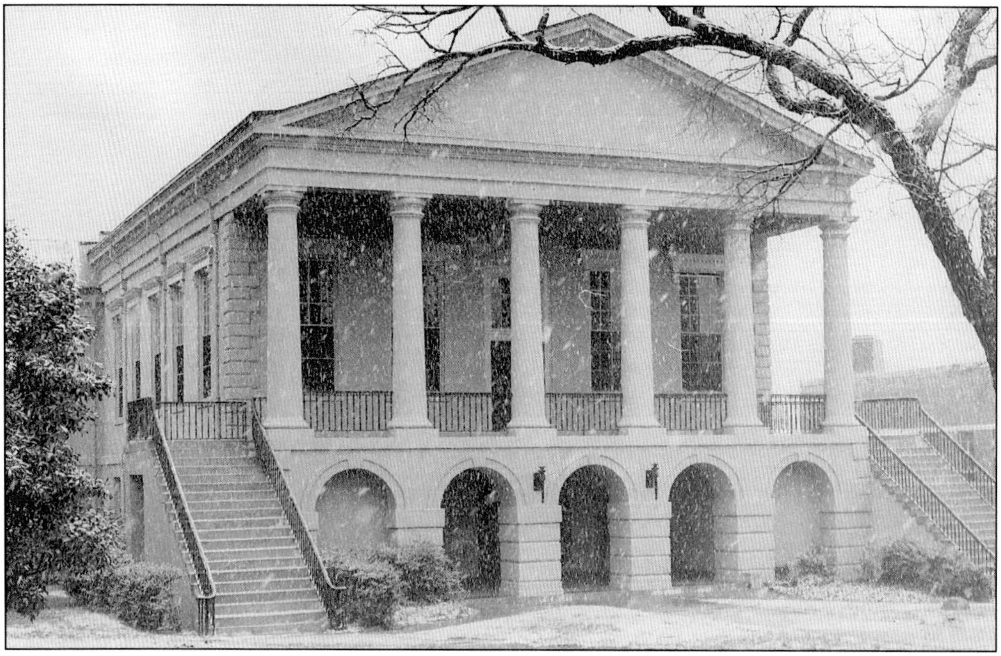

The Chester County Courthouse, built in 1852, was designed by Edward Brickell White (1802–1888) of Charleston, whose work was greatly influenced by Robert Mills. Additions were made to the building in 1896, 1928, and 1994.

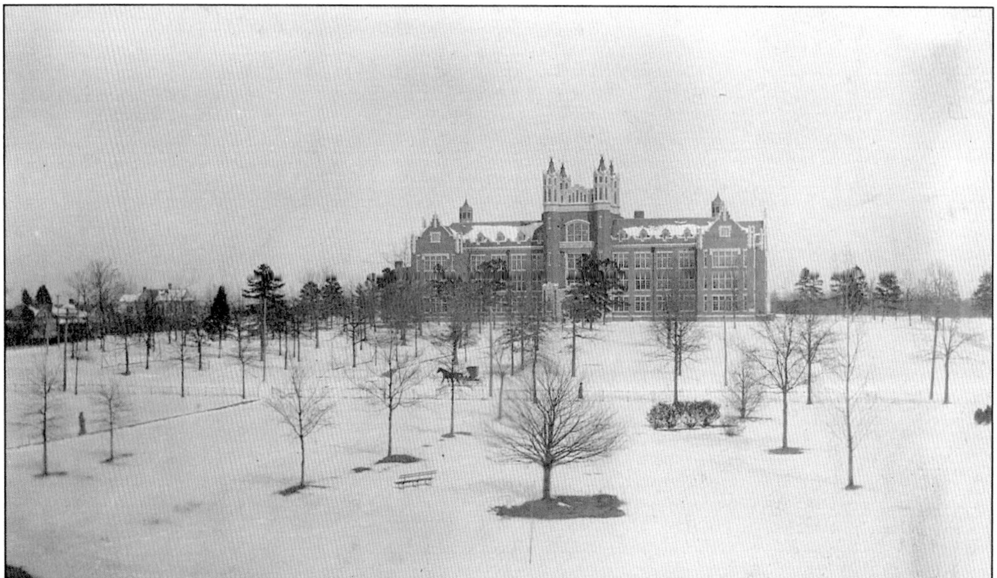

The Winthrop Training School building at Winthrop College in Rock Hill was constructed in 1912 to house a model school in which Winthrop students could practice teaching. This photograph was taken shortly after the training school was built.

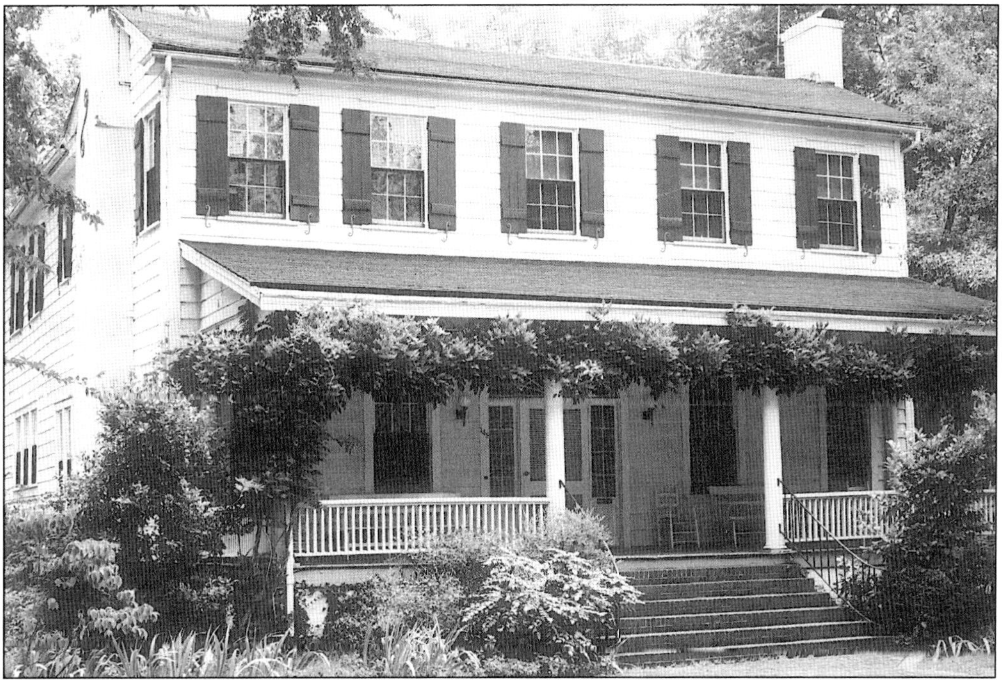

The Brawley House on York Street in Chester was built in 1838 by Hiram C. Brawley.

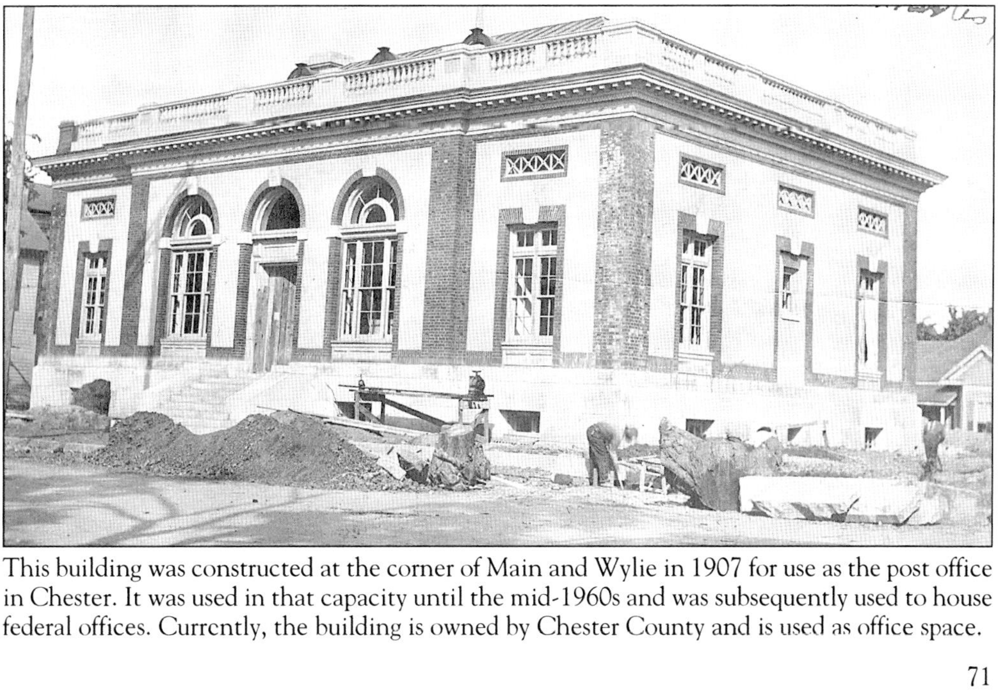

This building was constructed at the corner of Main and Wylie in 1907 for use as the post office in Chester. It was used in that capacity until the mid-1960s and was subsequently used to house federal offices. Currently, the building is owned by Chester County and is used as office space.

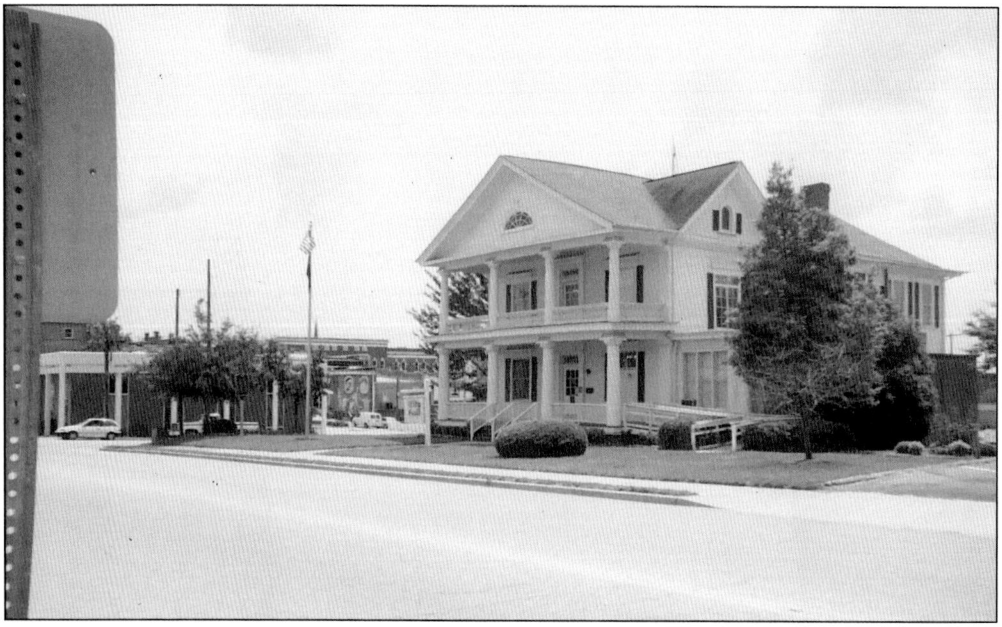

Lancaster City Hall was built as a residential home between 1828 and 1835 by Robert W. Gill. Elliott Springs was born in the house in 1896 and sold the house to the City in 1957.

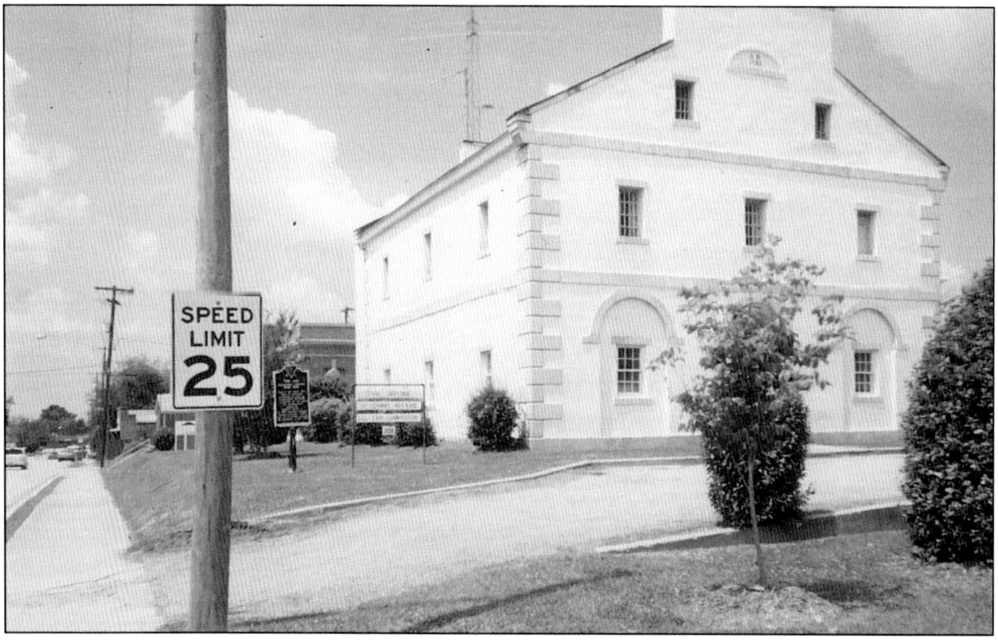

The old Lancaster County Jail was built in 1823 and was designed by Robert Mills, the famed architect and designer of the Washington Monument in Washington, D.C.

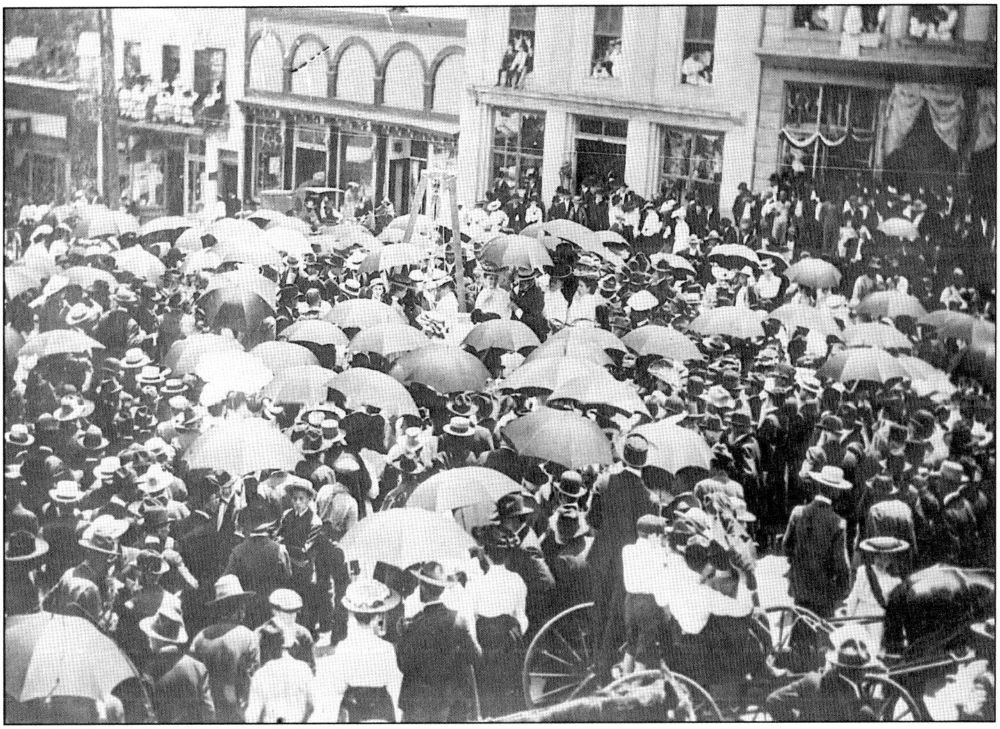

The laying of the cornerstone of the Confederate Monument in Chester took place on May 10, 1905. The 48-foot-high monument stands on top of the hill in downtown Chester.

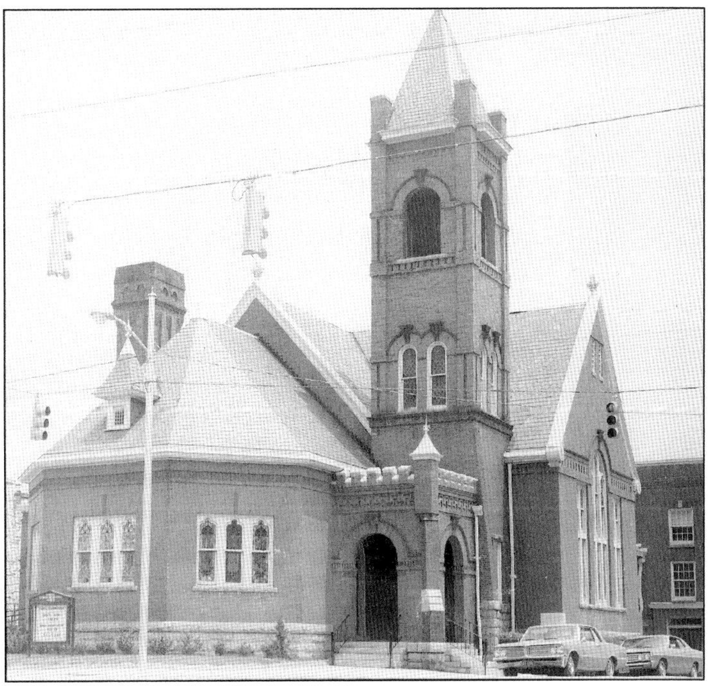

The Chester Associate Reformed Presbyterian Church was organized in 1869 with 14 members. This building was constructed in 1897–1898 and is still in use.

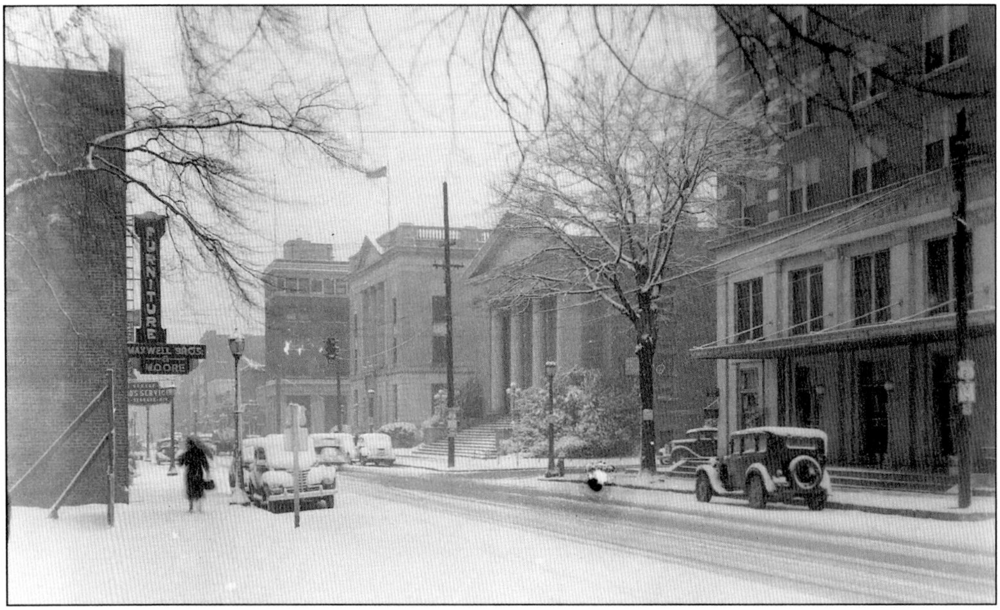

Pictured here is Main Street, looking west, in Rock Hill about 1940.

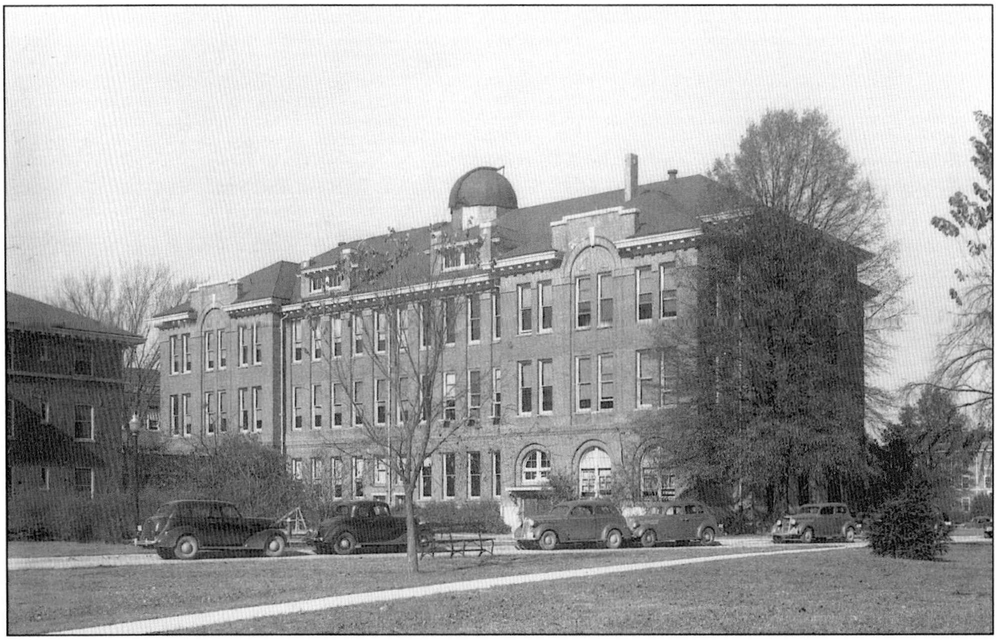

This is Tillman Science Building on the Winthrop campus in Rock Hill. Built in 1913, the building was razed in 1961. It housed science classrooms, laboratories, a museum, and an observatory.

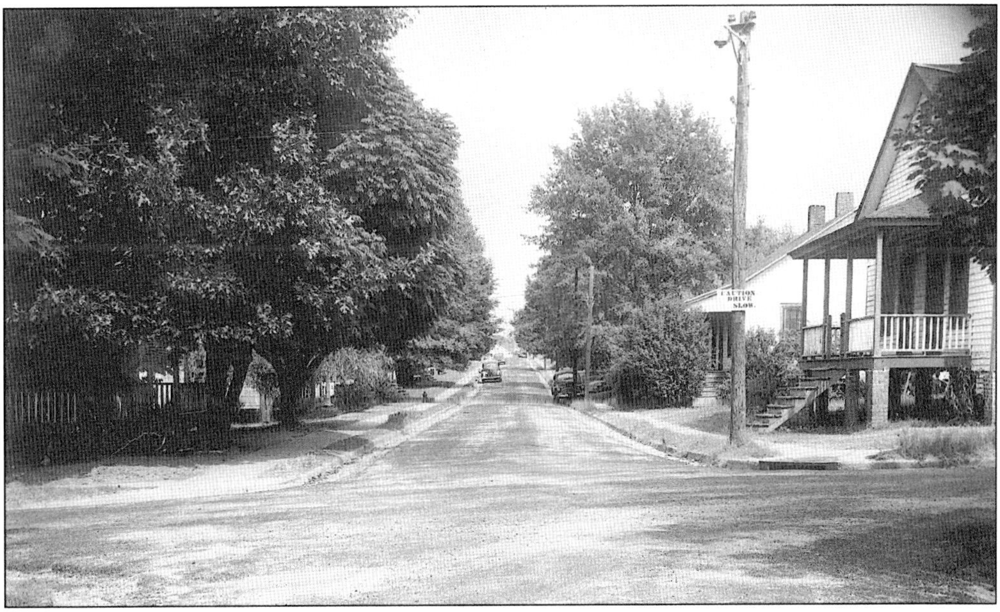

A street in the Gayle Textile Mill village in Chester is pictured here in 1948.

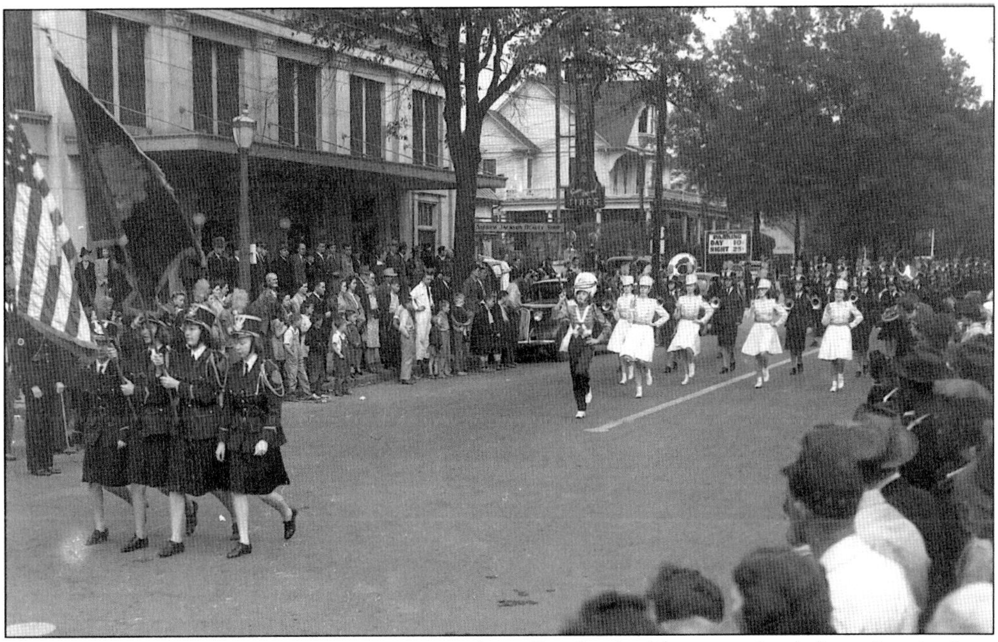

A parade travels down Main Street in Rock Hill. The building on the left is the Andrew Jackson Hotel.

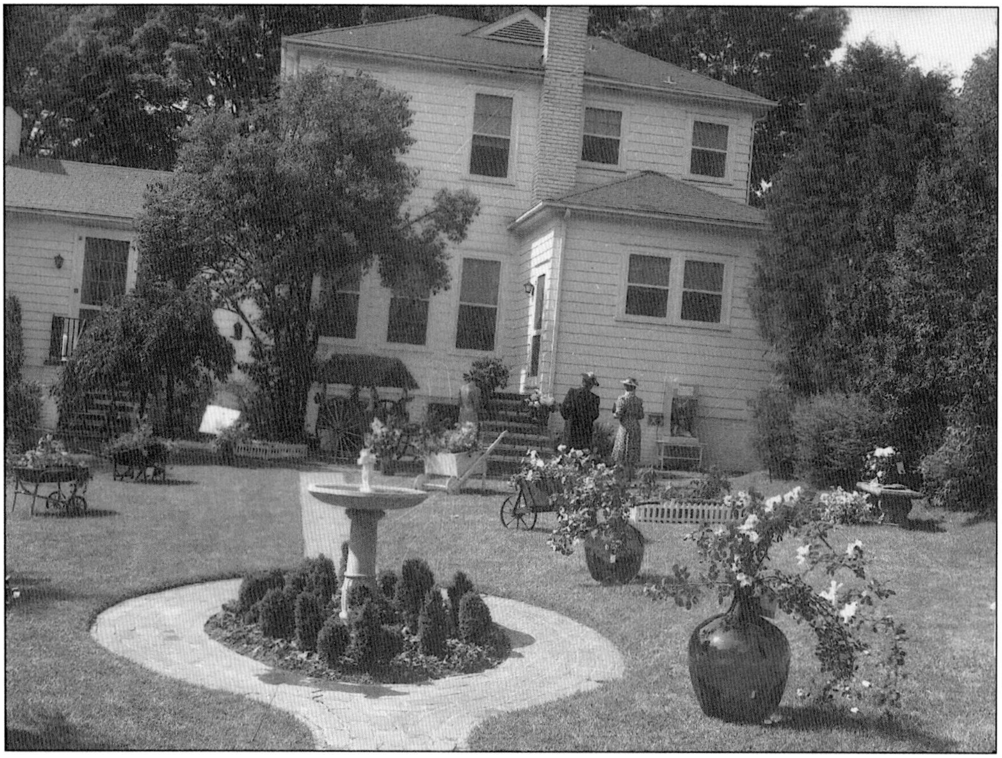

This lovely backyard garden belongs to a house on Aiken Street in Rock Hill.

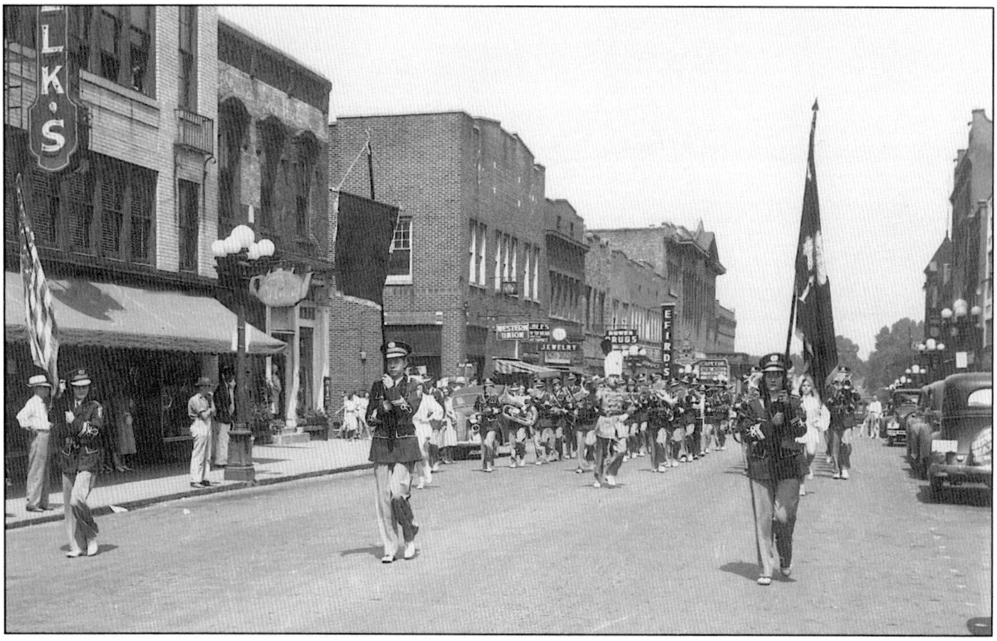

Rock Hill had a busy Main Street in the 1940s. This view is looking west from midway down the street.

Four

ARTS, SPORTS, AND ENTERTAINMENT

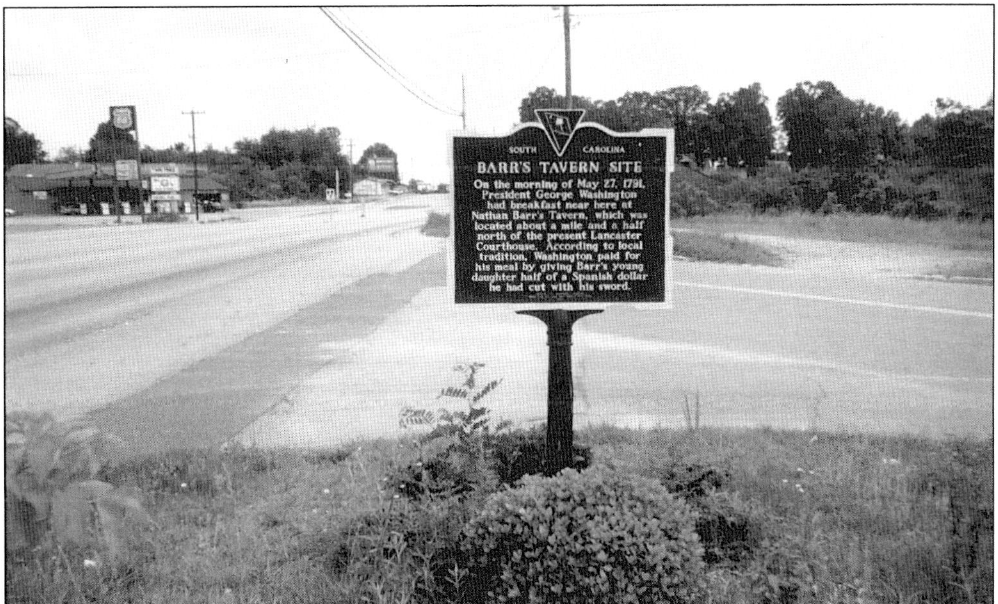

Typical of the numerous taverns and inns that once entertained travelers was Lancaster's Barr's Tavern. In 1791, George Washington visited this establishment during his tour of the South.

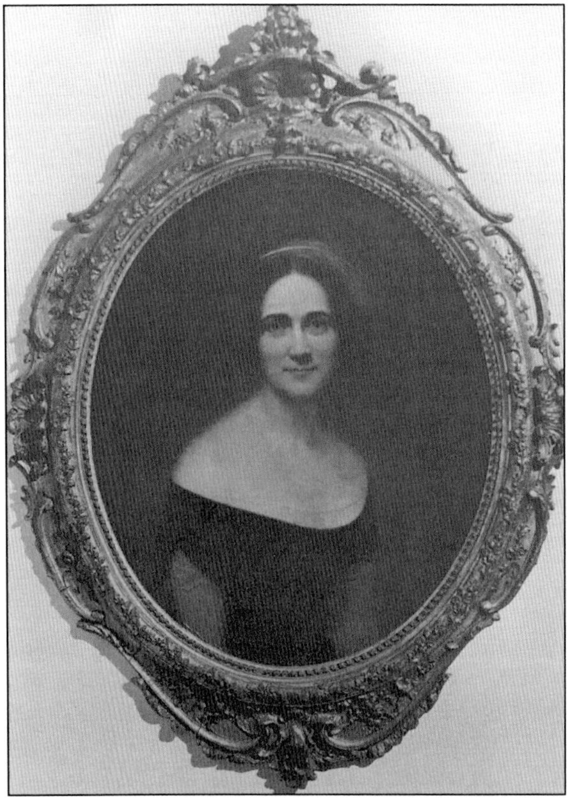

Famous Civil War diarist Mary Boykin Chestnut's father, Gov. Stephen Decatur Miller, once lived in Lancaster.

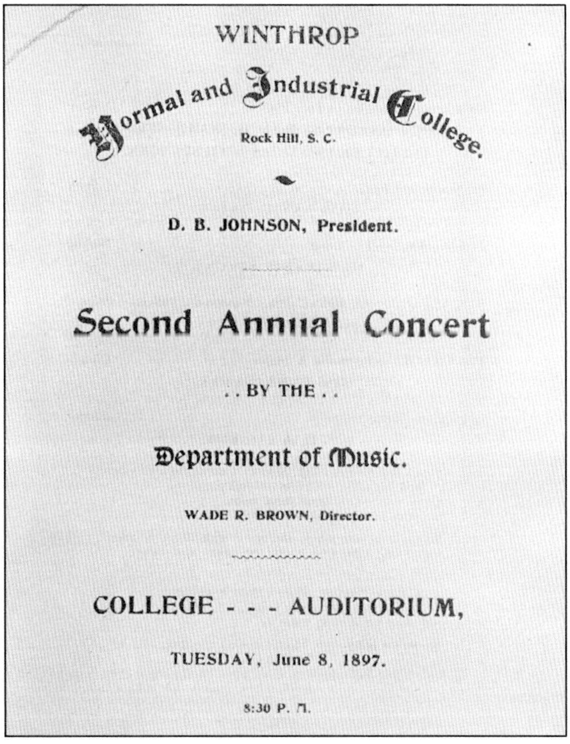

WINTHROP

Normal and Industrial College.

Rock Hill, S. C.

D. B. JOHNSON, President.

Second Annual Concert

. . BY THE . .

Department of Music.

WADE R. BROWN, Director.

COLLEGE - - - AUDITORIUM,

TUESDAY, June 8, 1897.

8:30 P. M.

Winthrop College's fine arts program is well known throughout the nation. This is the 1897 announcement of the Music Department's annual concert.

One of the most valuable holdings of the Winthrop University Archives is the Eleanor Burts Children's Book Collection.

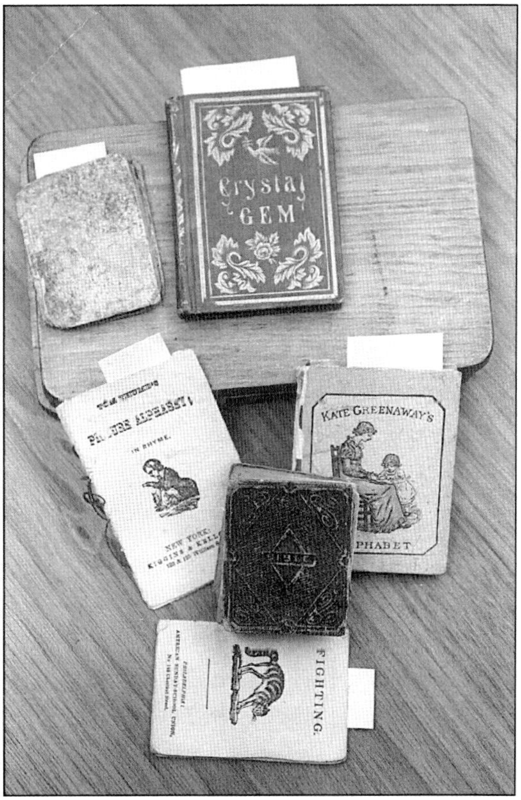

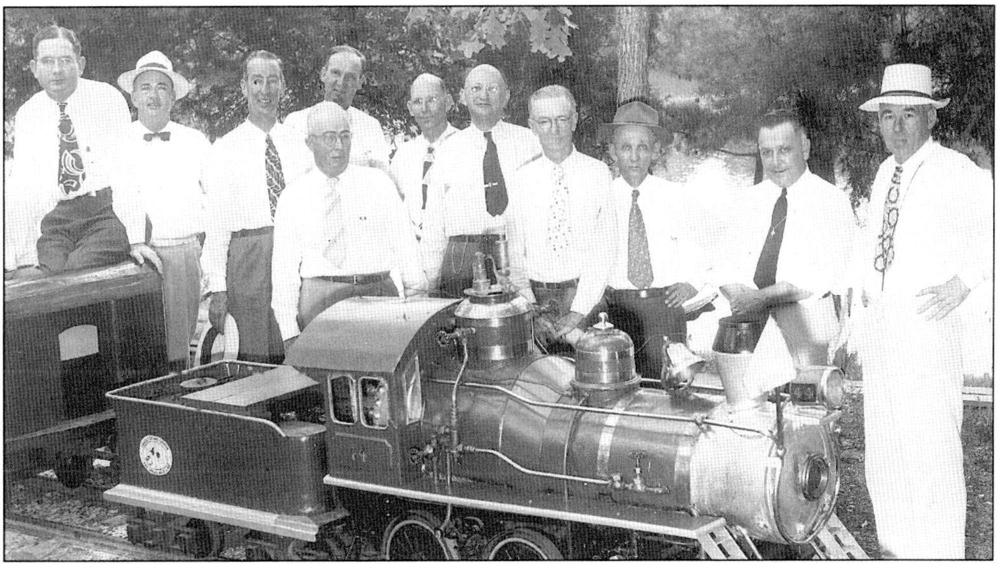

Springs Park, sponsored by the Springs textile company, operated a park for decades on the border between Lancaster and Chester Counties. On the right is Col. Elliot White Springs, president of the company.

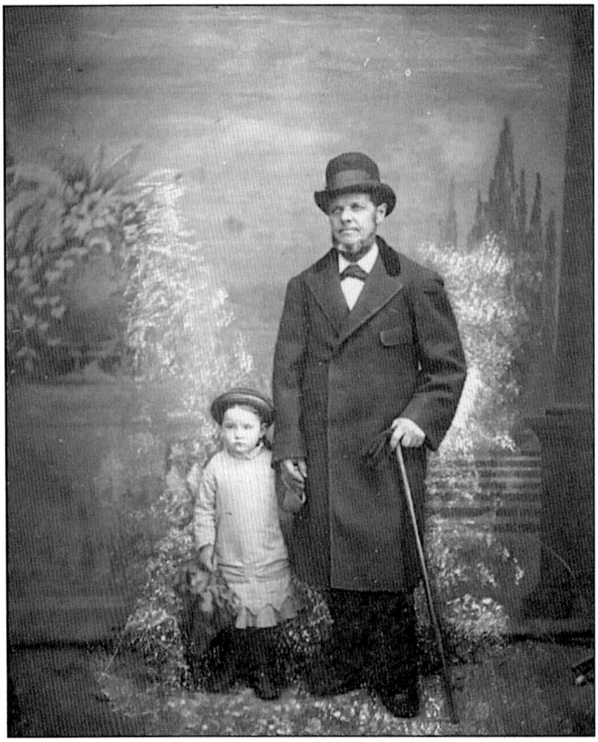

In turn-of-the-century Yorkville, John R. Schorb's photographs were valuable records of the community's activities.

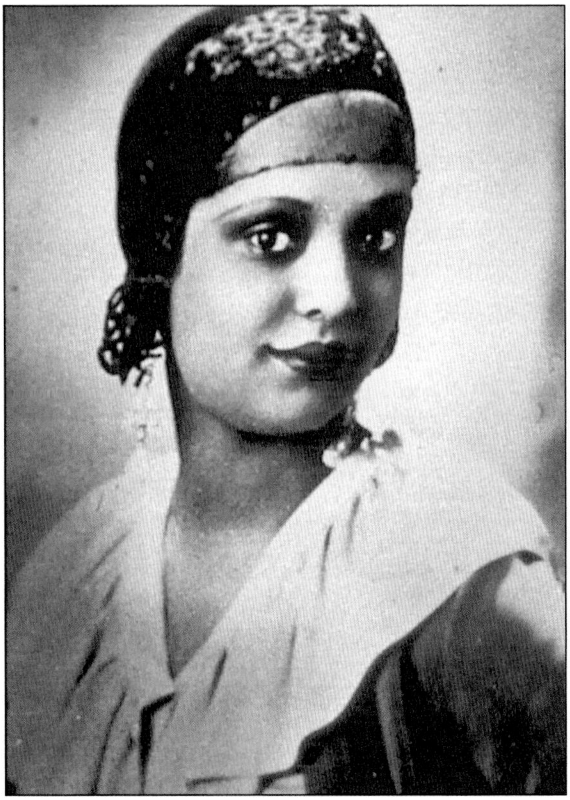

Nina Mae McKinney, one of Lancaster's most accomplished actresses, poses in this early 20th-century photograph.

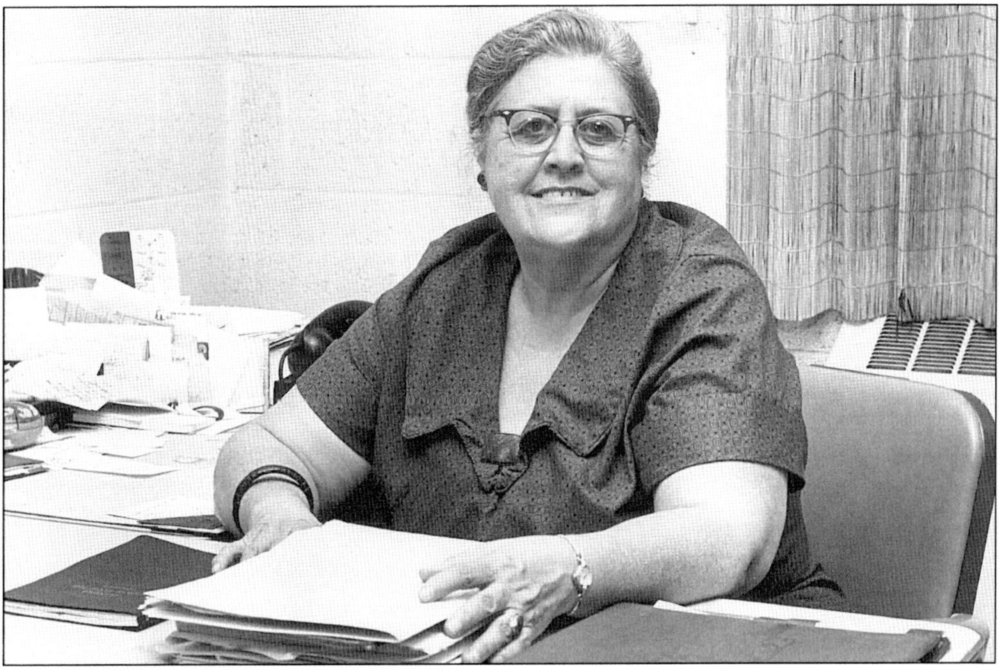

In the early 1960s, Julia Post, the head of Winthrop's Physical Education Department, became a pioneer in new ways to exercise.

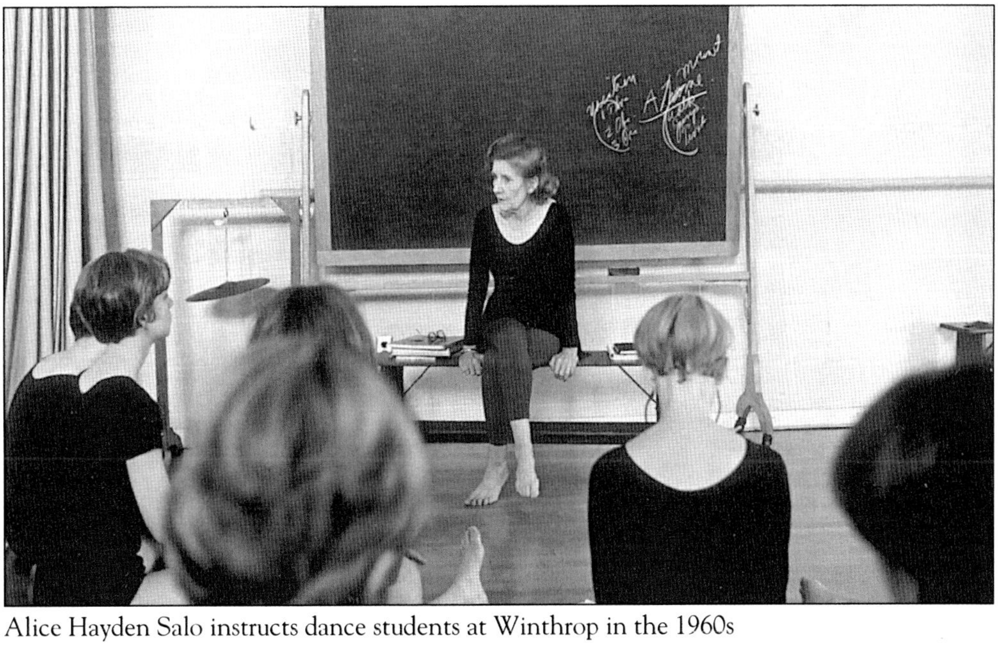

Alice Hayden Salo instructs dance students at Winthrop in the 1960s

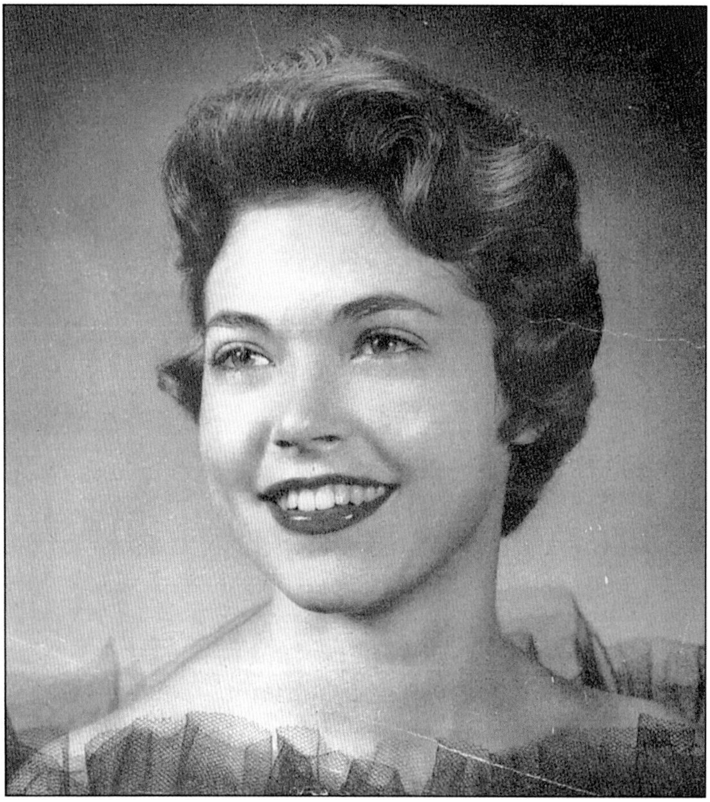

With her musical talents and beauty, York's Pat Moss became Miss Universe of South Carolina in 1959.

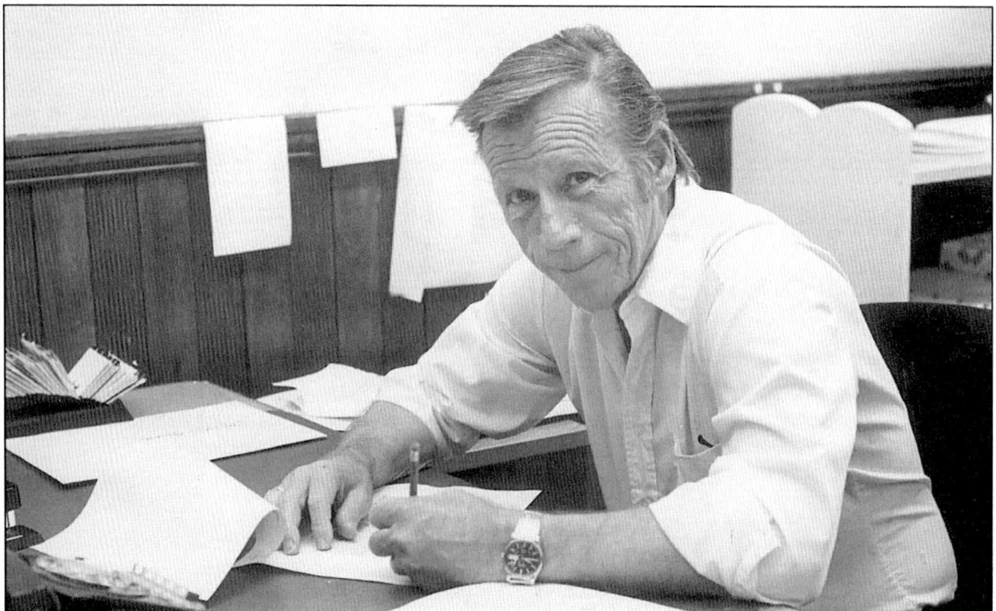

Winthrop's writer-in-residence, Prof. Bob Bristow, was the author of several well-received literary works in the 1970s.

Grace Beacham Freeman of Rock Hill was South Carolina's poet laureate in the mid-1970s.

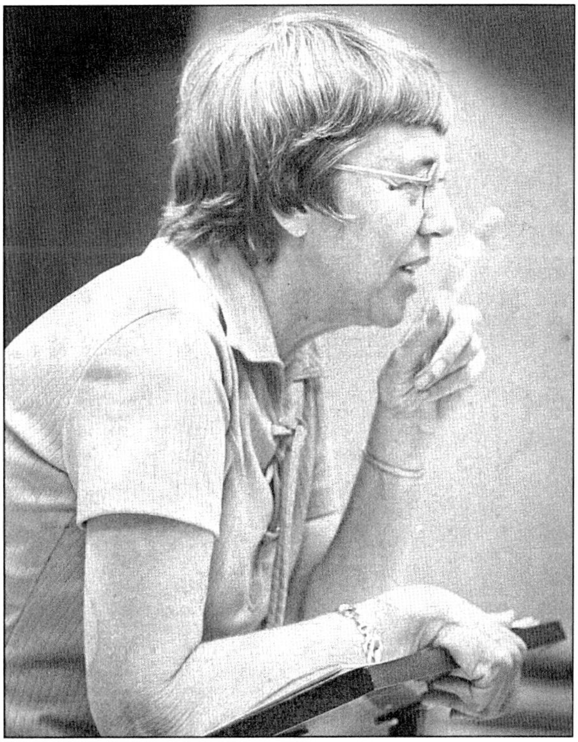

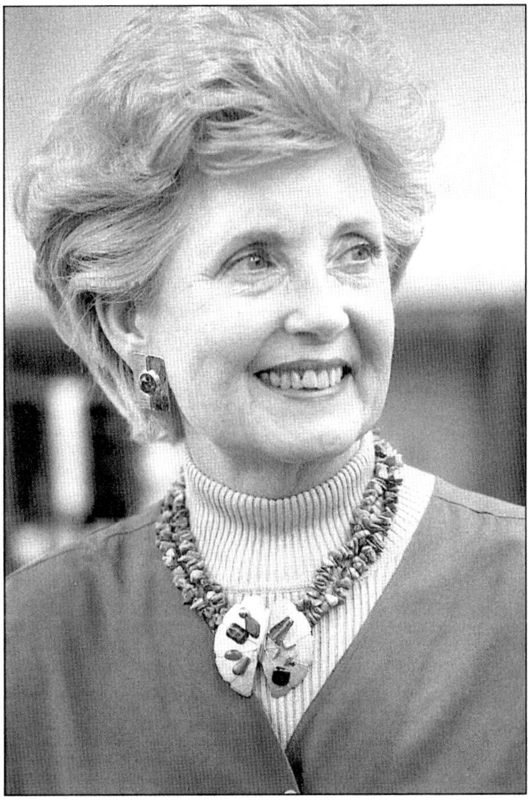

One of the area's most accomplished authors is Rock Hill native Frances Patton Statham.

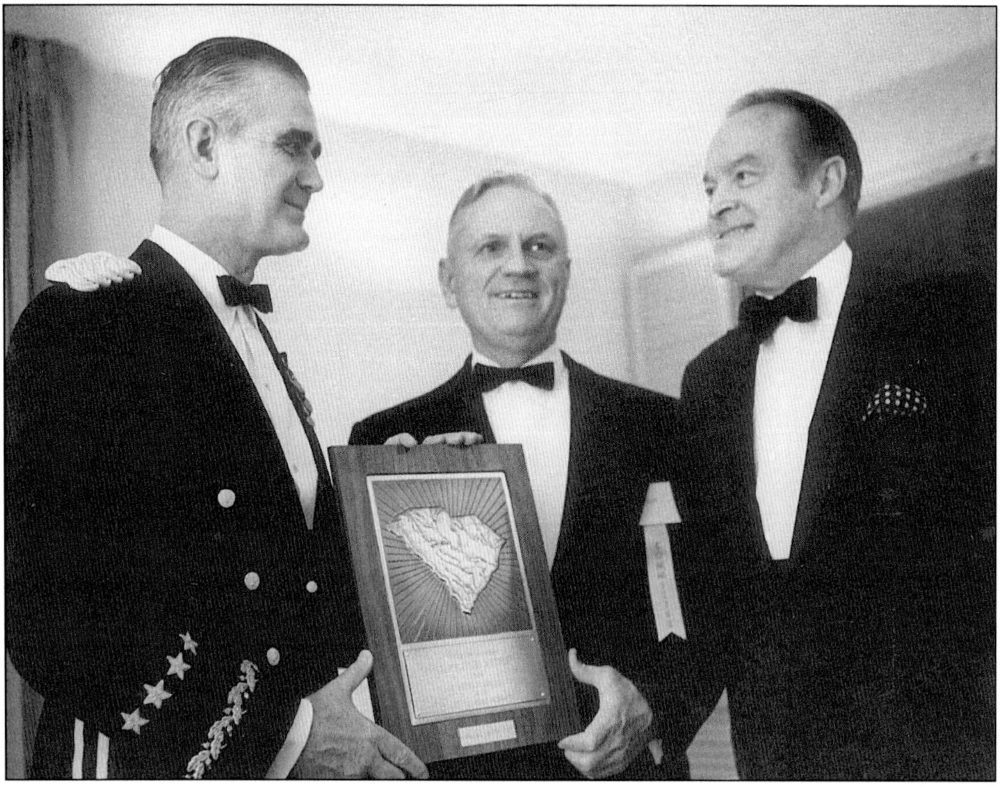

National performers frequently visit the Catawba region. On the right is comedian Bob Hope with Gen. William Westmoreland (left) and Fort Mill's Francis M. Mack Sr.

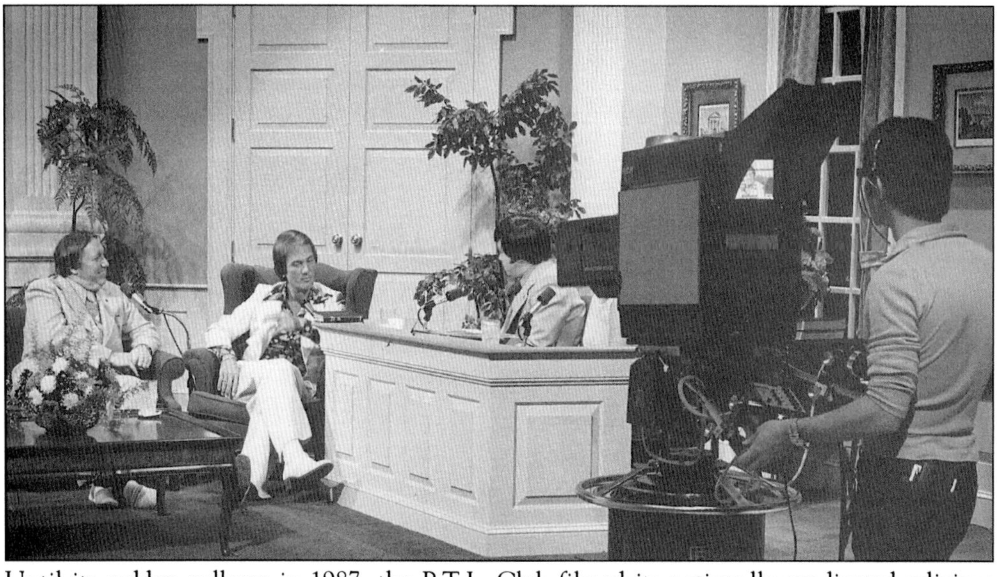

Until its sudden collapse in 1987, the P.T.L. Club filmed its nationally syndicated religious show from its Fort Mill studio. Singer Pat Boone (center) confers on the set with Rev. Jim Bakker (right).

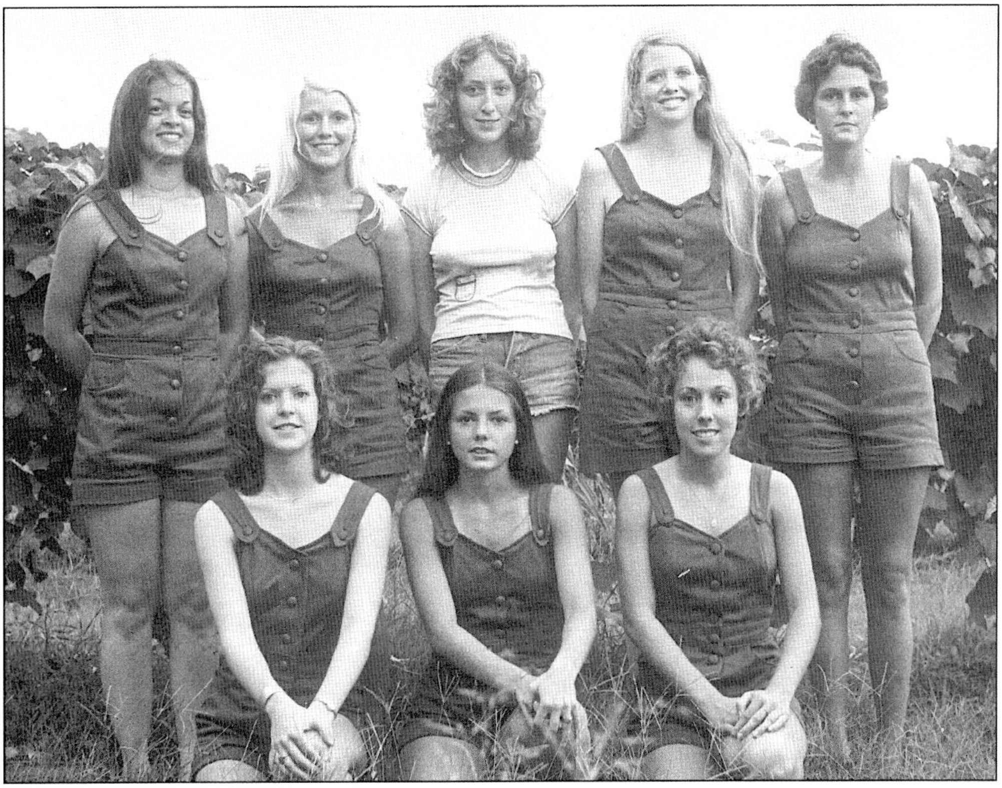

An annual festival in York featured performers like the 1976 Grapettes.

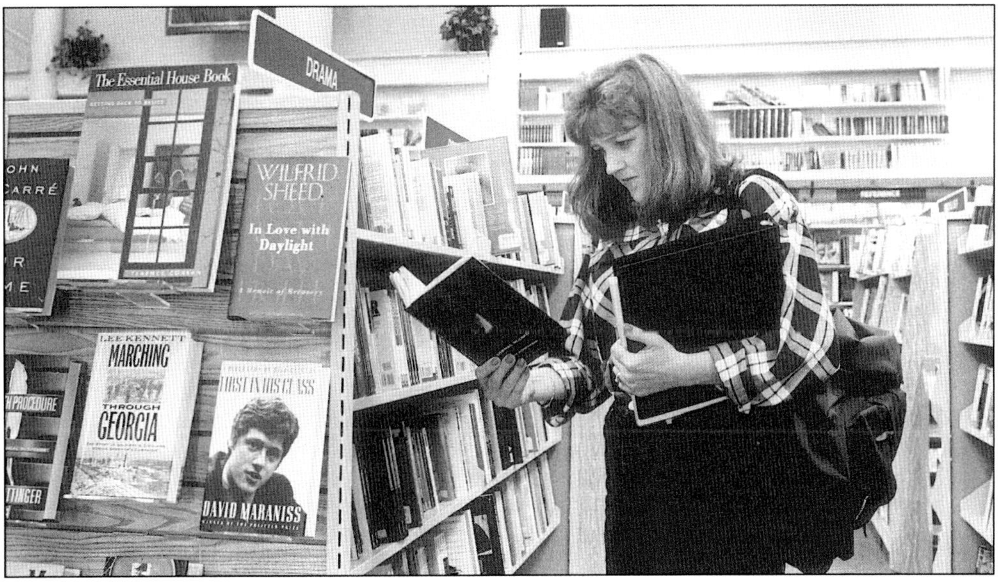

Books on virtually any topic are readily available at Rock Hill's Bookworm.

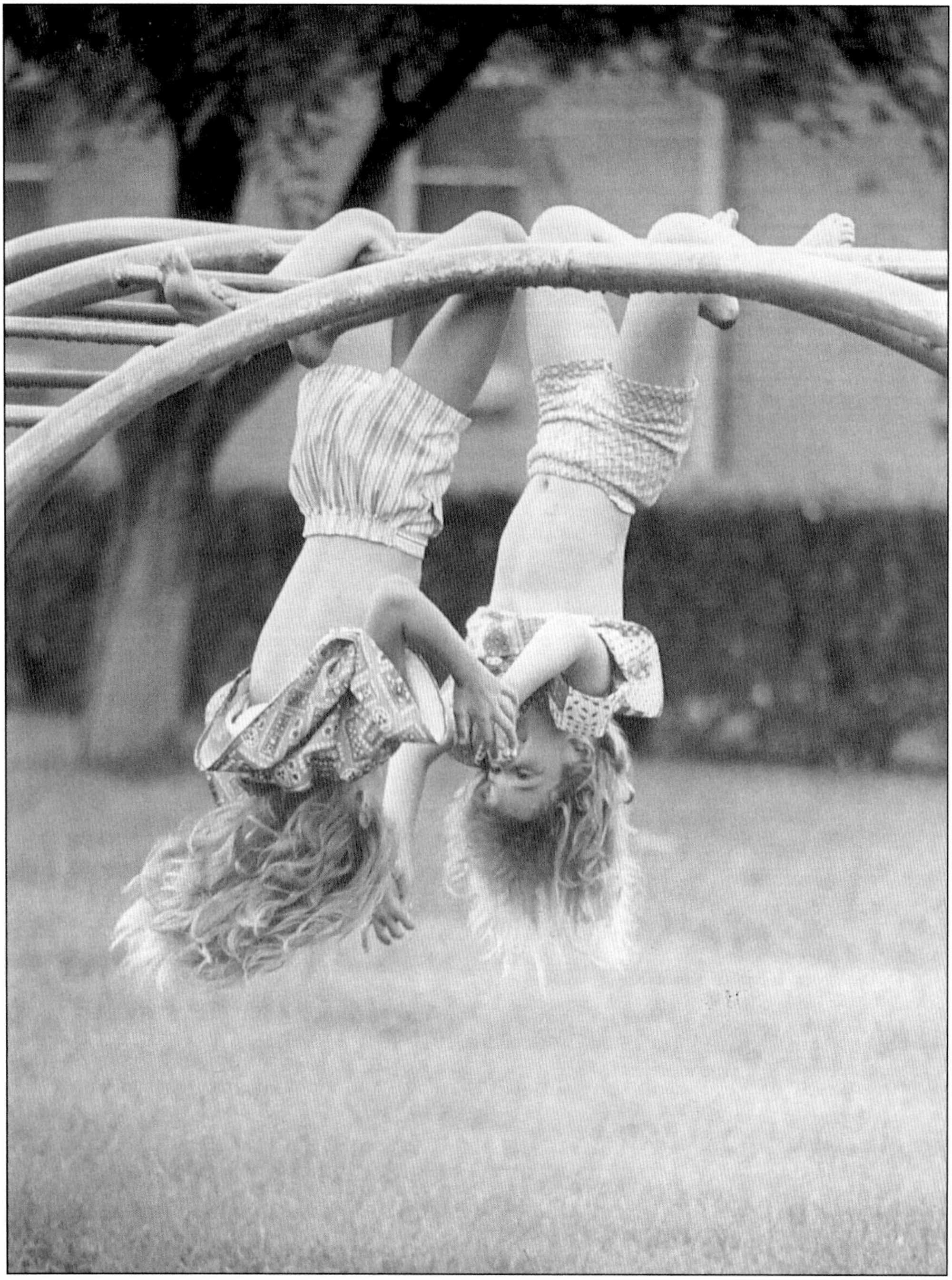

Kelly and Kim Bowers, two Rock Hill sisters, entertain themselves in one of the region's parks in the summer of 1976.

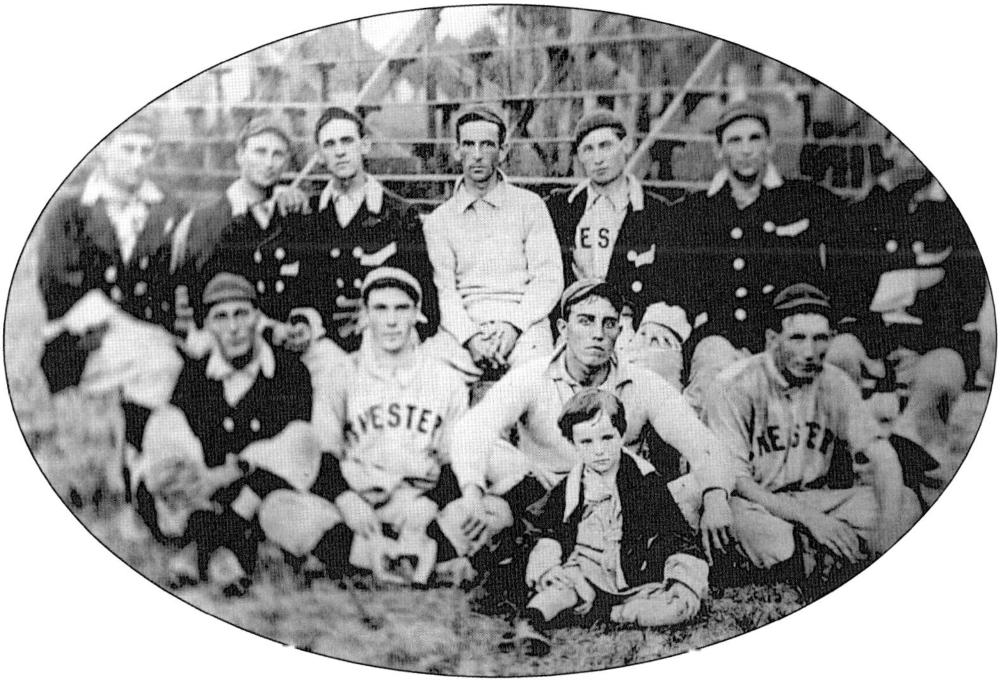

Baseball has been part of the Catawba region's heritage since the dawn of this century. Pictured here is one of Chester's early teams.

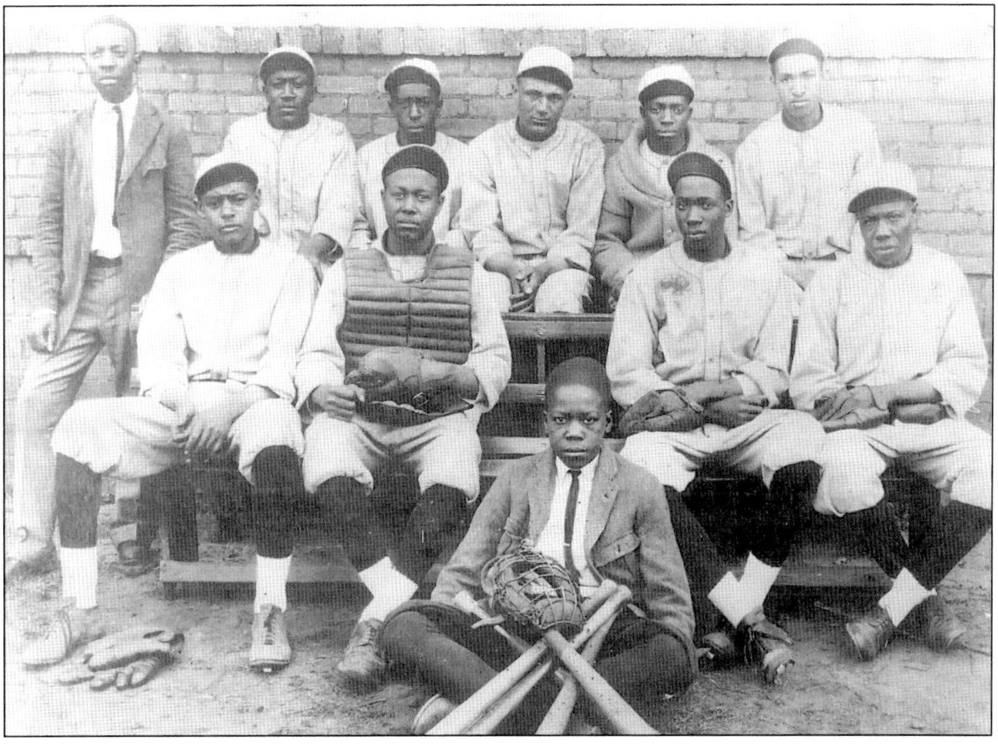

This African-American baseball team played in York around 1915.

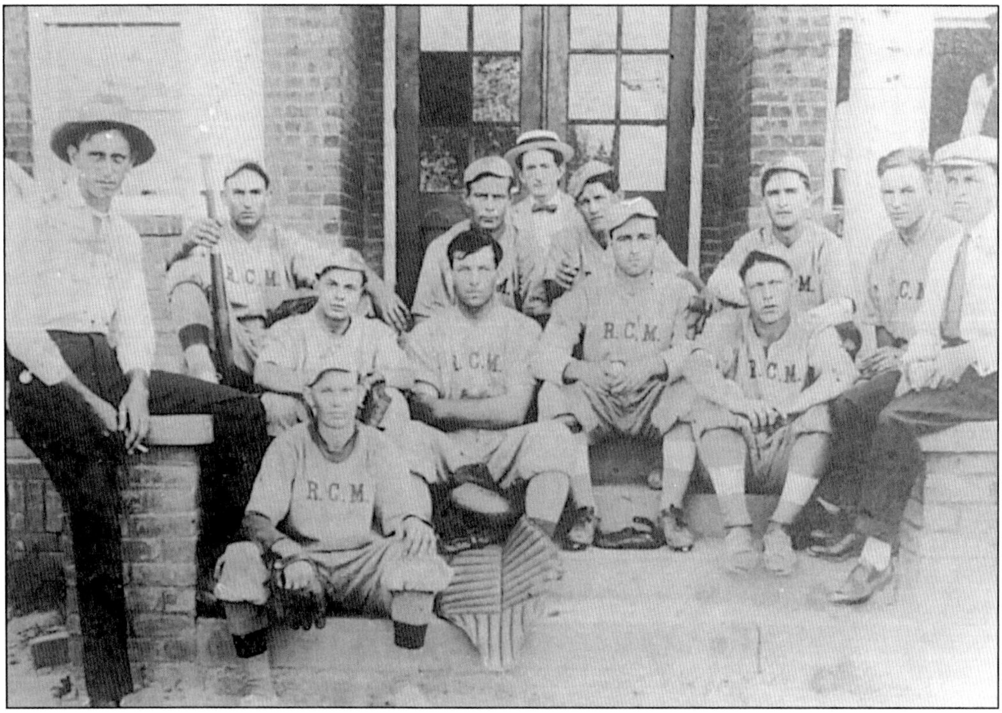

Mills often sponsored athletic teams. This one was the Republic Cotton Mill Squad in 1916.

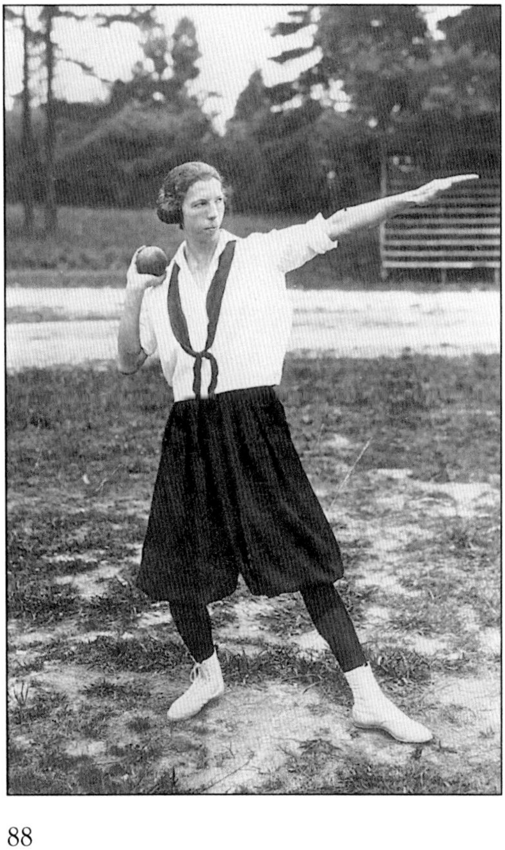

Lucille Godbold, a Winthrop College track star, won two gold medals and four other medals in Paris in 1922 at the First International Track Meet for Women. In 1961, Godbold was the first woman to be inducted into the South Carolina Athletic Hall of Fame.

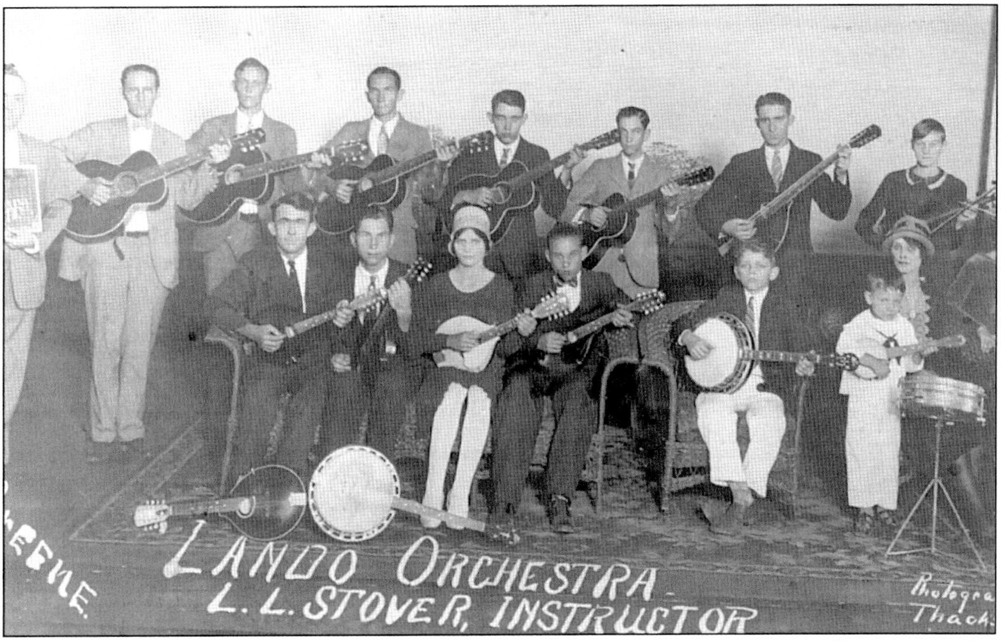

In the 1920s, orchestras appeared in virtually all of the region's communities. This group is the 1927 Lando Orchestra.

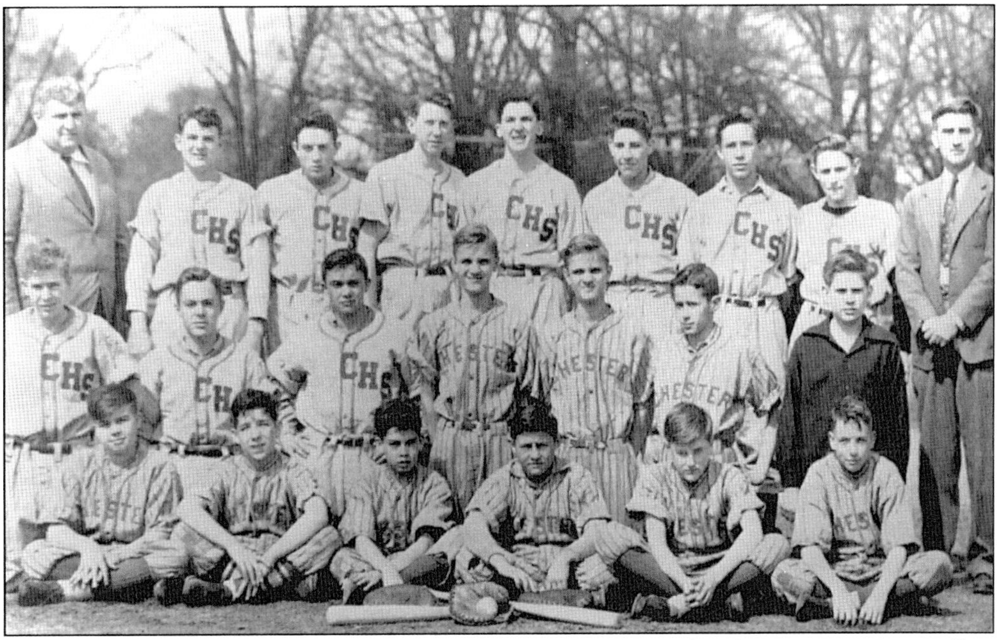
Even in the World War II years, sports continued to fill people's leisure time. Joe Collins (top left) and Al Shealey (top right) coached the 1944, 10-2 season, Chester High School baseball team.

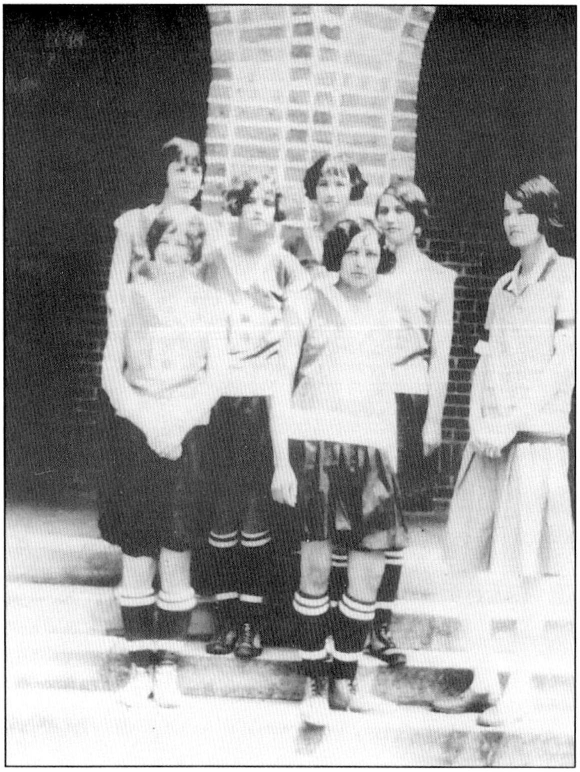

Even rural communities made sure that their children participated in sporting events. These girls were members of the Bethany 1920s team.

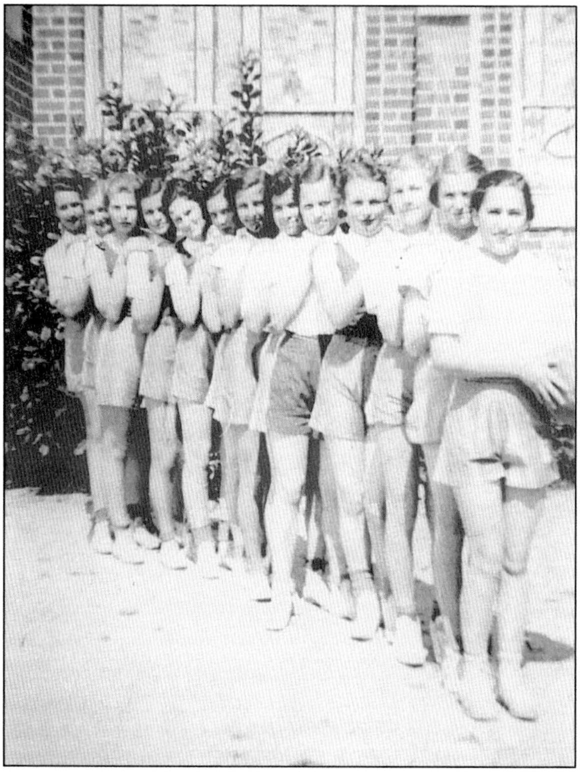

A decade later, in 1938, Bethany's team had doubled in size.

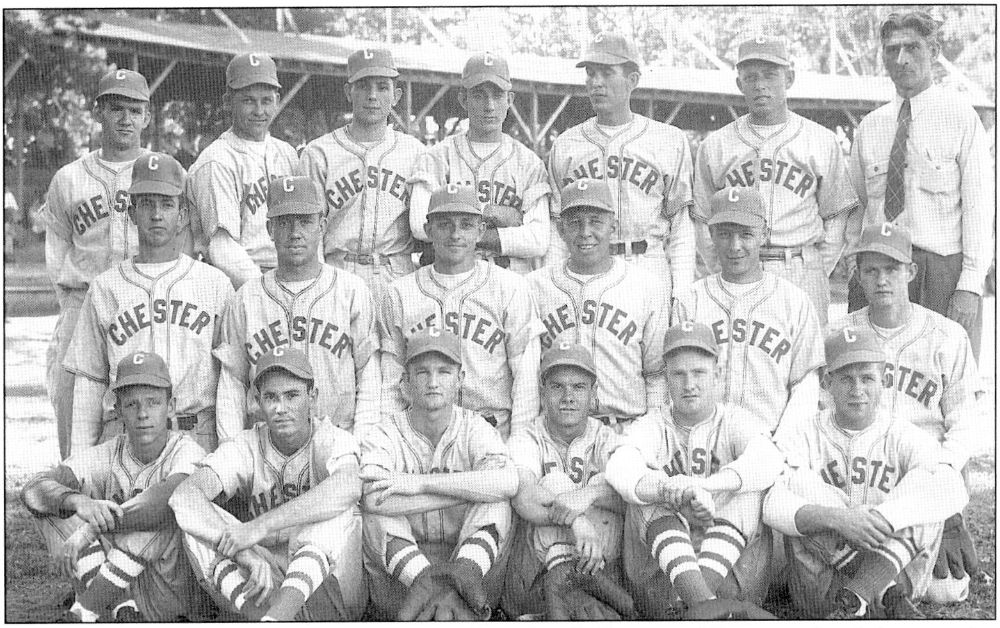

Coach Al Shealey continued to field excellent baseball teams. This one faced foes on the diamond in 1948.

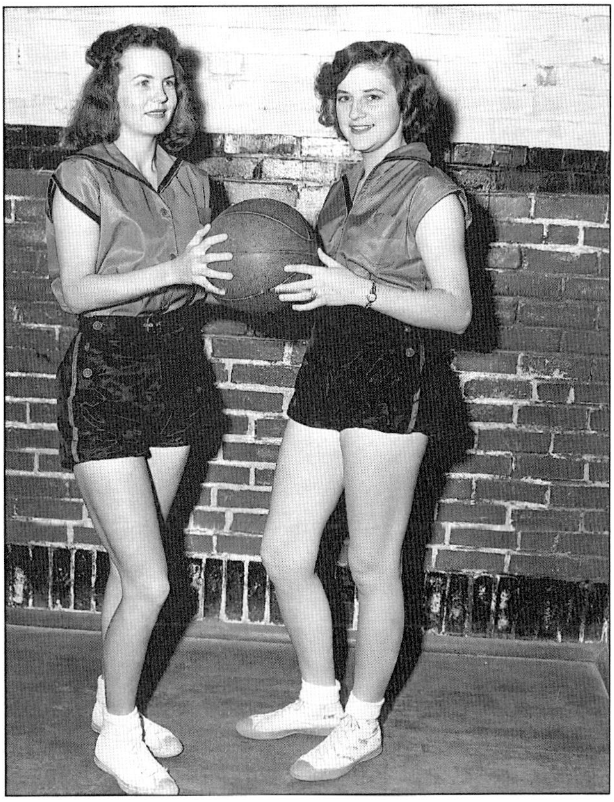

Elizabeth Morris and Vivian Collins were star players on the Gayle Mill basketball team in Chester.

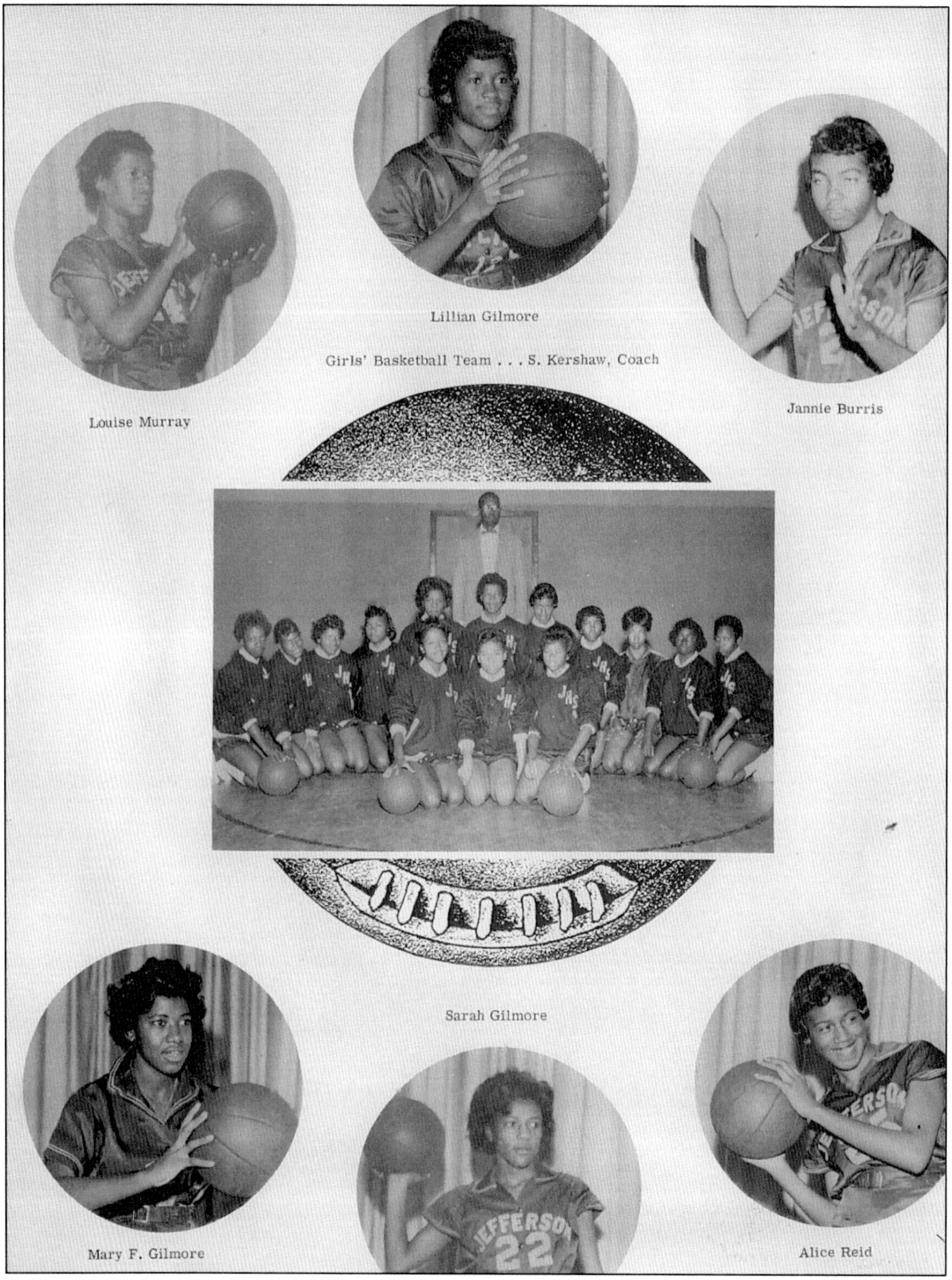

Jefferson High School's girls' team was showcased in this York County yearbook from the 1950s.

Evans "Buck" George of Rock Hill was a star athlete at Clemson College and later played professional football for the Washington Redskins.

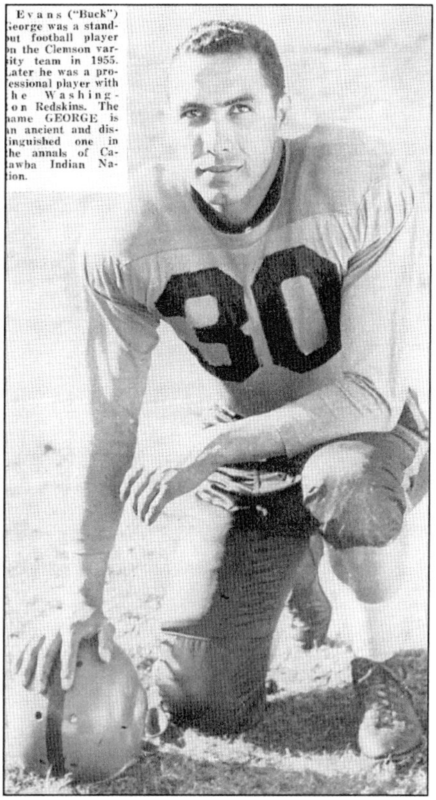

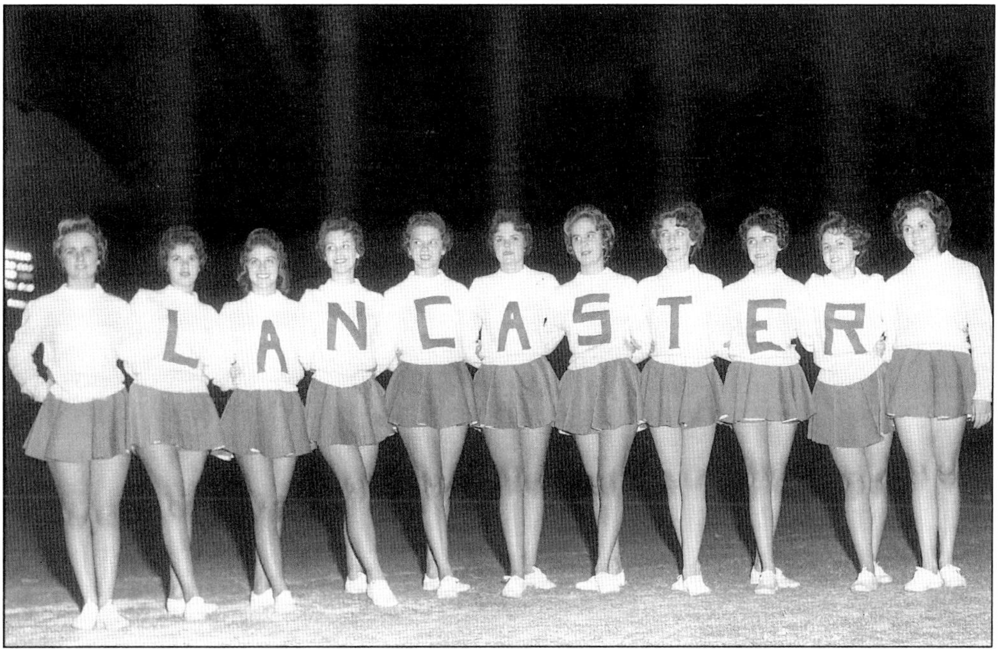

These Lancaster cheerleaders led the fans at gridiron games in the 1960s.

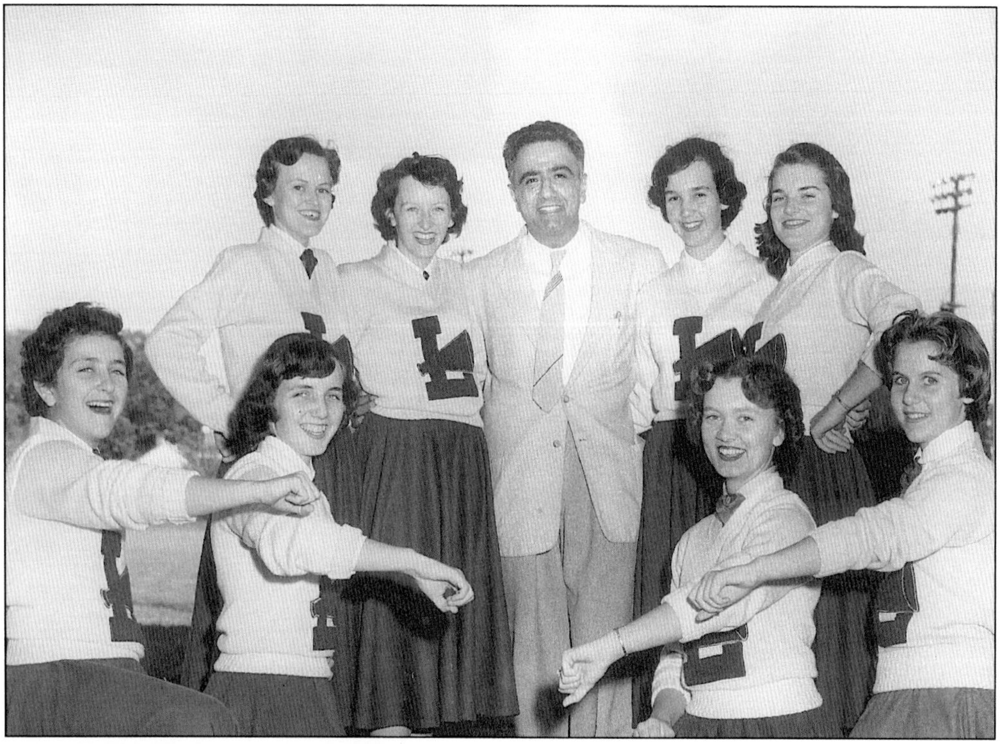

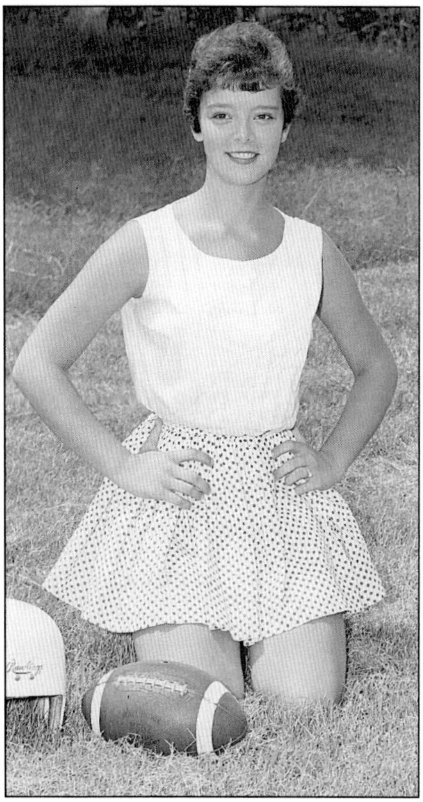

Well-known photographer Joe Azer posed with some of Lancaster High School's cheerleaders in the late 1950s.

Chester cheerleader Kay Lusk pauses before a game in 1960.

Majorette Jan Murray prepares to lead the Chester High School band onto the field in 1970.

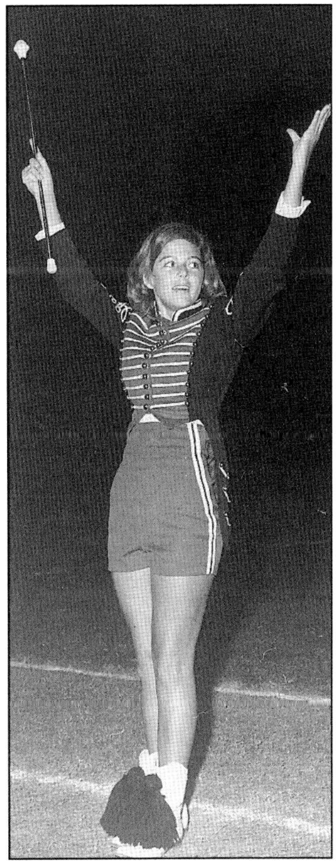

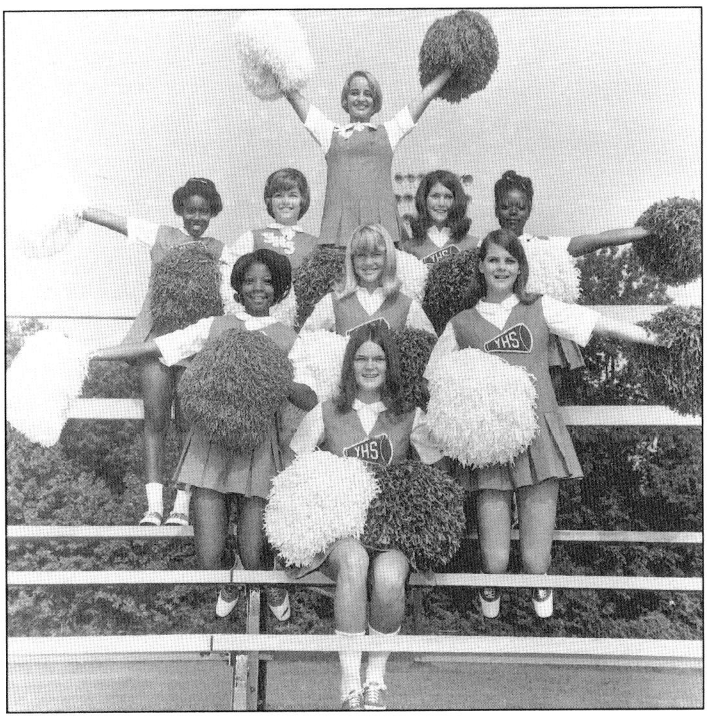

York High School's cheerleaders wave to the fans in 1971.

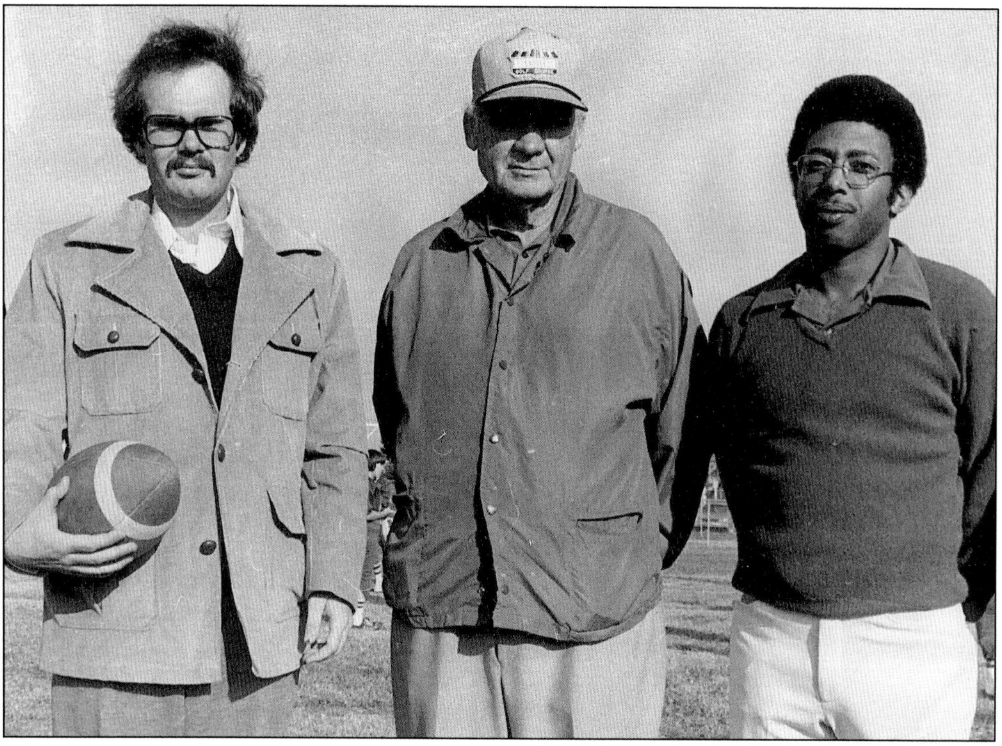

The Chester Junior High School coaches celebrate their undefeated 1976 football season. From left to right are Edward Lee, Tom McConnell, and Ron Sewell.

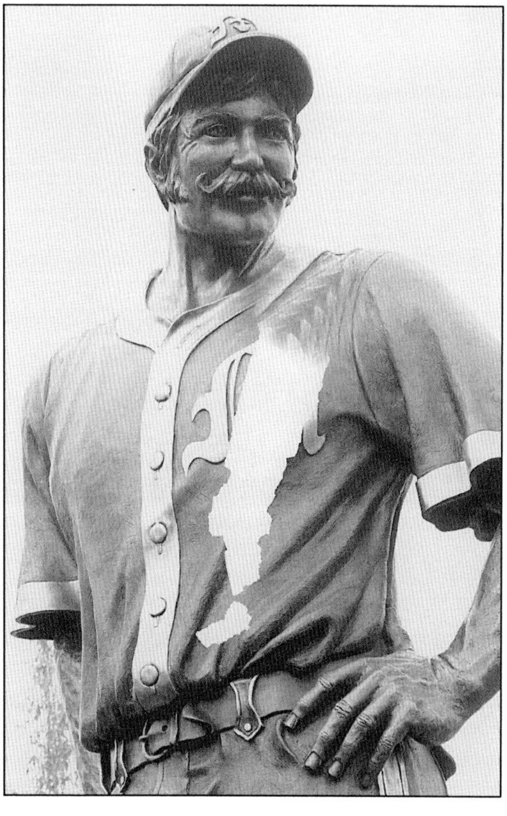

Mighty Casey is poised at the bat in Rock Hill's Cherry Park.

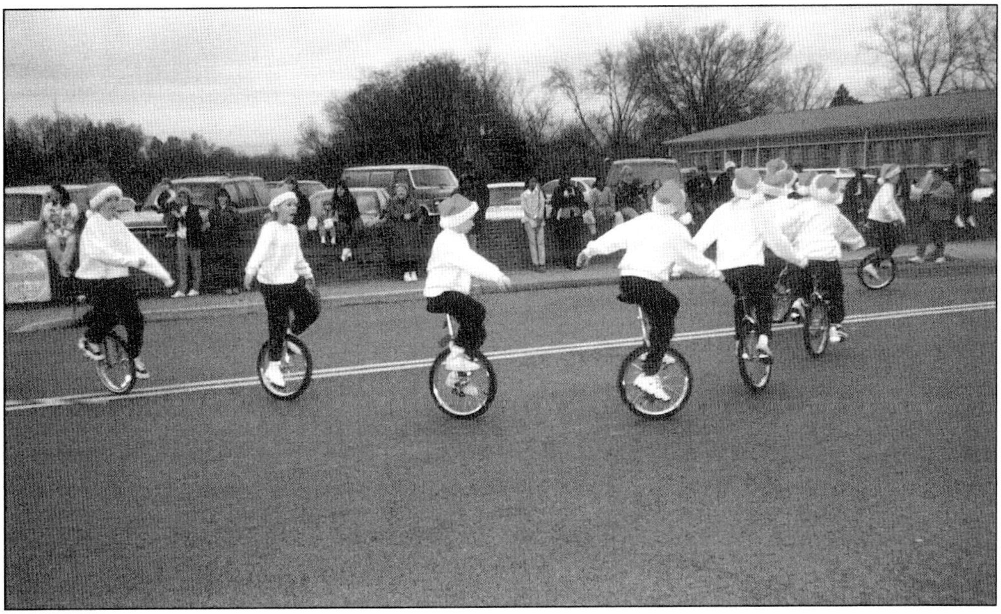

York's unicycle team performs at the 1997 Christmas parade.

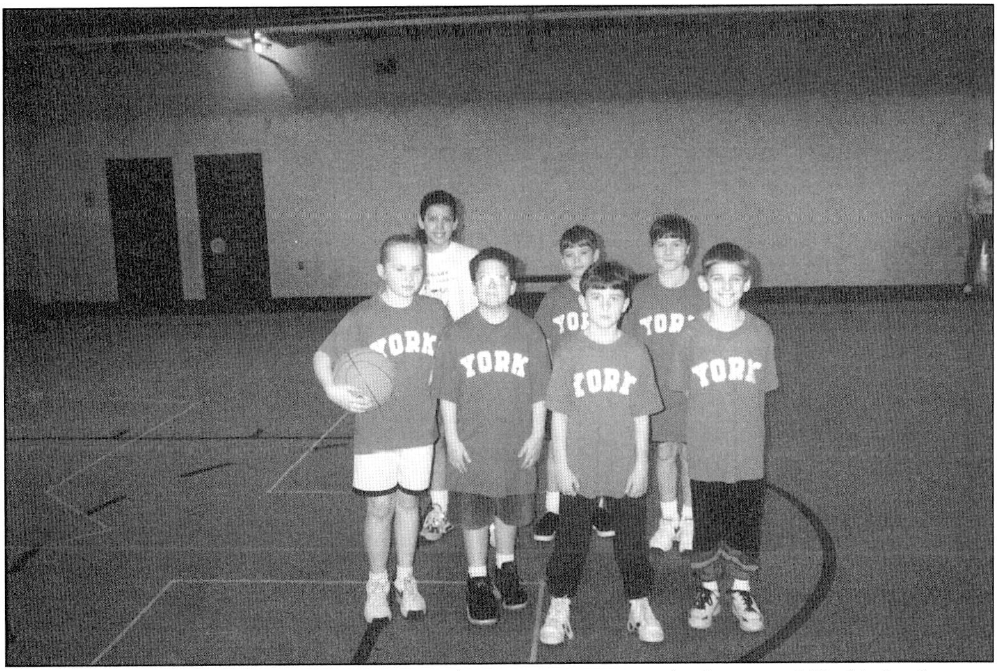

Churches often sponsor athletic teams. This one is comprised of some of York's Lutherans, Methodists, and Presbyterians.

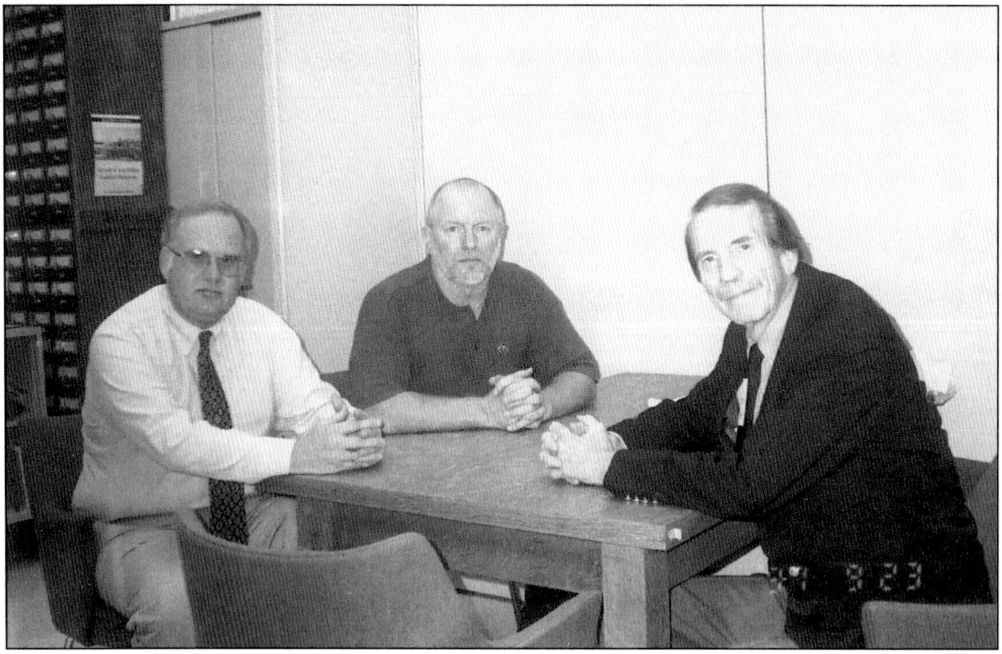

Three Winthrop professors, Edward Lee, Ron Chepesiuk, and Haney Howell, collaborated on a book that contained interviews with some of America's top investigative journalists. The program was a product of the Archives Senior Research Associate Program, which brings together Winthrop Archives staff and faculty in collaborative scholarly and outreach efforts.

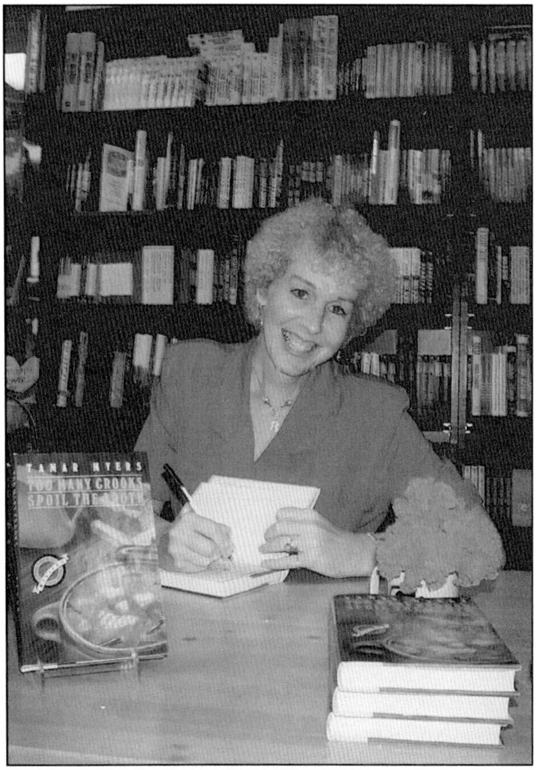

Author of more than 14 mysteries, Rock Hill's Tamar Myers signs copies of *Too Many Crooks Spoil the Broth*.

Five

Business and Industry

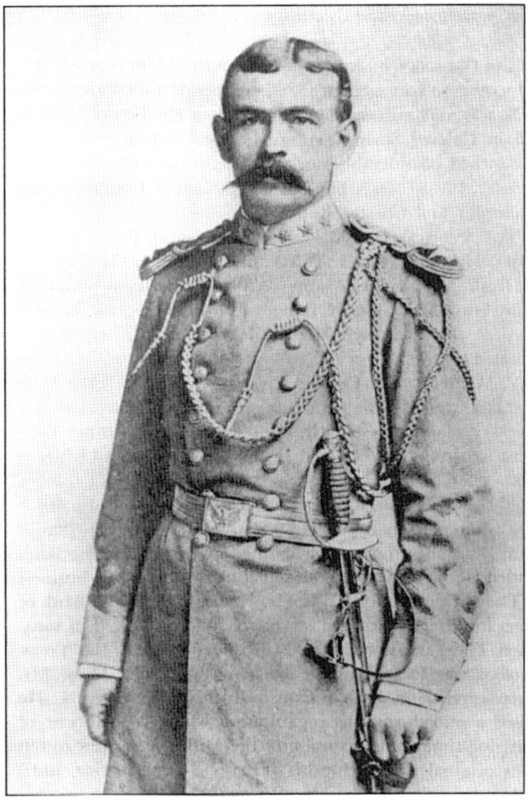

No person played a more prominent role in the early industrial development of the Catawba region than Leroy Springs (1861–1931), the founder of what is now Springs Cotton Mills. Colonel Springs is shown here in 1887 as a colonel on the staff of Gov. John Peter Richardson.

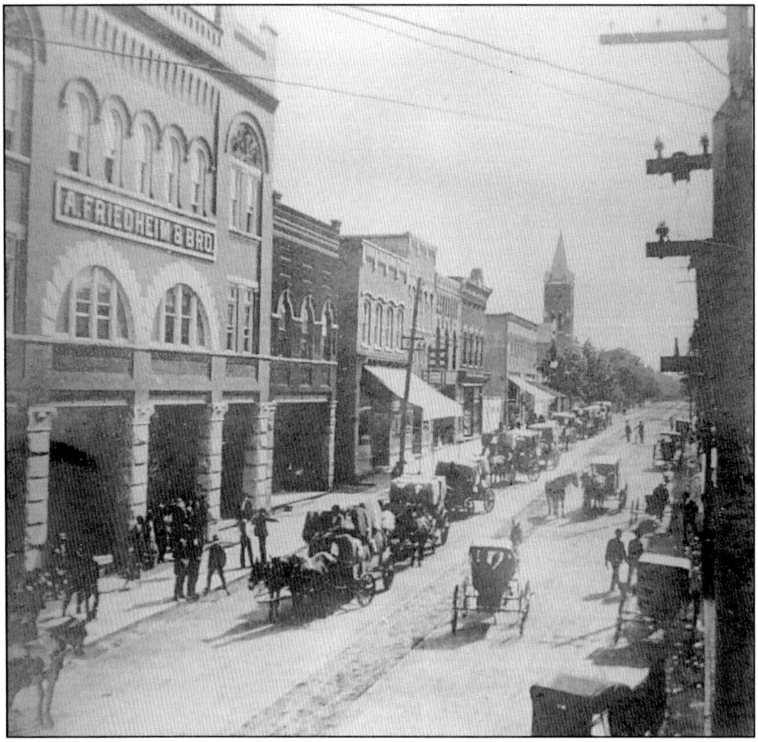

This is the way Main Street in Rock Hill looked in 1902. Notice Friedham's Department Store, one of Rock Hill's first businesses, on the left. The store closed in 1965.

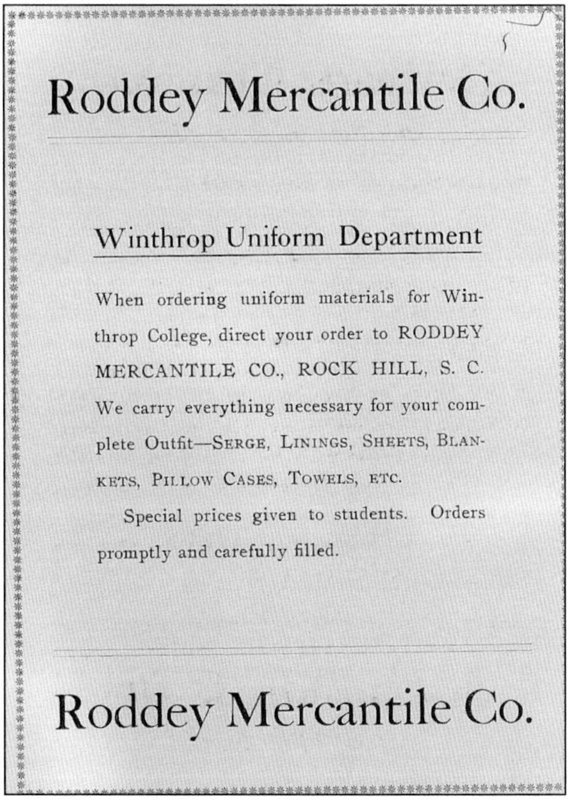

The Roddey Mercantile Company was a thriving Rock Hill business in the early part of the 20th century.

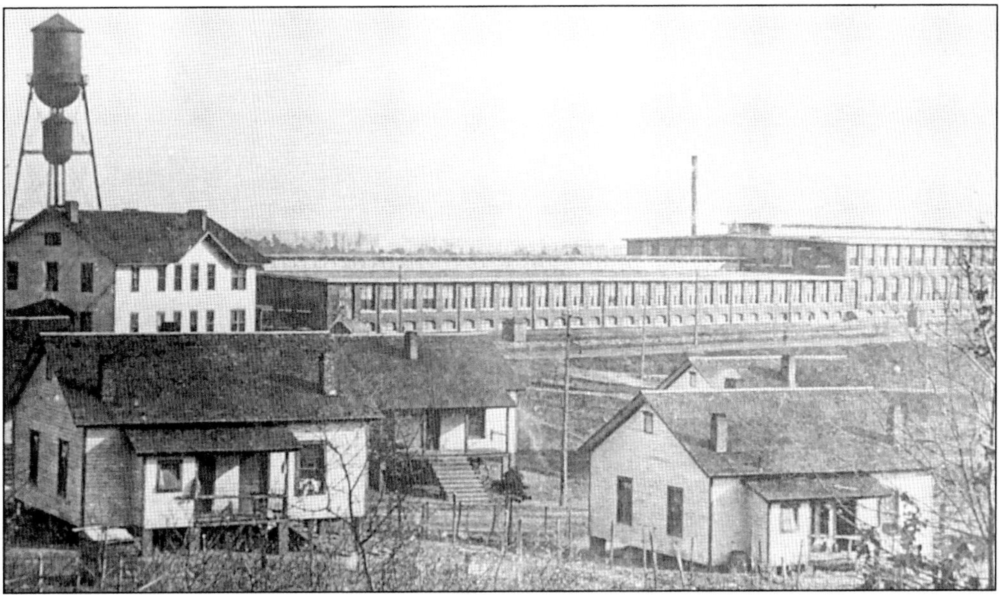

By 1909, the power plants on the Catawba River were providing more power than the area could use. James Buchanan Duke foresaw that the surplus electricity could be harnessed to manufacture textiles. Duke, along with some business associates, organized the Republic Textile Mills Company at Great Falls. The plant shown here officially became known as the Republic Plant One in 1948 when Republic Textile Mills merged with J.P. Stevens Company.

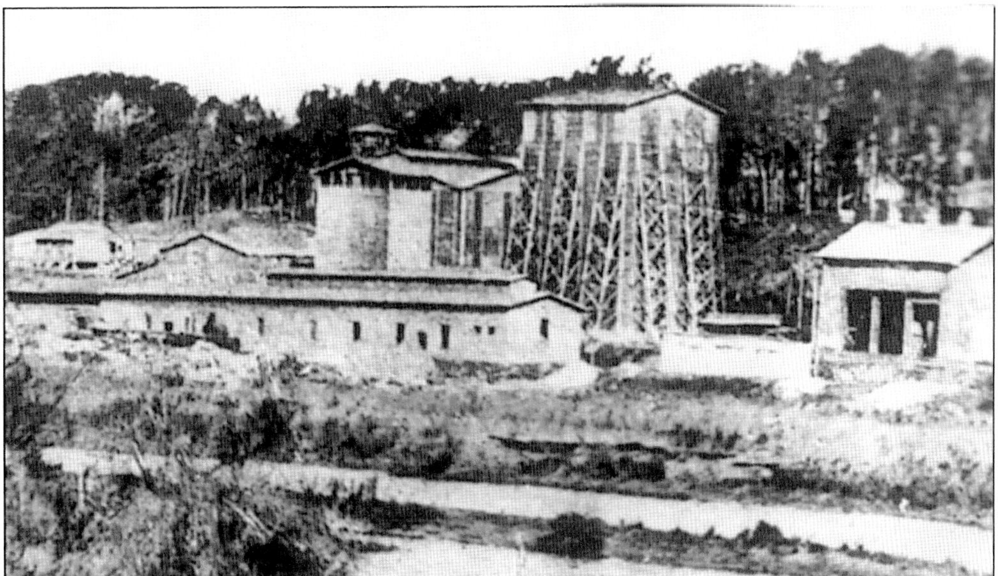

Built in 1916 at the intersection of Fishing Creek and the Catawba River, the Nitrolee Plant of Great Falls was the first plant in the United States that extracted nitrogen from the air for use in the manufacture of fertilizer.

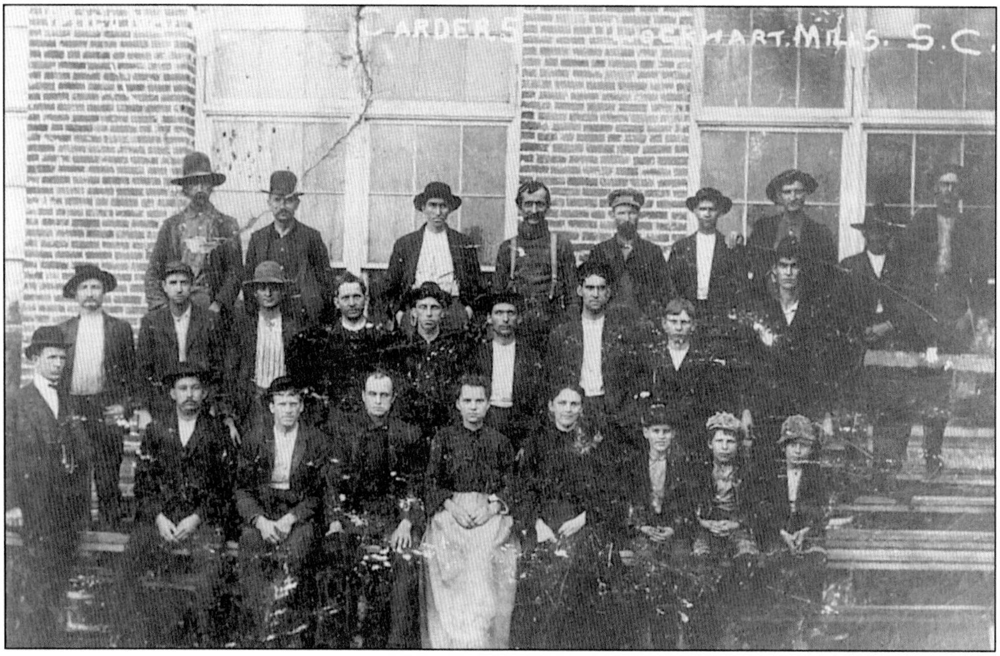

Carders from Lockart Mill No. 1 pose for this photograph.

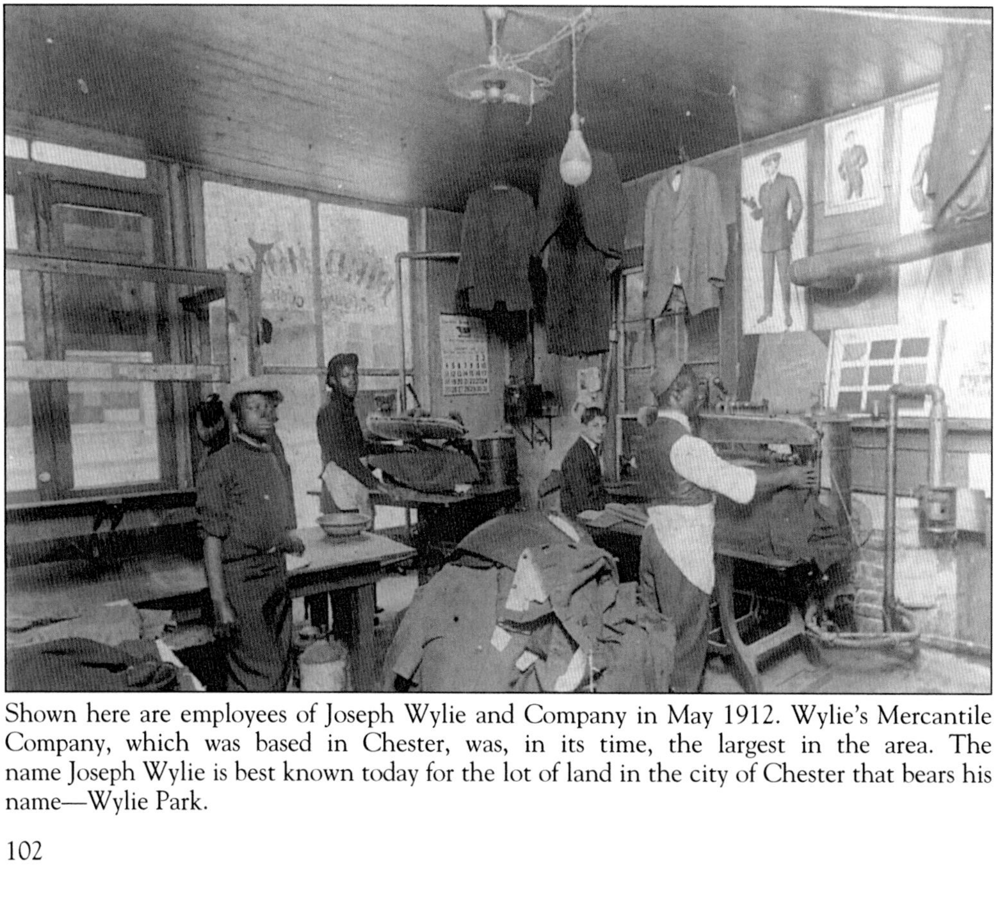

Shown here are employees of Joseph Wylie and Company in May 1912. Wylie's Mercantile Company, which was based in Chester, was, in its time, the largest in the area. The name Joseph Wylie is best known today for the lot of land in the city of Chester that bears his name—Wylie Park.

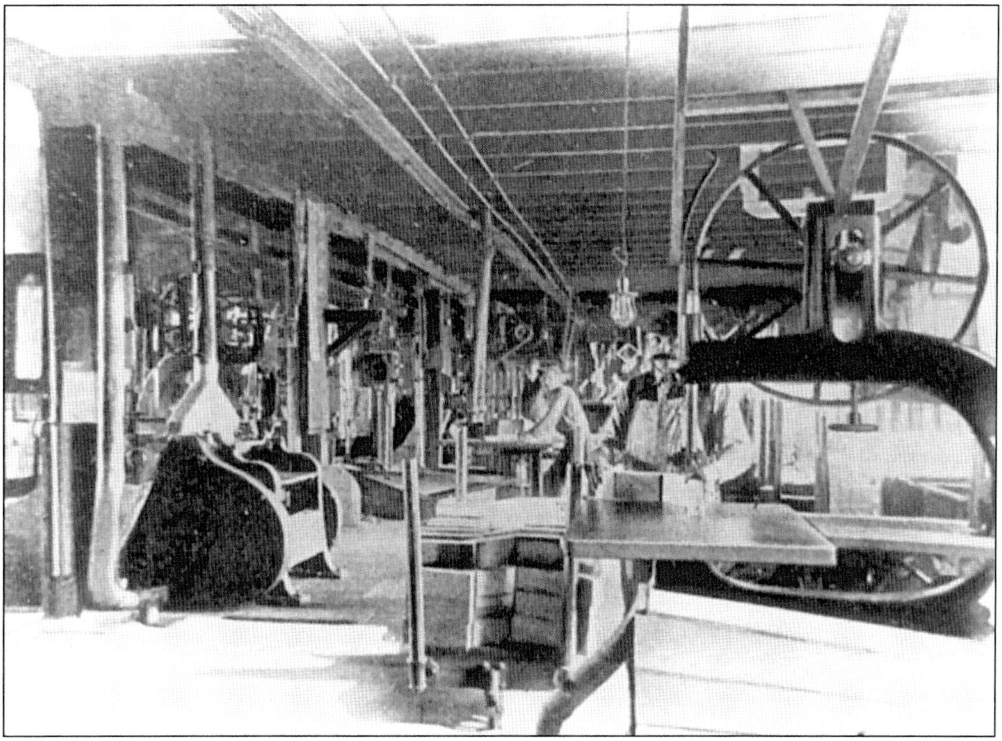

This view shows the interior of the Rock Hill Buggy Company *c.* 1910. The company was started by John Gary Anderson, Rock Hill's most famous entrepreneur. As the South's largest buggy manufacturer, the company sold more than 80,000 carriages worth $6 million.

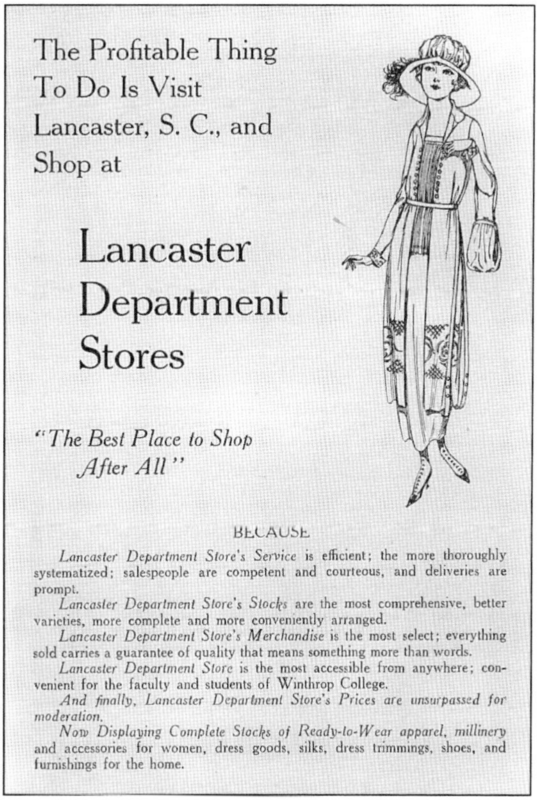

Lancaster Department Stores were popular shopping spots for many people in the Catawba region in the early twentieth century.

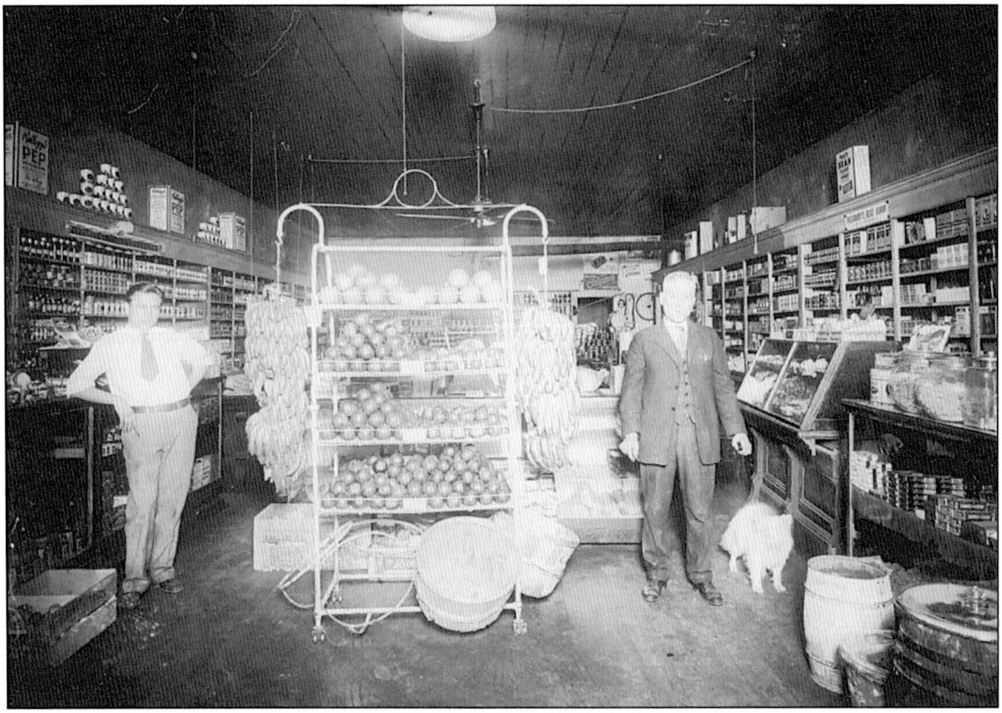

This interior view of the Cash and Carry Store that Wyche Elder opened in York in 1921 includes, from left to right, Roy Shillinglaw and Wyche Elder.

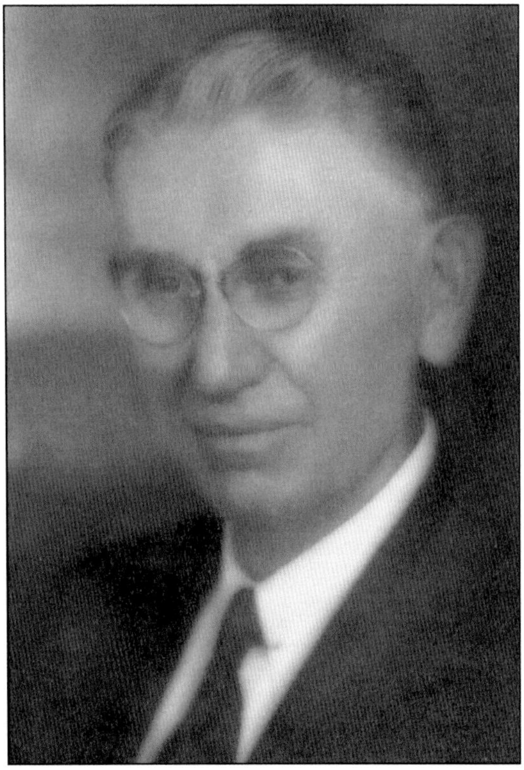

John Gary Anderson was one of the Catawba region's most interesting personalities. He became famous for manufacturing the Anderson Car, which he sold during the 1910s and 1920s. Anderson was an innovator who left his mark on the American automobile industry, but his own company went bankrupt. In 1929, the Anderson Motor Company's buildings and plant were sold to M. Lowenstein and Company.

Grady Ernandez and some Lando friends strike a daring pose for this early 1930s photo.

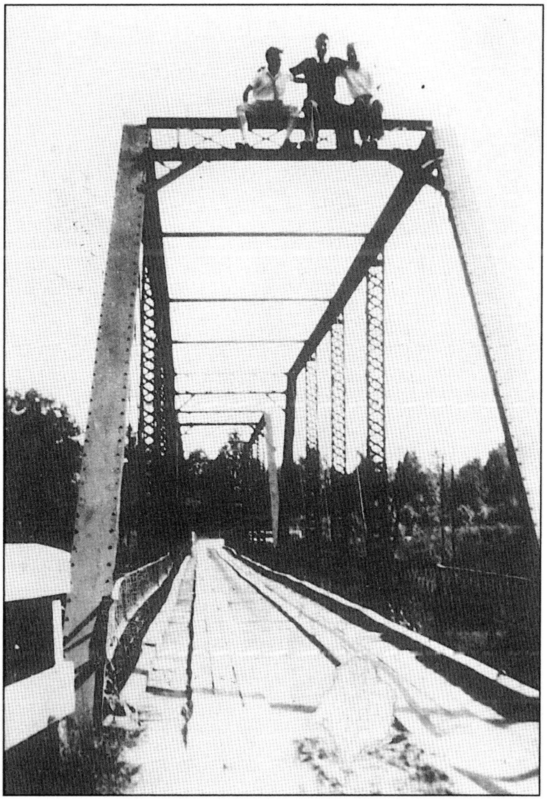

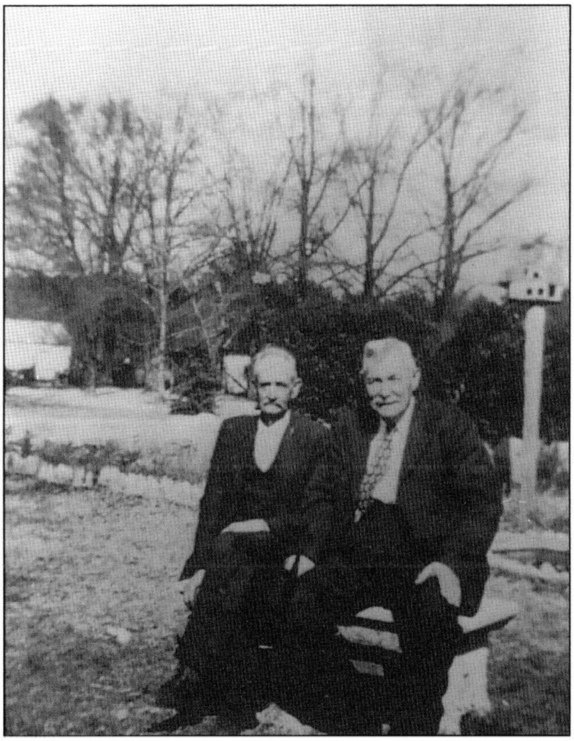

Joseph Walter Bankhead, on the right in this photo, was a prominent Lowrys farmer and the People's Free Library's first librarian. On the left is Robert Edward Lee, a prominent farmer of the Blackstock community in Chester County.

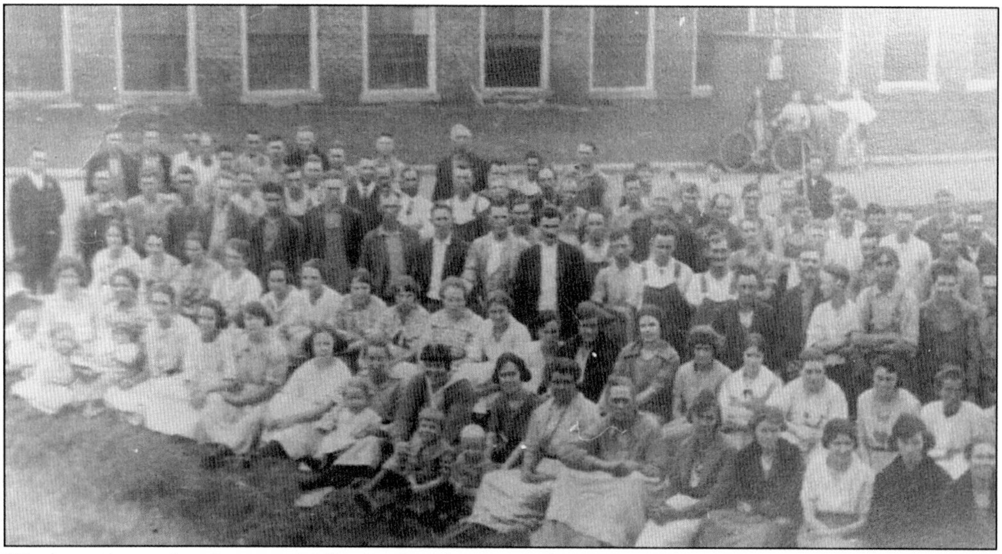

Workers from the Springs Mills Gayle Plant in Chester County pose for this 1930s photo. Organized in 1900 as the Wylie Mill, the Gayle plant did not become part of the Springs organization until 1933, when it was purchased by Elliott Springs in an effort to strengthen the operations of the Springsteen and Eureka plants. The Gayle Plant closed in 1981.

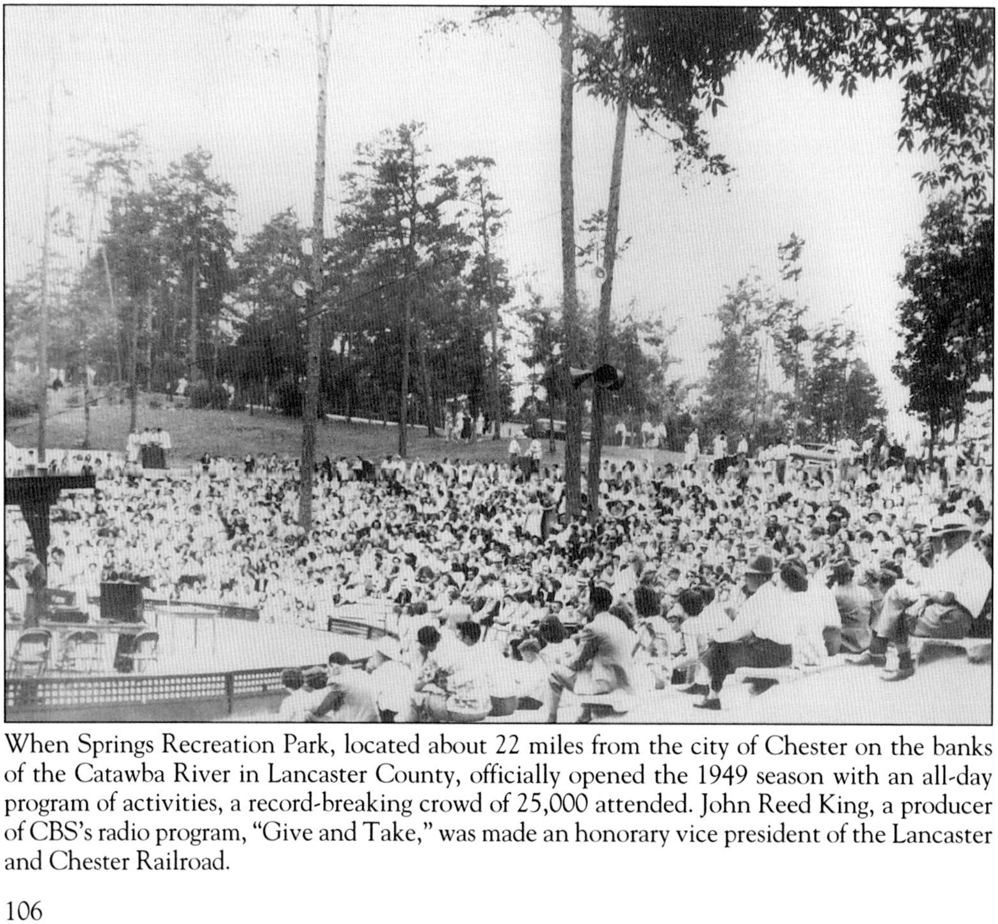

When Springs Recreation Park, located about 22 miles from the city of Chester on the banks of the Catawba River in Lancaster County, officially opened the 1949 season with an all-day program of activities, a record-breaking crowd of 25,000 attended. John Reed King, a producer of CBS's radio program, "Give and Take," was made an honorary vice president of the Lancaster and Chester Railroad.

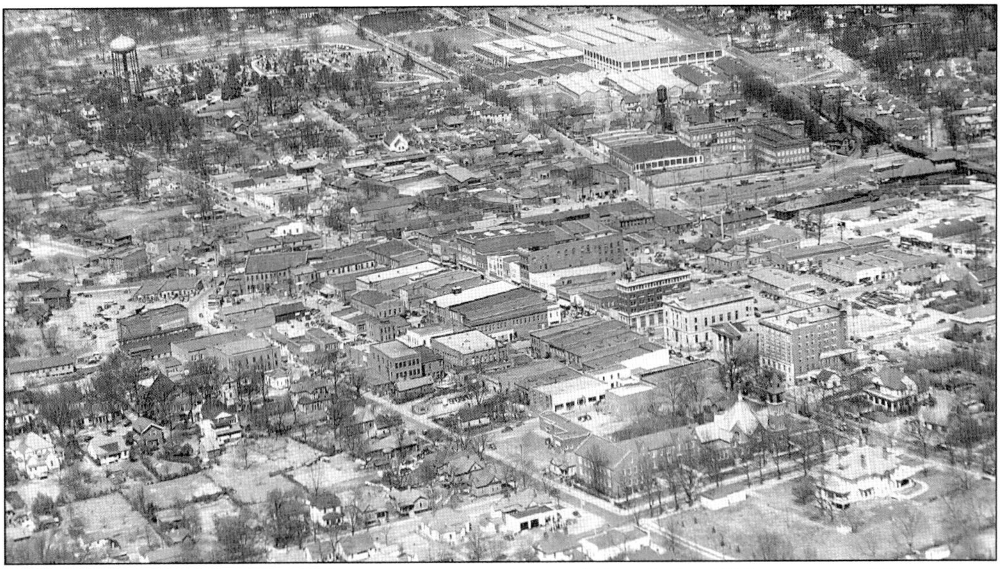

This aerial view of Rock Hill was taken in the middle of the 20th century. Times have certainly changed.

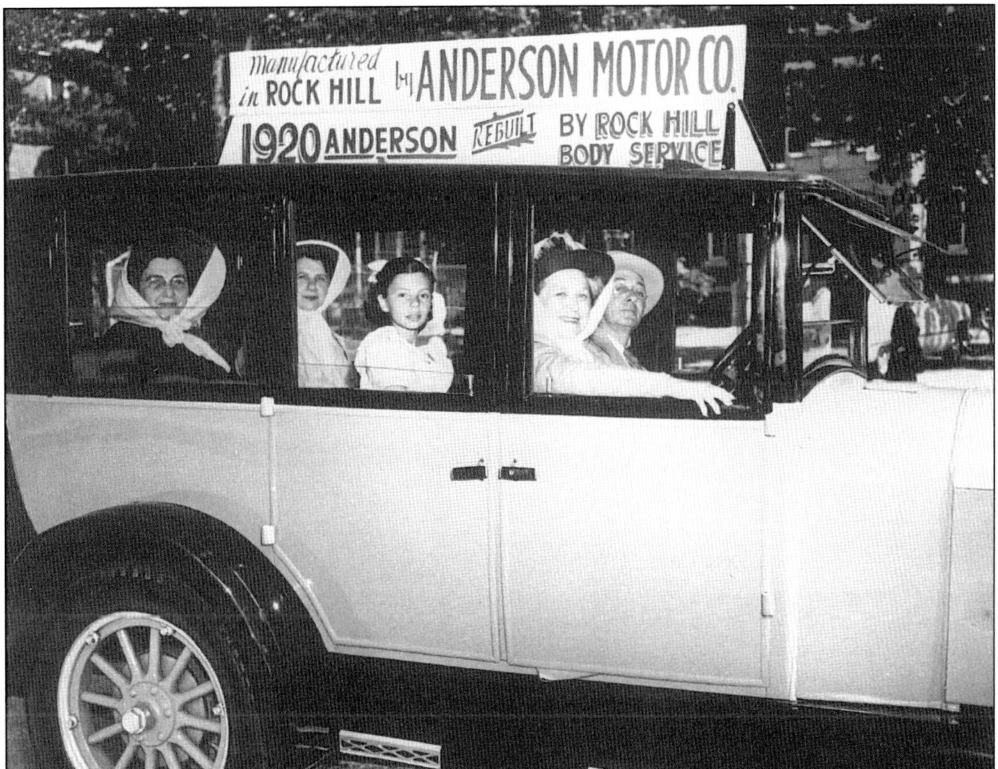

The Anderson Car is displayed during Rock Hill's centennial celebration in May 1952. Pictured, from left to right, are (front seat) Jenks Johnston Anderson and John Wesley Anderson Sr.; (back seat) Carrie Anderson Johnson, Alice Anderson Gill, and Martha Hardin.

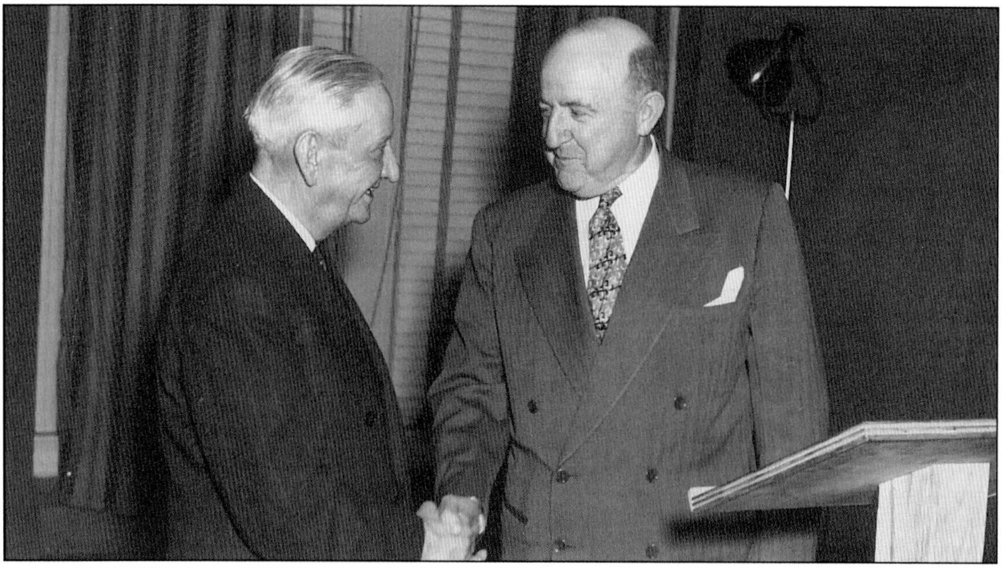

On the left, Charles L. Cobb of Rock Hill greets guest speaker Elmer R. Oliver, vice president of the Southern Railway System. The occasion was the annual meeting of the Rock Hill Chamber of Commerce on January 31, 1953. Cobb was one of the Catawba region's most prominent bankers.

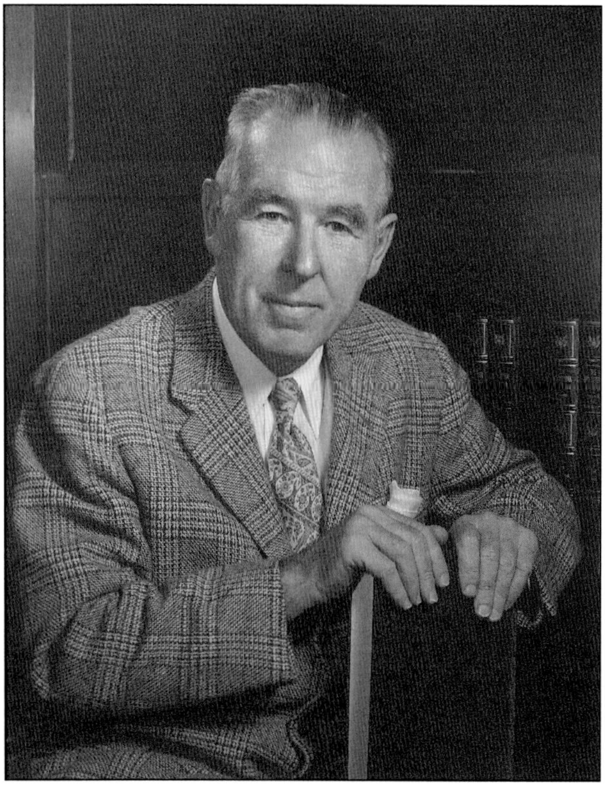

Perhaps no individual exerted more influence over the economic development of the Catawba region in the 20th century than Elliot Springs (1896–1954). When he took over the presidency of Springs, he inherited a company that consisted of five obsolete cotton mills. Company property was valued at $7,476,000, and annual sales were $8,555,000. At his death in 1959, the company property was valued at $114,546,000, and sales for that year totaled $184,340,000.

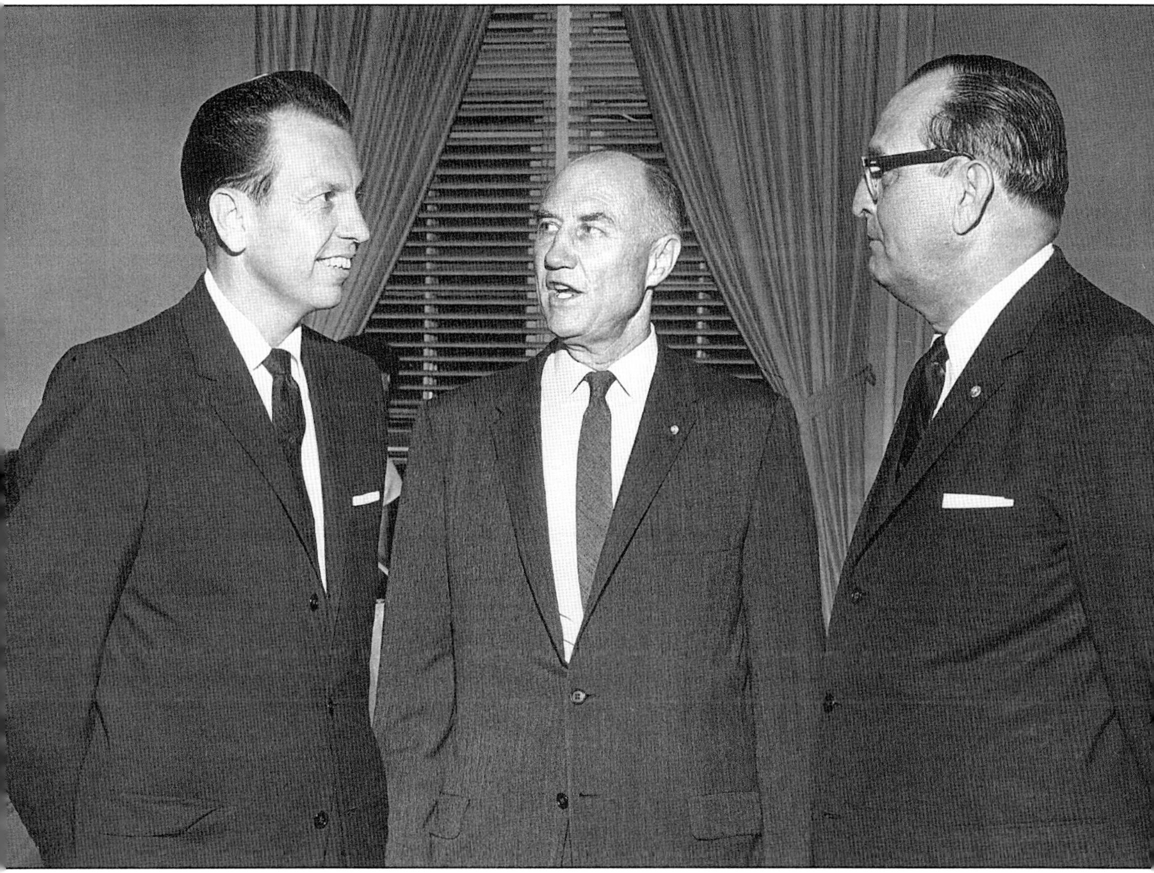

Two of Rock Hill's most prominent citizens, John Hardin (at left) and C.H. "Icky" Albright (at right), meet with South Carolina political legend Strom Thurmond in 1959. Hardin is a prominent banker, and Albright a realtor. Both are former mayors of Rock Hill.

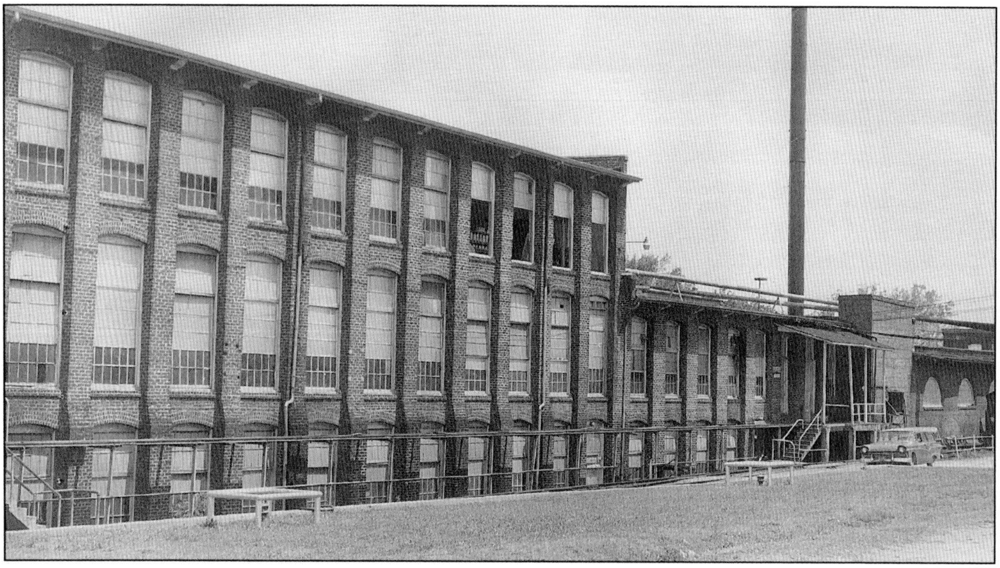

This is a view of the Manetta Mills plant in Lando that is no longer in operation.

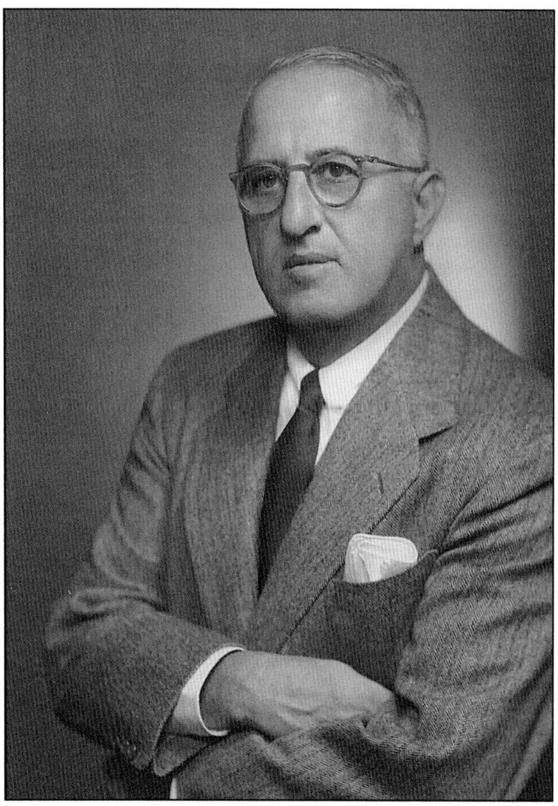

Archie O. Joslin was the president of the New York-based M. Lowenstein and Sons Finishing Division Inc. Formerly known as the Rock Hill Printing and Finishing Company, the business had a big impact on the region.

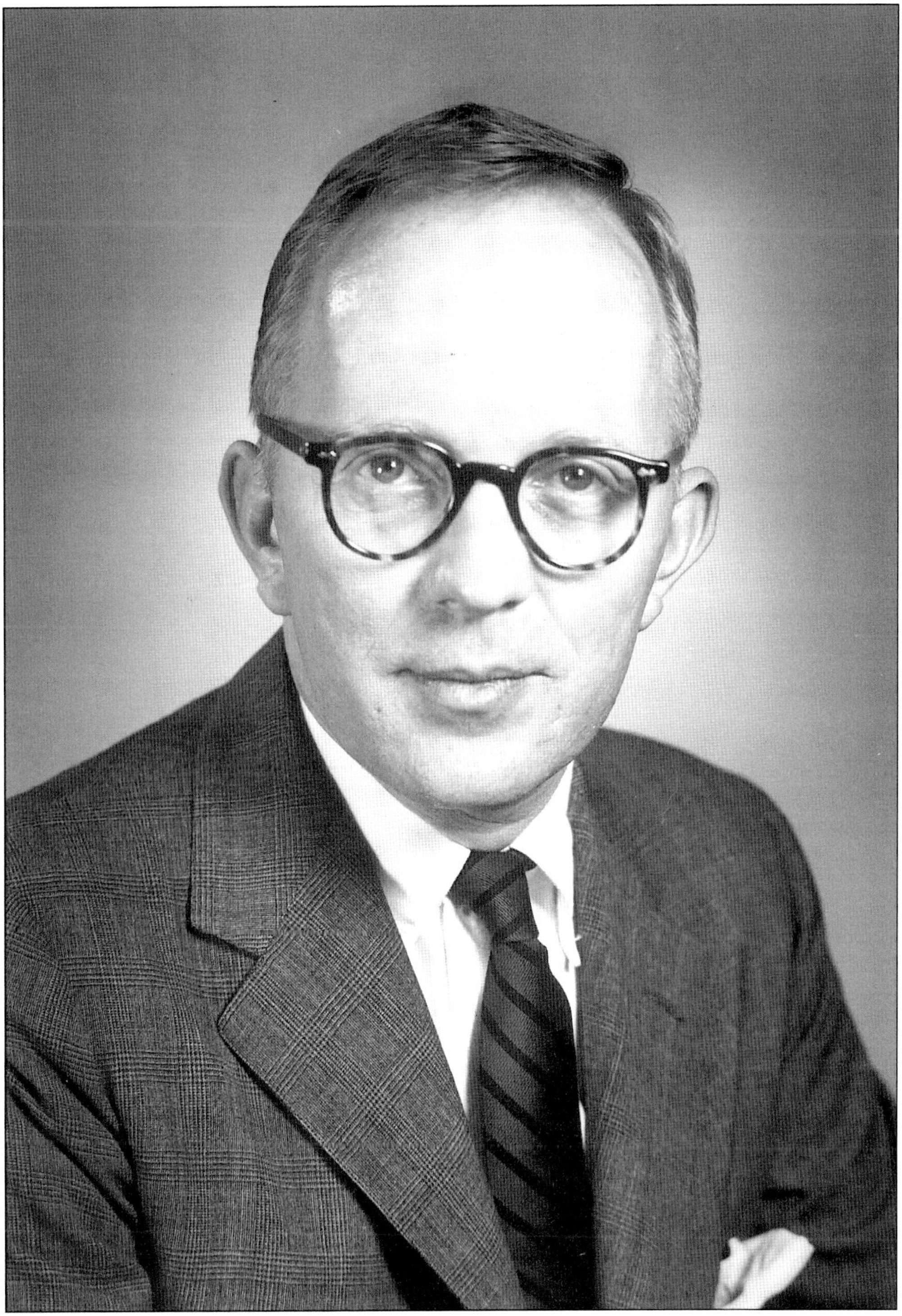

Upon the death of Elliott Springs in 1959, H.W. Close assumed the leadership of Springs Cotton Mills. Close was also an active leader in the textile industry and an advocate of public service. He died in 1983.

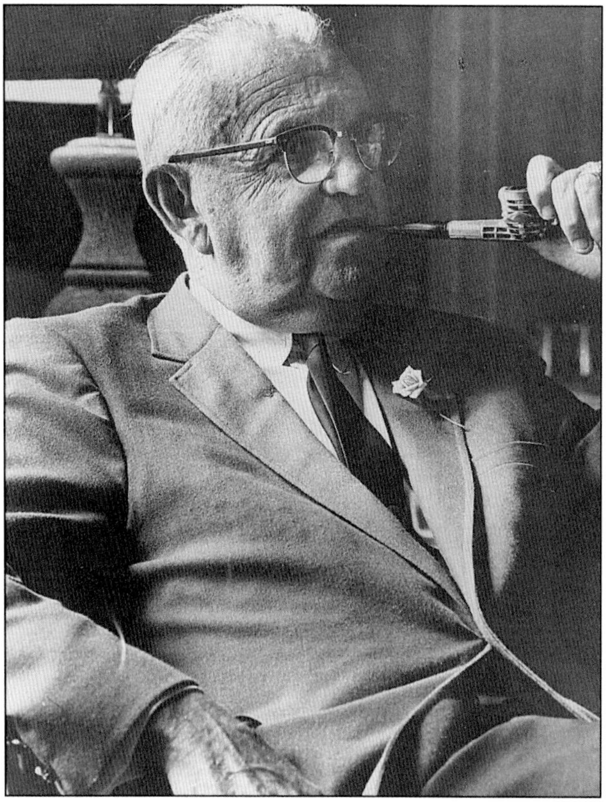

William H. Grier (1903–1984) was the president of M. Lowenstein and Sons Finishing Division (formerly Rock Hill Printing and Finishing). Grier was the first man to receive an honorary doctorate from Winthrop for his work as a Winthrop trustee.

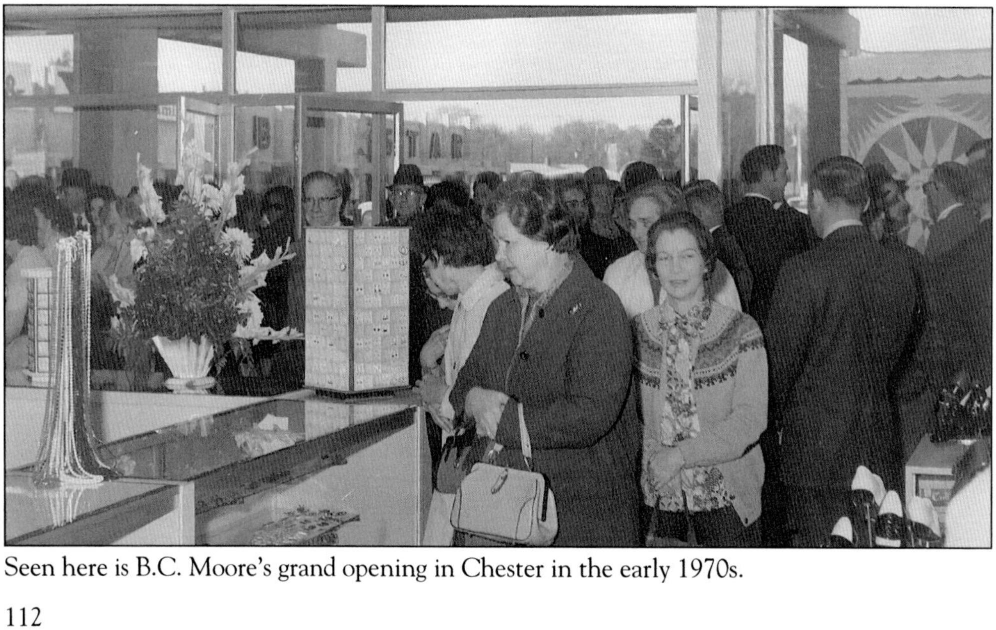

Seen here is B.C. Moore's grand opening in Chester in the early 1970s.

Six

Politics and Community Service

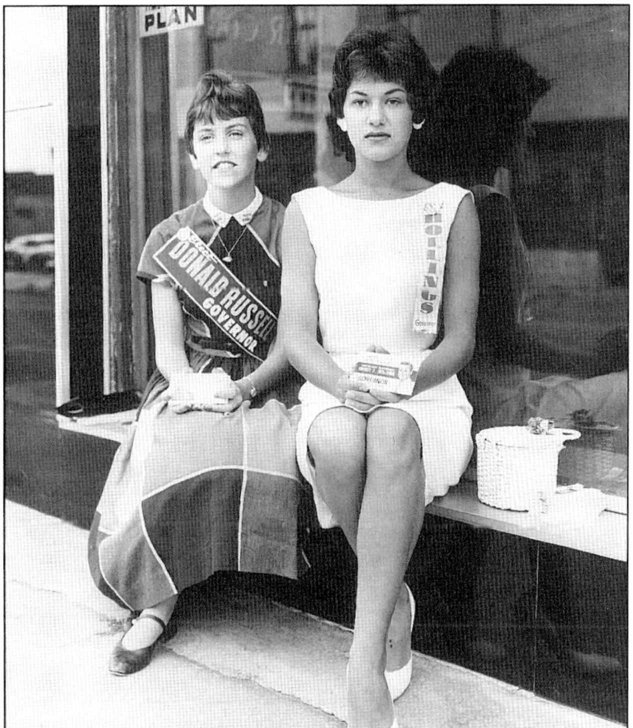

In the summer of 1958, these two Rock Hill women campaigned for different candidates seeking the Democratic Party's gubernatorial nomination. It was a battle between the Upstate's Donald Russell and the Low Country's Ernest Hollings. Hollings defeated Russell, a native of Chester.

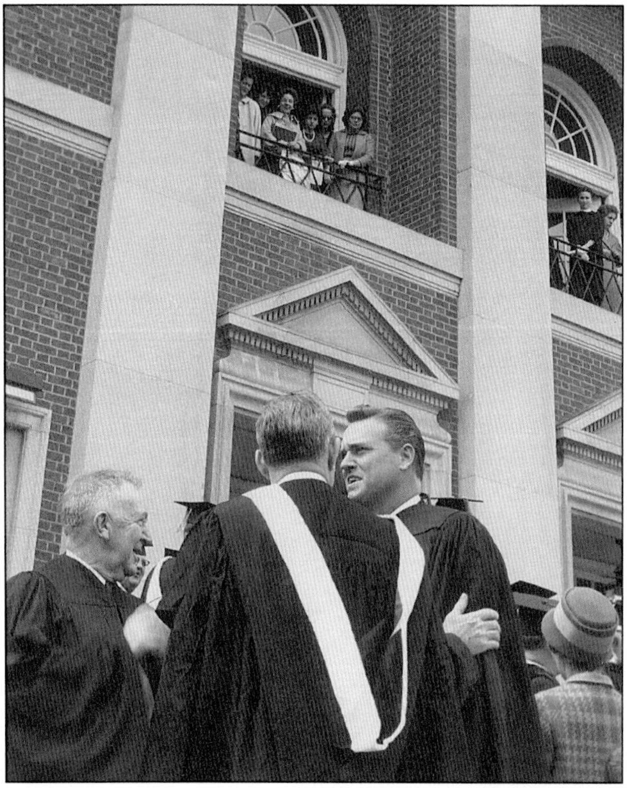

Governor Hollings (right) came to the 1960 inauguration of Winthrop president Dr. Charles Davis.

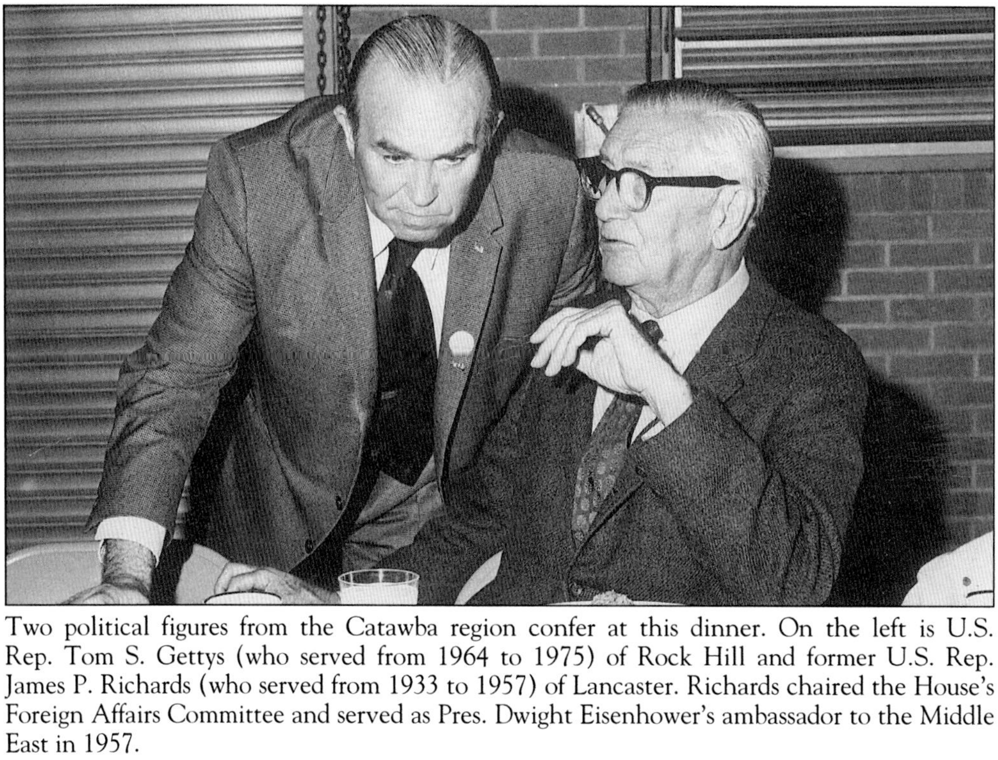

Two political figures from the Catawba region confer at this dinner. On the left is U.S. Rep. Tom S. Gettys (who served from 1964 to 1975) of Rock Hill and former U.S. Rep. James P. Richards (who served from 1933 to 1957) of Lancaster. Richards chaired the House's Foreign Affairs Committee and served as Pres. Dwight Eisenhower's ambassador to the Middle East in 1957.

U.S. District Court judge Robert Hemphill of Chester served as a member of Congress from 1957 to 1964 when Pres. Lyndon Johnson appointed him to the federal bench.

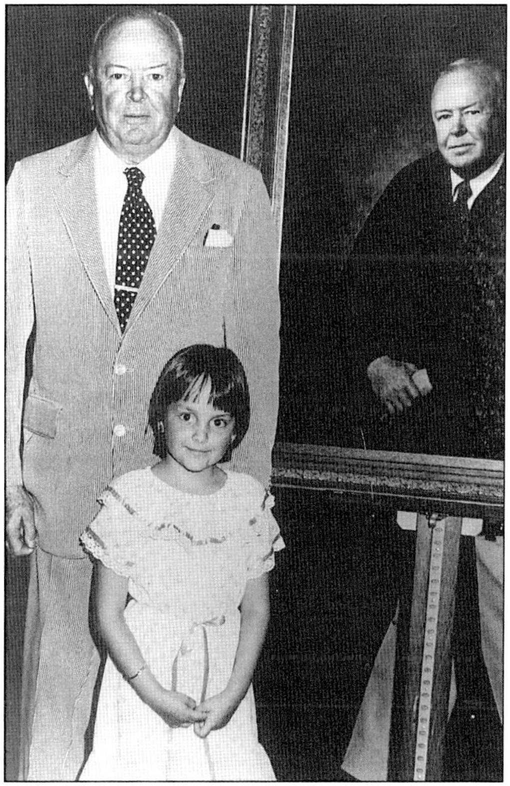

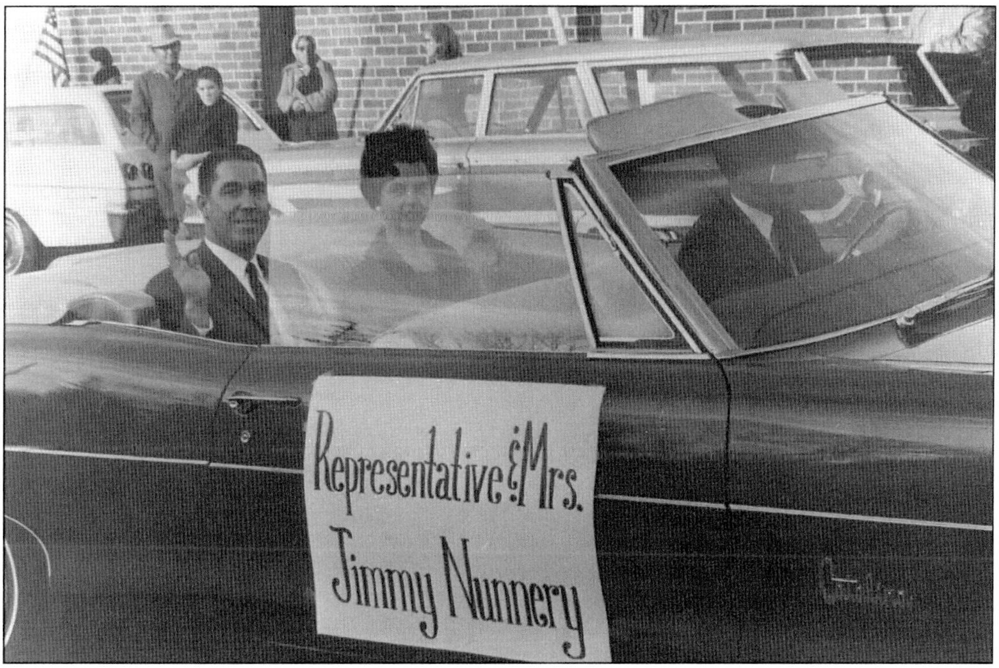

Christmas parades always feature political figures. In this mid-1960s photograph, State Rep. and Mrs. Jimmy Nunnery of Chester wave to the crowd.

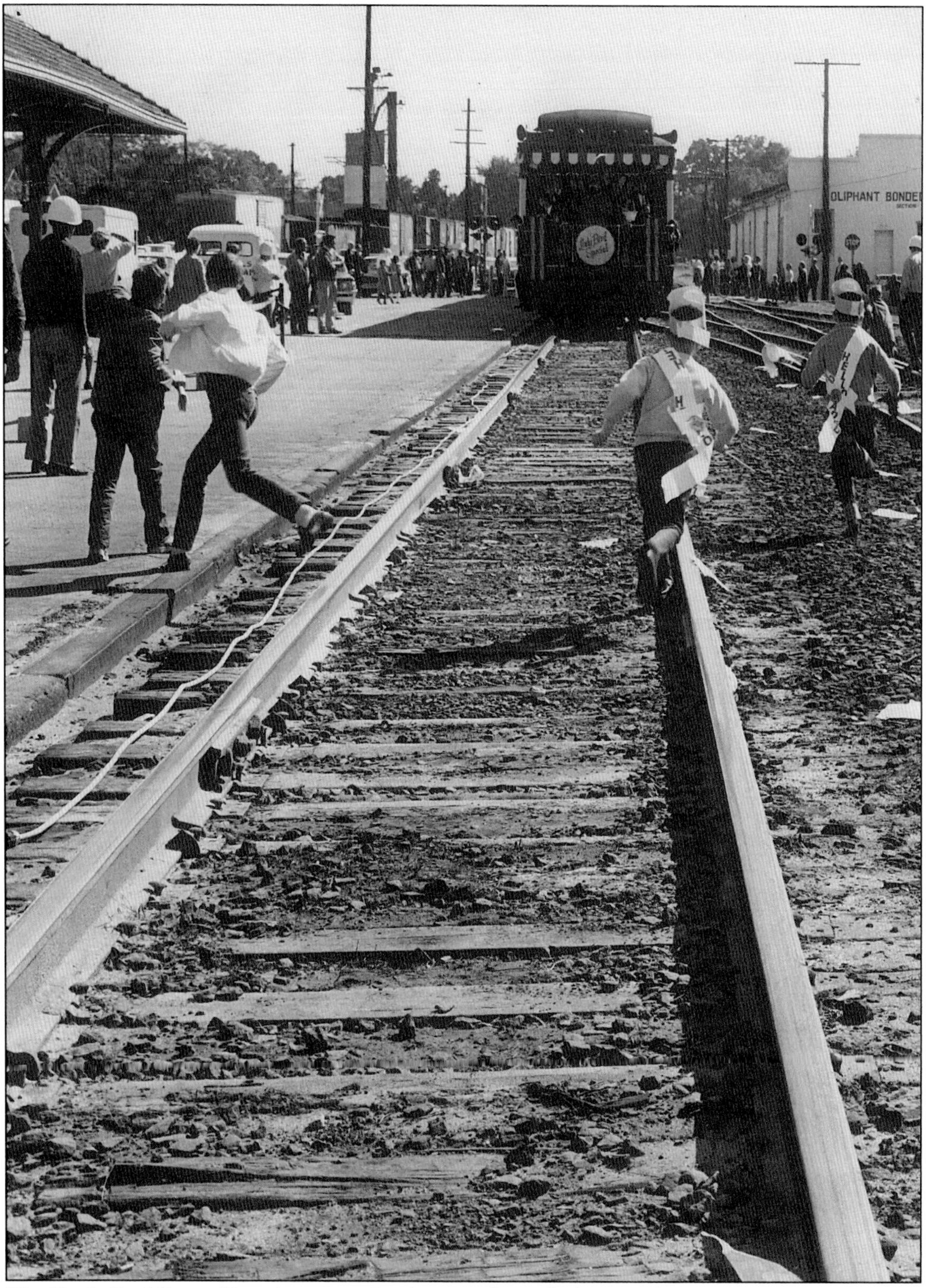

The "Lady Bird Special" made many whistle stops through the area during the 1964 presidential campaign. Here, the train arrives in Chester with the First Lady on board.

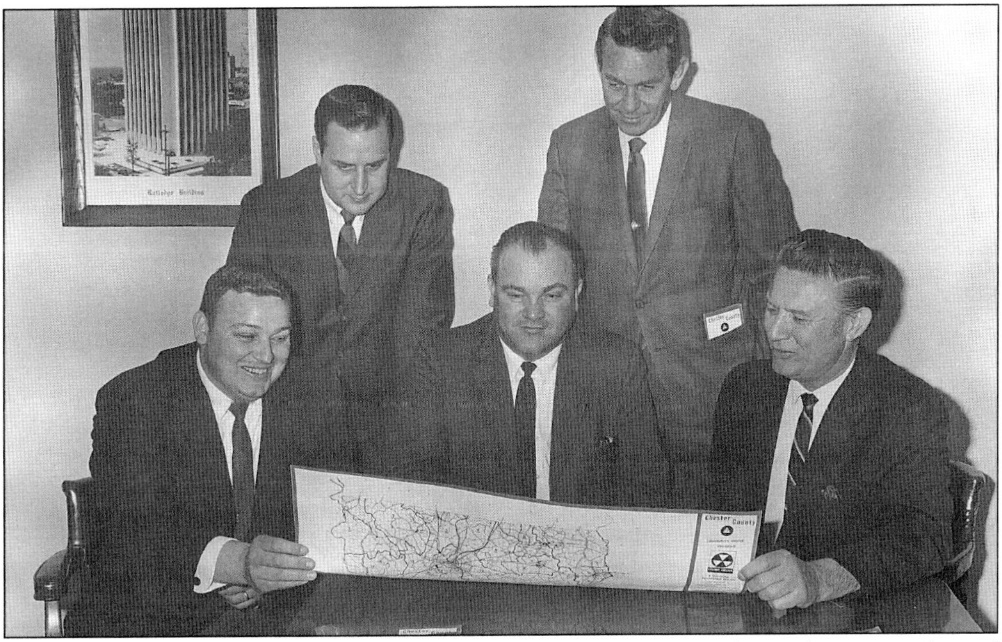

"All politics is local," and in this picture State Sen. John Martin (center) meets with civil defense officials and Chester legislators Billy Hare (second from left) and L.C. Wright (second from right).

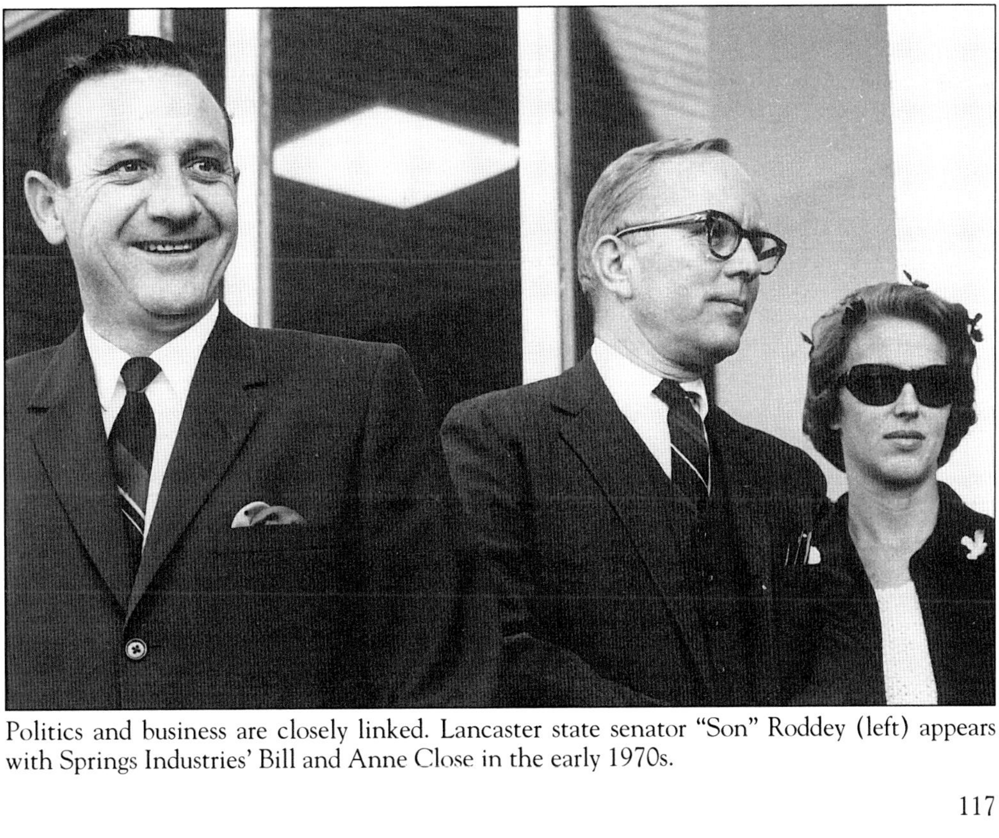

Politics and business are closely linked. Lancaster state senator "Son" Roddey (left) appears with Springs Industries' Bill and Anne Close in the early 1970s.

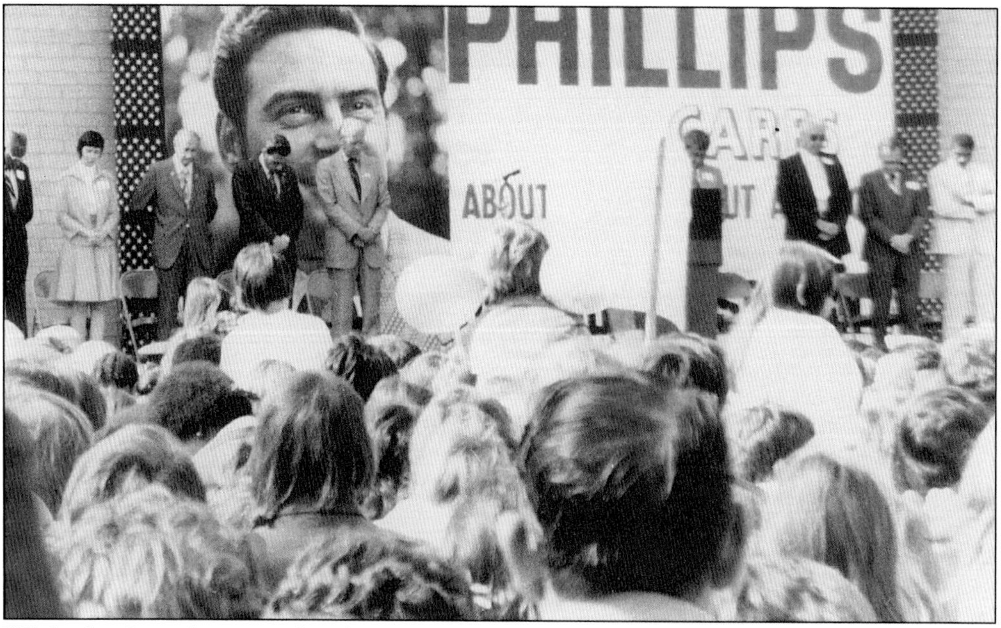

While the Catawba region has deep Democratic Party roots, winds of political change began swirling in the mid-1970s. With the help of Pres. Gerald Ford, Republican challenger Len Phillips of Lancaster made a shiny bid for the U.S. House.

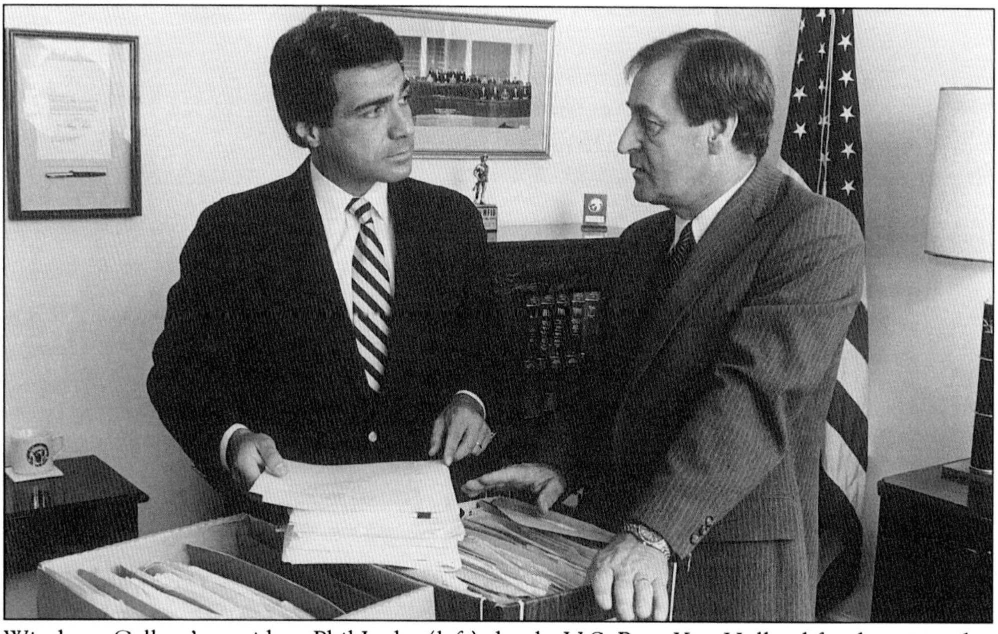

Winthrop College's president Phil Lader (left) thanks U.S. Rep. Ken Holland for depositing his papers in the archives in 1983. Lader left the presidency of Winthrop in 1984 to seek South Carolina's governorship. Today, Lader is the United States ambassador to the United Kingdom.

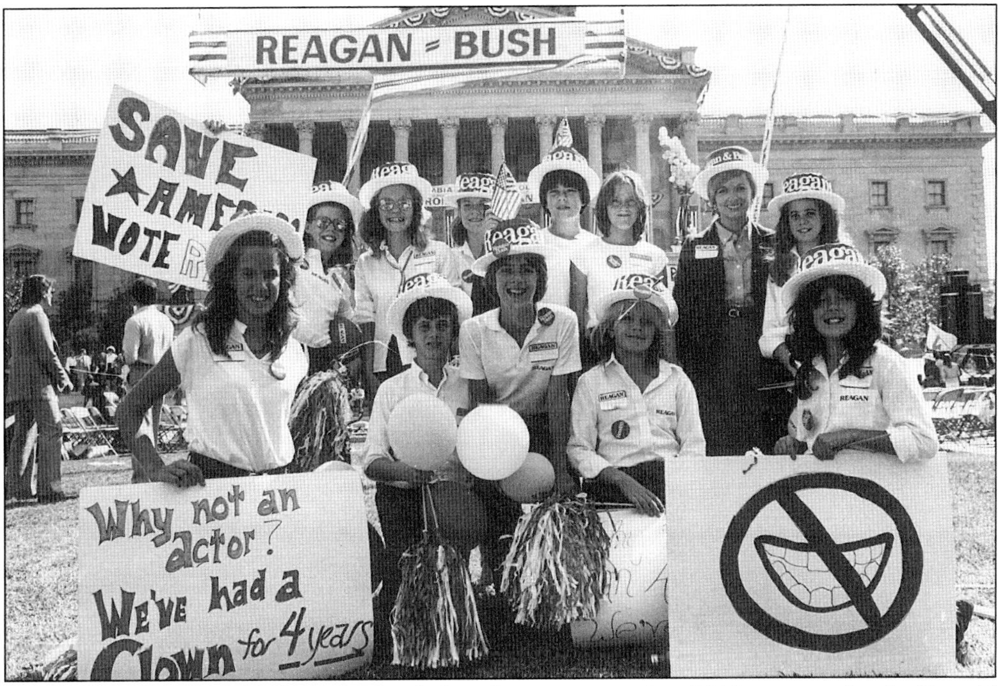

Republican women from the area traveled to the state capital in 1980 to campaign for Ronald Reagan and George Bush.

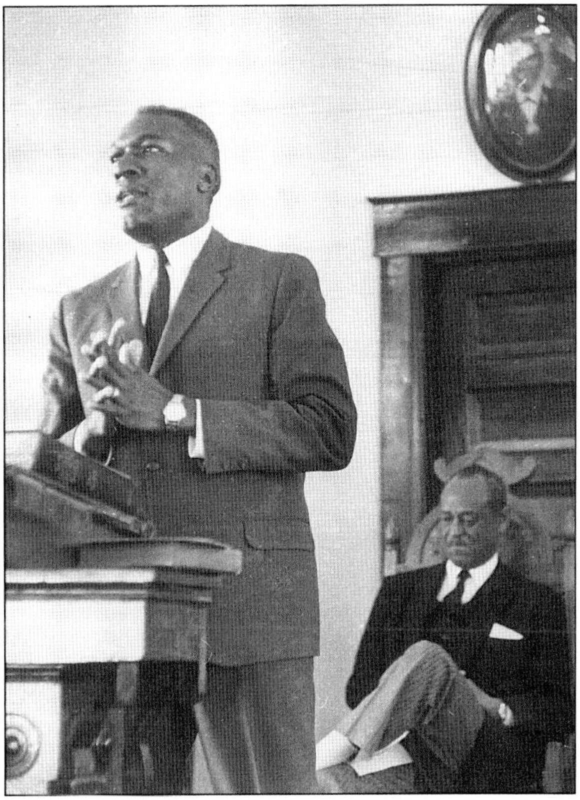

Local NAACP leader Lloyd Morris (left) introduces state NAACP executive director I. DeQuincey Newman, who later became South Carolina's first African-American senator since Reconstruction.

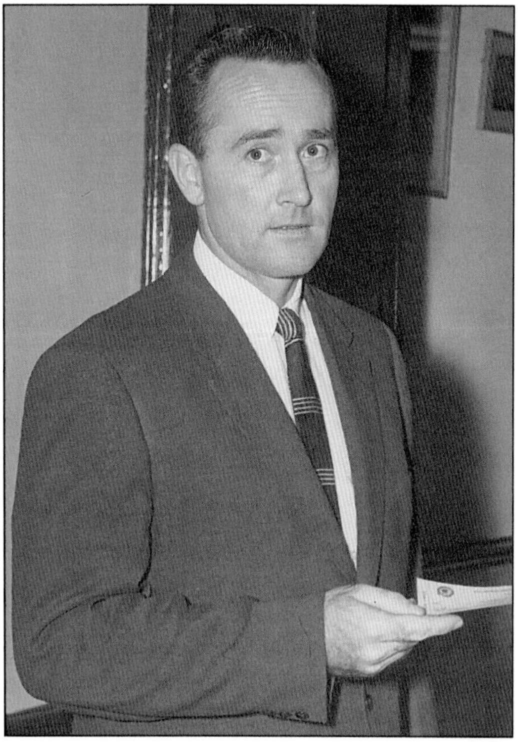

Chester mayor James F. Funderburk served from 1975 until his death in 1983.

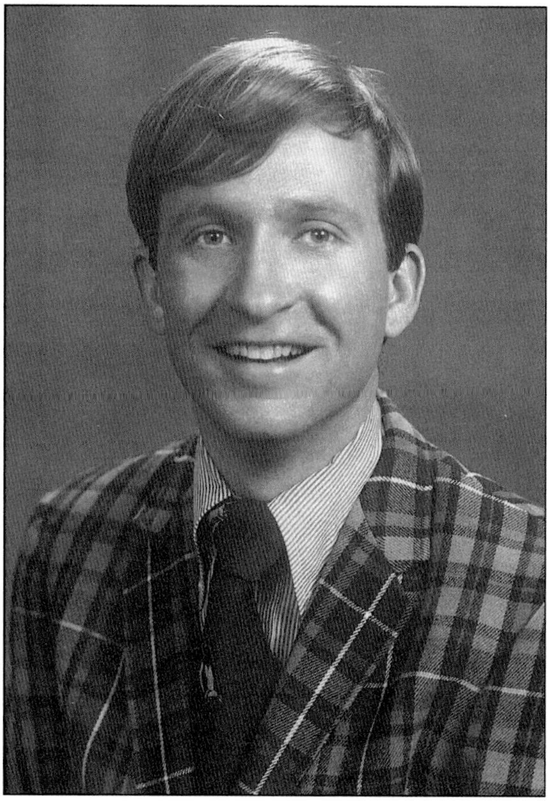

USCL professor Ralph Garris serves as magistrate.

After a series of disappointing elections and a long court battle, Chris King became Chester's first African-American mayor in 1998 and then lost his fight against cancer.

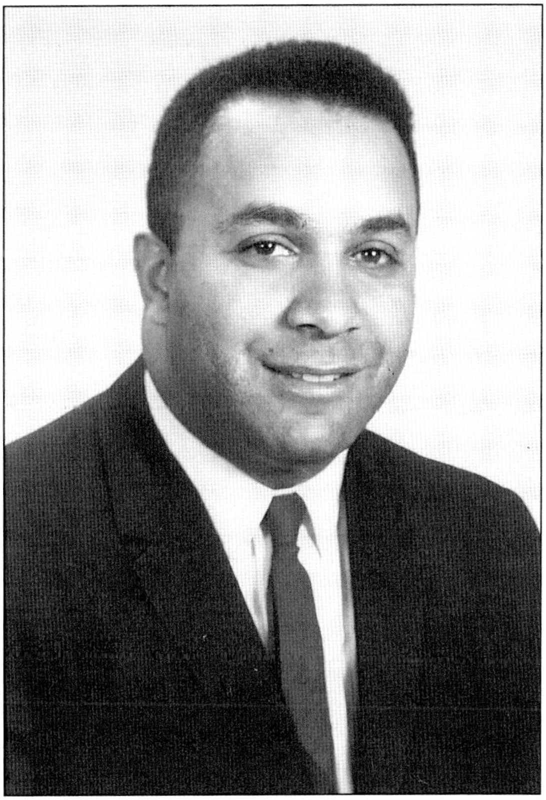

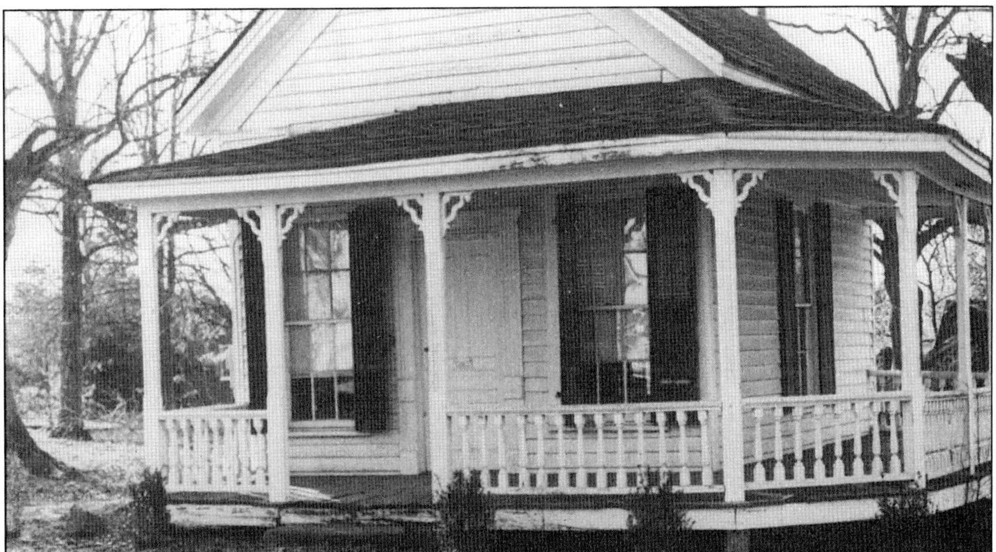

In 1905, Chester County farmer Walter Bankhead delivered books from the People's Free Library to rural families in Chester and York Counties.

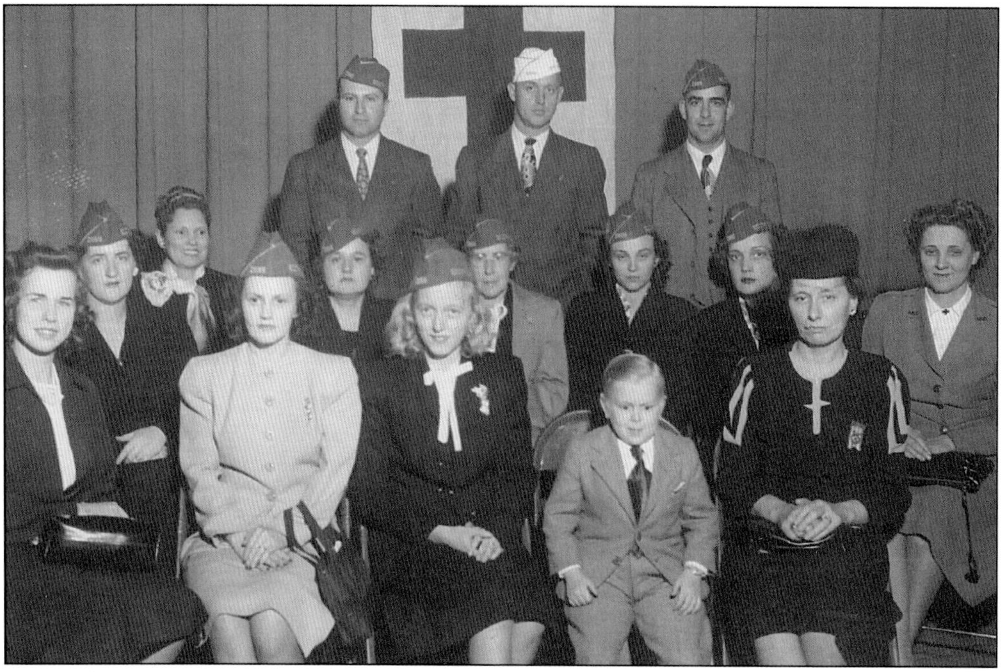

The Red Cross has always had strong community support in the Catawba region. Here, a group of volunteers gather after World War II.

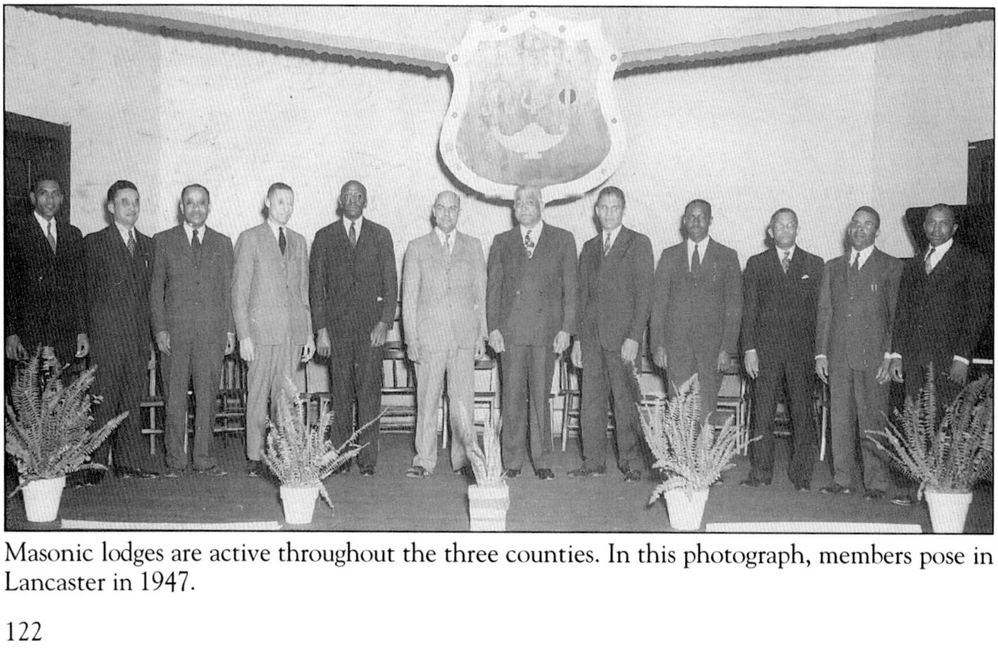

Masonic lodges are active throughout the three counties. In this photograph, members pose in Lancaster in 1947.

In the African-American community, funeral homes provide a number of services for the families of the deceased. York's Wright's Funeral Home, founded by Issac Wright, is a well-respected and multi-purpose establishment.

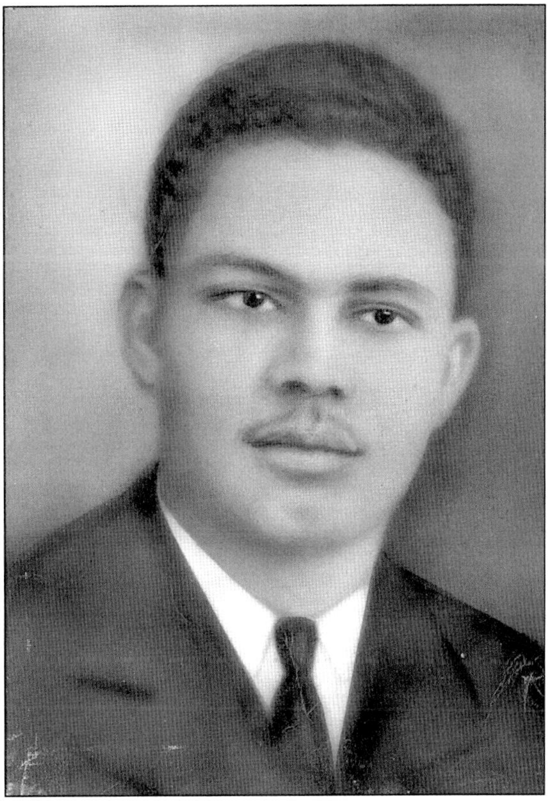

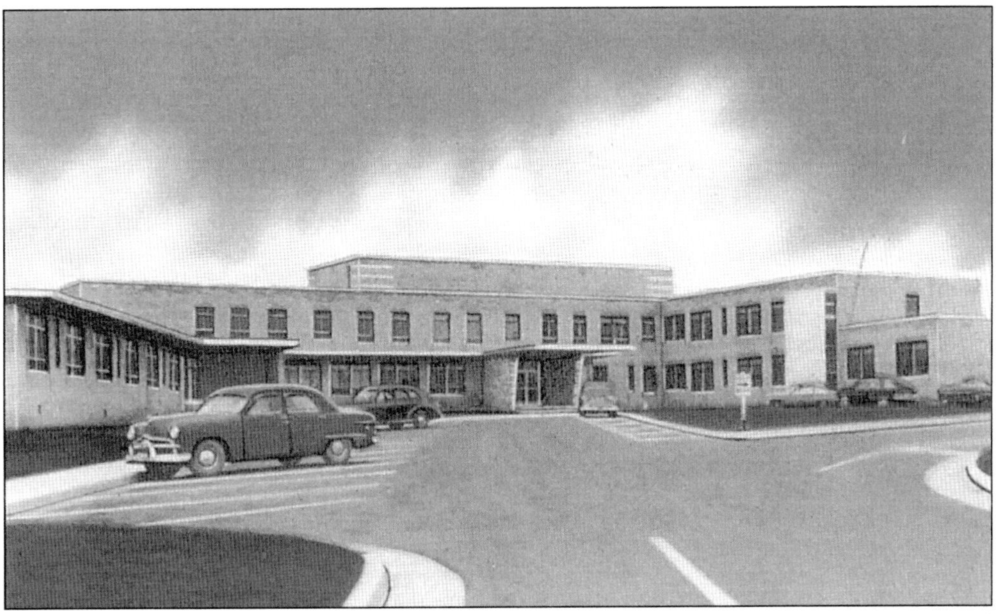

By the early 1950s, modern hospitals, such as this one in Chester, had replaced home-based medical care.

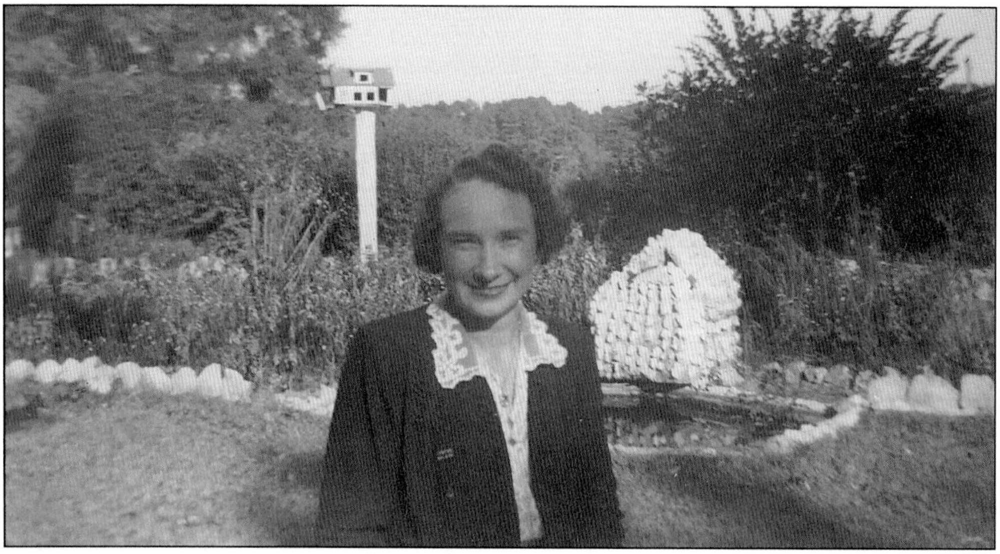

Kindergarten teacher Ola Bankhead Lee was an active leader in early childhood education in the Catawba region, guiding the South Carolina Association on Children Under Six.

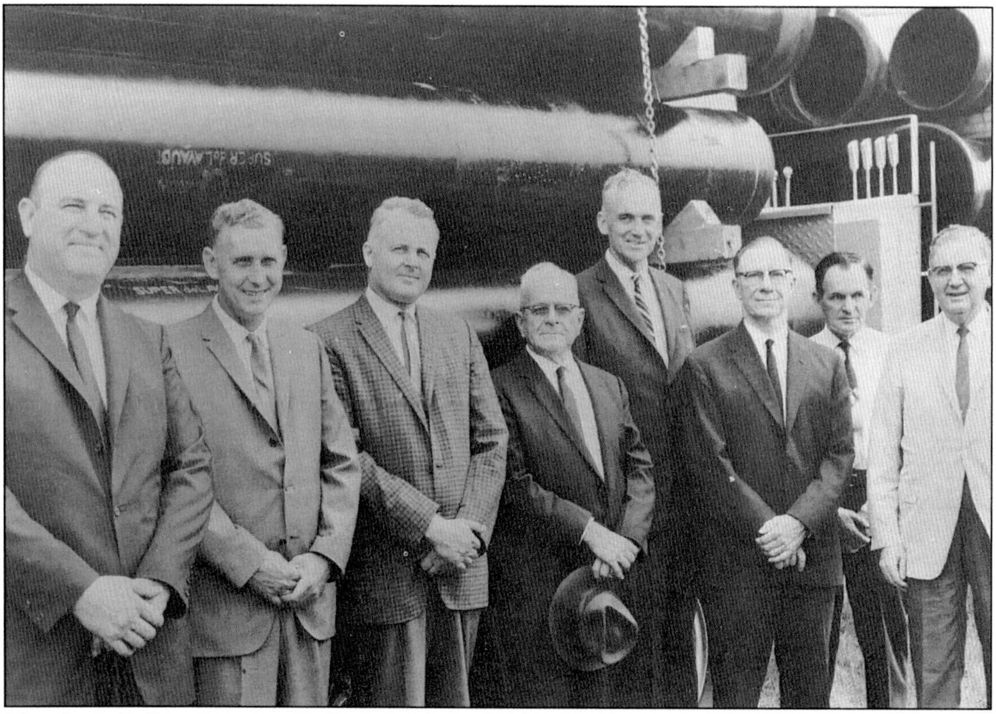

The Catawba River's water was harnessed in 1963 by the Chester Metropolitan District in order to attract industries to the area. Above are the community leaders who founded the modern water system.

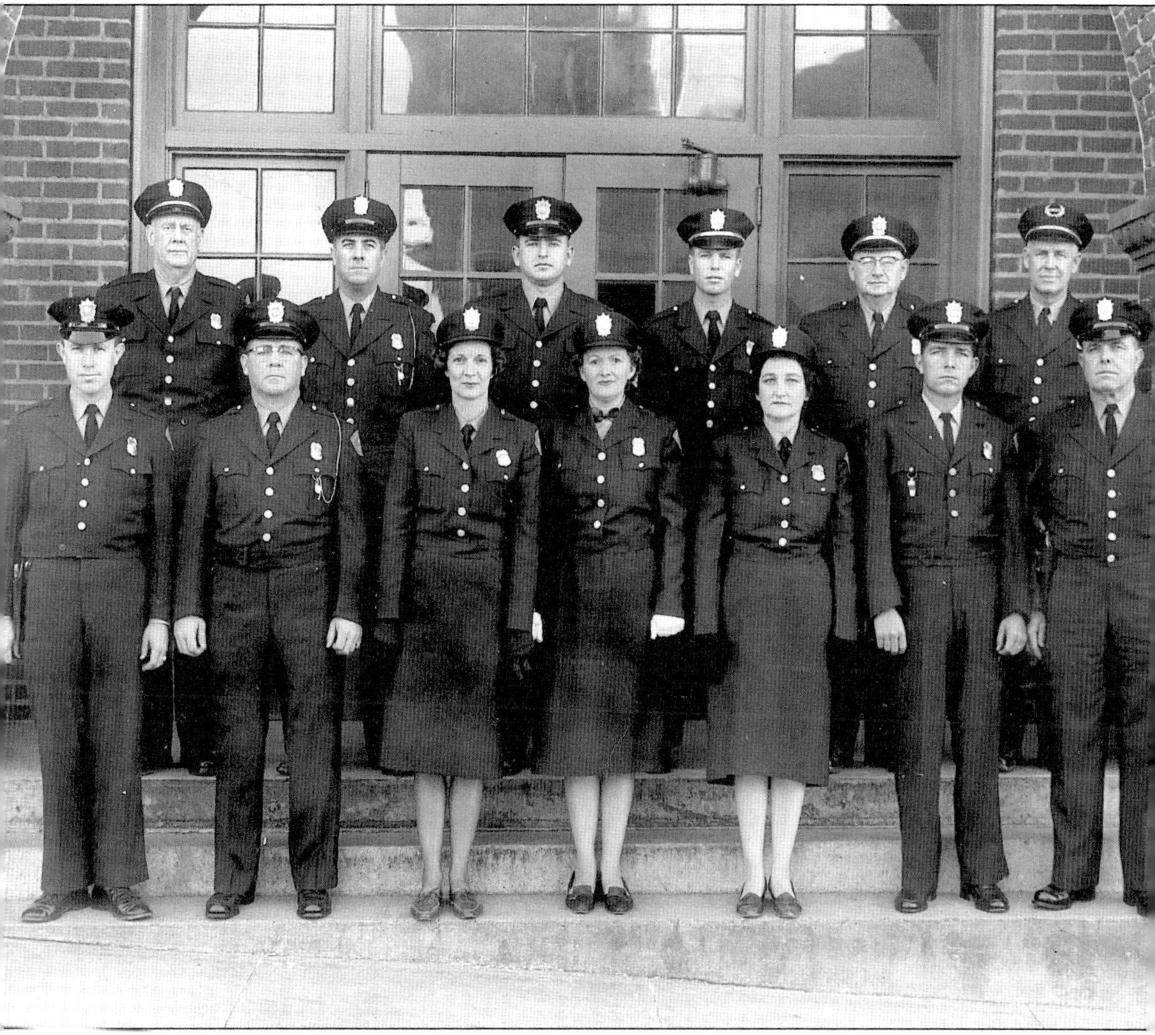

Chester's police department posed outside the city hall in the early 1960s. By this time, three women had been added to the force.

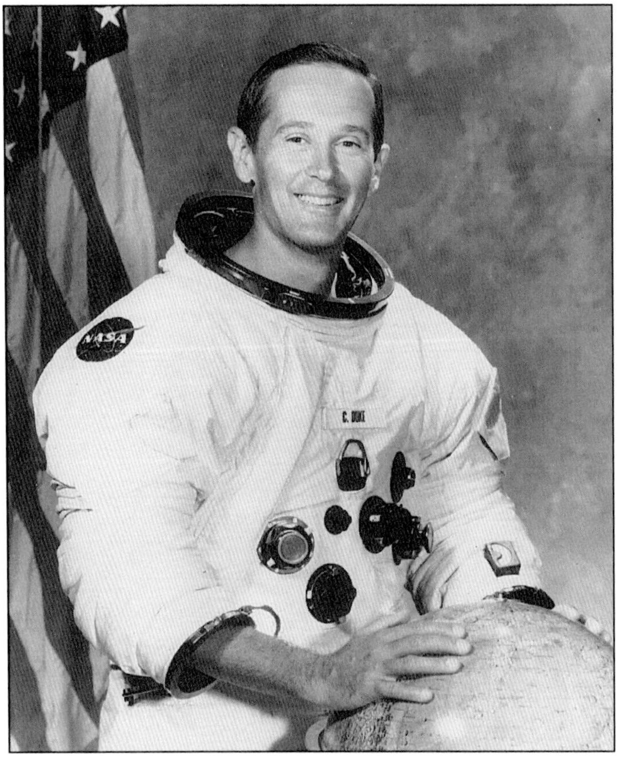

Lancaster's Charles M. Duke Jr. set foot on the moon in 1971 as part of NASA's Apollo Space Program.

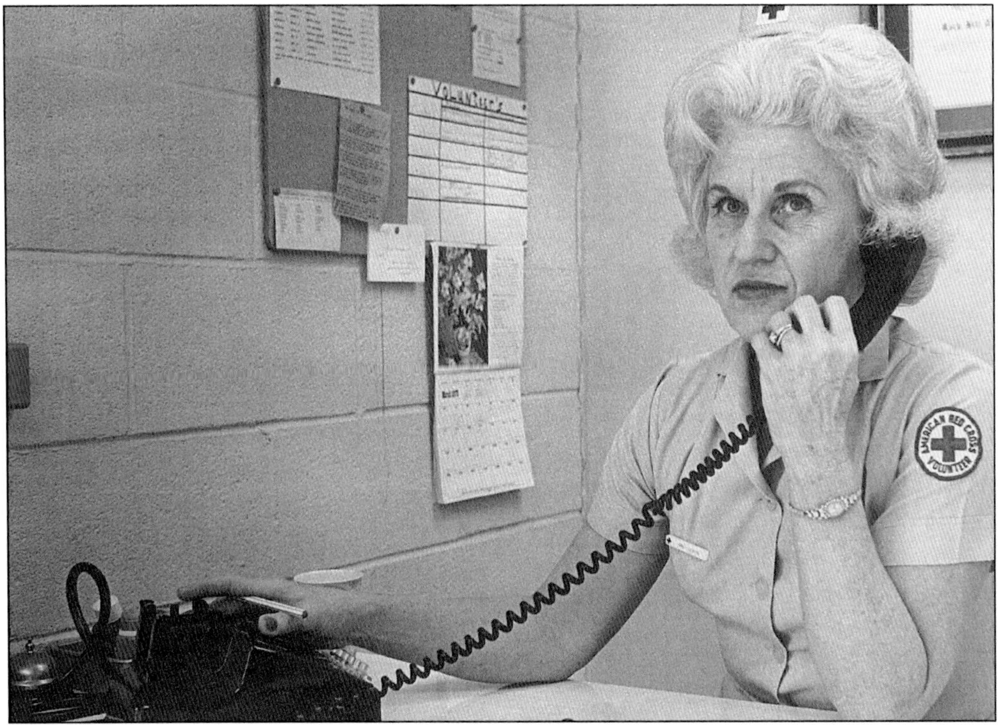

Rock Hill's Martha Martin handles the Red Cross phone lines in this 1973 photograph.

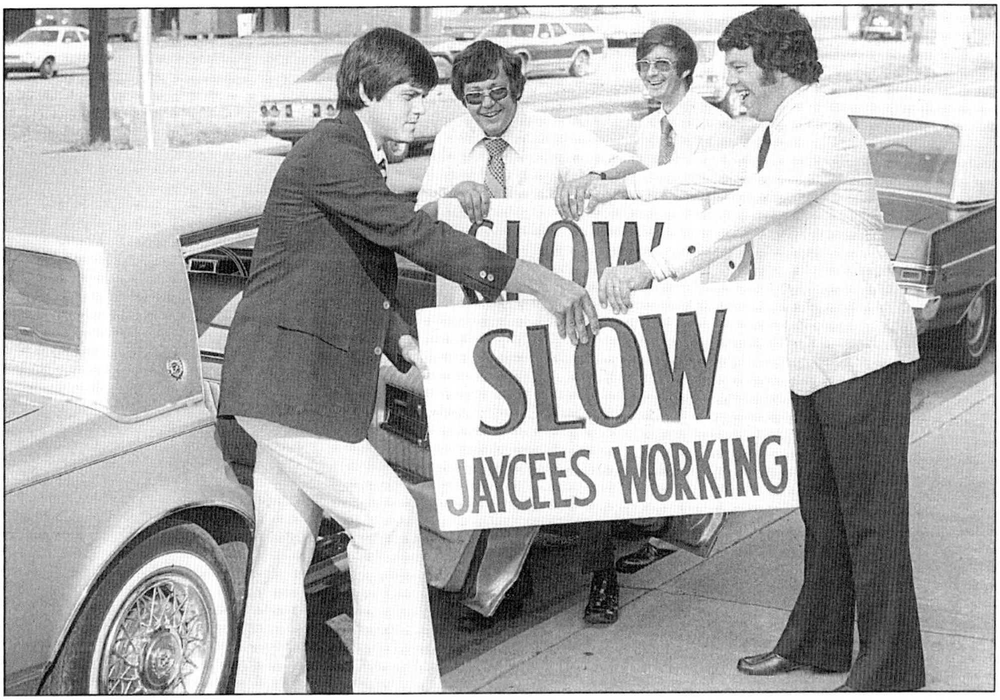

Throughout the region, Jaycees serve their communities while developing leadership skills among their members.

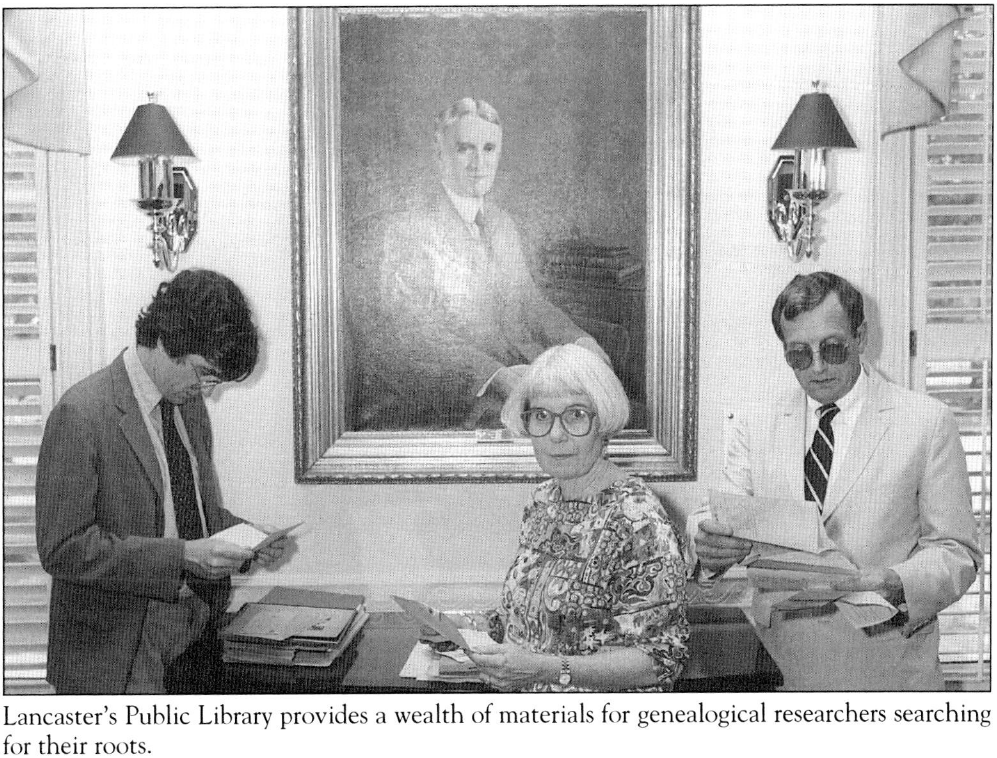
Lancaster's Public Library provides a wealth of materials for genealogical researchers searching for their roots.

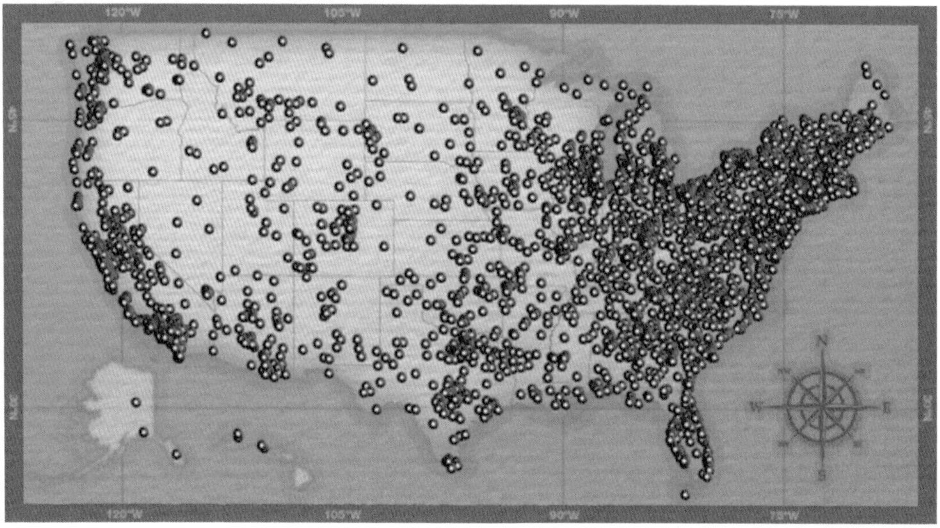